JESUS

The Forsaken, Occasional Christ

JESUS

The Forsaken, Occasional Christ

DONNA DILBECK

Jesus: The Forsaken, Occasional Christ

Trilogy Christian Publishers A Wholly Owned Subsidiary of Trinity Broadcasting Network

2442 Michelle Drive Tustin, CA 92780

Manufactured in the United States of America

10 9 8 7 6 5 4 3 2 1

Library of Congress Cataloging-in-Publication Data is available.

ISBN: 979-8-88738-009-4

E-ISBN: 979-8-88738-010-0

To Commemorate

In thankful appreciation to Almighty God for graciously giving us the son we named Clay.

Little did we know how very soon God would call him home again. God gives and takes away. Blessed be the Name of the Lord.

Clay Austin Dilbeck

1974–2012

Dedication

*When my people humble themselves—the ones who are called
by my name—and pray, seek me, and turn away from their
evil practices, I myself will listen from heaven, I will pardon
their sins, and I will restore their land.*

2 Chronicles 7:14 (ISV)

Each of these little lambs is eternally secure and comforted in the mighty arms of the Good Shepherd. Their imperishable souls live on forever in the everlasting kingdom of our God and Savior Jesus Christ.

Naveah Bravo, ten; Jackie Cazares, ten; Makenna Elrod, ten; Jose Flores Jr., ten; Eliahna Garcia, nine; Uziyah Garcia, eight; Amerie Jo Garza, nine; Jayce Carmelo Luevanos, ten; Xavier Lopez, ten; Tess Marie Mata, ten; Miranda Mathis, eleven; Alithia Ramirez, ten; Annabell Guadalupe Rodriguez, ten; Maite Rodriguez, ten; Alexandria Aniyah Rubio, ten; Layla Salazar, ten; Jailah Silguero, ten; Eliahana Cruz Torres, ten; Rogelio Torres, ten.

This book was written with the hope of preventing the very tragedy that occurred in Uvalde, Texas, on May 25, 2022. In the same hour this manuscript was approved for publication, I watched in horror at the unfolding reports of the massacre at Robb Elementary School, a place that should have been a haven of safety.

My heart aches for each family member whose precious treasure was violently torn from those who dearly cherished them. And secondarily, to all the many families who have suffered the lamentable loss of their children in a similar catastrophe. All America weeps in deep despair.

The reality of sin in America is all too frequent and painfully graphic. Again the world is stunned by the indefensible and recent murder of nineteen innocent children, now adjoined with all the other adolescents ripped from this life at the hands of a savage killer. Who, incidentally, was not much more than a child himself. Salvador Ramos, an impressionable lost soul, was also a victim. His powers of reasoning were ensnared by the diabolical influence of Satan, the greatest enemy of the mind and most powerful and debauched influencer in this sin-filled fallen world.

My heartfelt sympathy to all who grieve.

Foreword

It's time for the citizens of America to wake up and stop all the foolish pretense. It's time for the Christian hypocrites to return to their Savior Jesus and faithfully commit to their covenant. There is no time left for fence walking. These are truly the days of Elijah revisited. Other than the Lord Jesus, everything that you have grown accustomed to or believed in, is disintegrating at a pace never imagined. Once, this God-serving nation was an all-powerful fortress unto itself and a haven for many other people the world over. America was once a tribute to the Giver of Life for its uncompromising loyalty to God. But now, this nation under the sovereign hand of God has gone far adrift. Now sadly, America is no more than a dried branch severed from the fruitful Vine that provided enriched fitness and prodigious strength. The conduit of Living Water has been crushed, and soon that same branch will eventually fall to the barren ground. What once was a thriving tree of superior influence and efficacy is no longer of any God-fearing use. All that remains holy in America is a small flock of loyal saints keeping the passion of Christ aflame, thereby illuminating that darkened world closing in on every side of humanity.

Typically, most of us are interested in the daily weather conditions. We plan our weekends, parties, and various other celebrations around the climate. Today's weather forecasters have very sophisticated equipment that regularly informs the public of meteorological events such as wind, rain, or severe storms that may overshadow our social events. Thanks to modern technology, those warning signs help us prepare for severe conditions arising from a variety of unforeseen circumstances.

The Bible is significantly less hi-tech but patently futuristic and one hundred percent more factually accurate than any technical advancement we have to date. Many turbulent conditions were foretold by way of God's prophets. Some of those prophecies were for specific individuals, others for nations, but all were error-free. Everyone is curious about the future. Jesus Spoke clearly about the end-time events. The warning signs of future turmoil have been long established and well confirmed from the scriptural accounts of countless generations, many of whom suffered judgment from Almighty God for their rebellion. But the New Testament prediction given by Jesus in answer to His disciples' inquiry about the end times is the one all the world should be most concerned about today. *"When you hear of wars and insurrections, do not be terrified; for these things must take place first, but the end will not follow immediately." Then he said to them, "Nation will rise against nation, and kingdom against kingdom; there will be great earthquakes, and in various places famines and plagues; and there will be dreadful portents and great signs from heaven* (Luke 21:9–11, NRSVUE).

Has the Sovereign hand of judgment begun to press upon America and the world? Nation against nation is a familiar discipline in the Bible. Plagues, wars, drought, and famine are all indications of God's displeasure. There are many confirmed similarities taken from Scripture plainly revealing what happens to a nation in defiance of God. All of these circumstances in combination might be a reliable indication of much greater unrest to follow. It's time to stop all the foolish child's play. A make-believe Christian is no more a Christian than Satan himself. It's time to wake up and think critically! Open your eyes. Living a life in the flesh means that you are spiritually dead. You must seek the Lord while He may still be found, and His grace remains upon your life. The Words of the Lord Jesus are simple to understand and straightforward in the following Scripture. *And no one can be my disciple who does not carry his own cross and follow me* (Luke 14:27, TLB).

Jesus does not play games with words as some do today. What Jesus has to say is right to the point and final. The Proclamation from the mouth of our Lord has made His ordinances plainly understood by everyone who has ears to hear. Whoever does not regard Jesus as their Master is fooling themself by thinking their spirit-man is saved, when in all actuality, the insincere soul might spend eternal Life in the torrid lake of fire. Professing to be a Christian does not make you one. You must be spiritually transformed from the inside out. This kind of supernatural transformation is only consummated by God's will, and absolute fidelity to His will is vital. Jesus was Savior first, but after that, He became your Master. And now, being seated at the right hand of the Father, Jesus is the Christian's High Priest and Lord overall.

The Son of God gave us the pattern for righteous living. Every soul that is purchased and cleansed by the redeeming blood of Jesus no longer has proprietary rights over their life. Their absolute allegiance for all eternity must be to their Savior and Benefactor Jesus. To the reader, let me offer this prudent council from one of the unswerving champions of the Lord Jesus. From the author of thirteen books in the New Testament, Paul's elucidated epistle speaks indisputably, "Follow me as I follow Christ." The forerunner of Jesus was John the Baptist, exclaiming to all, "Prepare the way of the Lord." And a final thought from the highly favored woman who gave birth to Him. The woman who was there for Him in every circumstance of early life and by His side until the conclusion of His incarnation. But it was her words at the marriage feast that spoke prophetically. His mother said to the servants, "*Whatever He says to you, do it*" (John 2:5, NKJV). Mary's far-sighted words are likewise for the servants of Jesus today, tomorrow, and until the Lord returns for the second time.

The Bible must be revered as a living document. It's a chronicle of prudent practices and Commandments that are beneficial to all mankind regardless of era, belief, nationality, or the color of one's skin. When the mandates of the Lord are applied, there is harmony and tranquility among the people wherever they dwell. God's directives served our ancient brotherhood well in their day, and that same guiding light is especially suitable for us, their modern counterpart. However, when whole societies disregard God's directives, chaos will inevitably be the result.

Table of Contents

BOOK 1: Jesus: The Forsaken, Occasional Christ.........15
   Chapter 1 It's All for Jesus or All in Vain.............15
   Chapter 2 Religion or Relationship...................23
   Chapter 3 Reckless Assumption or Fatal Reckoning 35
   Chapter 4 Embrace the Price of Living Righteously.....45
   Chapter 5 Building a Life on the Immovable Rock 53
   Chapter 6 The Diminished Light of Eternal Life.......61
   Chapter 7 Hear the Lord Speaking...................71
   Chapter 8 Freedom Means Accountability............79
   Chapter 9 Acknowledge Your Need for the Savior 85
   Chapter 10 Two-Thousand Years of Warning.........93
   Part 2: Chapter 11 Plant Wisely, Harvest Bountifully...103
   Chapter 12 If the Truth Is Told....................111
   Chapter 13 The Facts of the Matter 117
   Chapter 14 The Incomparable Jesus 127
   Chapter 15 Will Your Sin Be Judged or Forgiven? 133
   Part 3: Chapter 16 Peril, Risk, or Refuge.............143
   Chapter 17 The Lamentable Sinking of America 153
   Chapter 18 Lies, Fearmongering, and Ineptitude 163
   Chapter 19 The Trojan Horse 169
   Chapter 20 You Are Naked, Exposed, and Vulnerable ..181
   Chapter 21 Stand Firm for What You Believe 191
   Chapter 22 The Deadly Dangers of Doubt and Delay ..201
   Chapter 23 From a High Horse to a High Calling.....213
   Part 4: Chapter 24 When God Chooses to Test Your
   Faith 219
   Chapter 25 Glorifying God in the Ashes of Life 225
   Chapter 26 Never Jump to Conclusions 233
   Chapter 27 Last Will and Testament 241
   Epilogue...251
BOOK 2: Fundamental Pillars of Honorable
Wholesomeness....................................255

Chapter 1 Pillar of Faith 257
Chapter 2 Pillar of Virtue 267
Chapter 3 Pillar of Knowledge 273
Chapter 4 Pillar of Self-Control 279
Chapter 5 Pillar of Patience. 283
Chapter 6 Pillar of Kindness 291
Chapter 7 Pillar of Love 299

Postscript. 309
Open your heart to God... 309
About the Author 311
Bibliography 313

BOOK 1:
Jesus:
The Forsaken,
Occasional Christ

Chapter 1

It's All for Jesus or All in Vain

Whether someone gave you this book as a gift or you chose to invest your own hard-earned money in this written work, I can only conclude that deep within you, there is a yearning for the candid truth of something that has long eluded you. Then be assured, God is fully aware of that yearning. Although I have no way of knowing what those thoughts might be, it's my hope to enlighten you in some small way. Or at least brighten your outlook for the future by shedding some light on the pathway to a more abundant life in the Lord Jesus.

Just as life is a journey, Christianity is a journey also, through a maze of twists and unexpected turns, high mountains to climb, and deep valleys to cross. The Christian lifestyle is often called a race—not because Christians are in competition with anyone. It's because there will be many different challenges, hurdles, deterrents, and trials to overcome in a predetermined period of time. It's not an easy road to travel. And no one reaches the finish line until God gives His approval or makes a sovereign decision on their behalf. *And let us not be weary in well doing: for in due season we shall reap if we faint not* (Galatians 6:9, KJV).

For those reasons and a great many more, most people do not

enter Christian life with the proper perspective. Therefore, let's get those undesirable obstacles right out in the open. Most so-called Christians have an entirely wrong concept of how a genuine, faithful Christian ought to live and contribute to the kingdom of God. Unfortunately, that's because there are too few confirmed Christians around to make a rightful comparison. Hopefully, you were made aware beforehand what would be the cost of becoming a follower of Christ. Most self-described Christians haven't a clue what it means to be a disciple of Jesus. And moreover, they don't have any desire to give their heart, soul, mind, and strength to God. Oh, sure, many people want to be seen as Christ's faithful followers, but they don't want to endure any of the discrimination, tribulation, or sacrifices that accompany the life of a dedicated disciple of the Savior Lord. Jesus told us, a servant is not greater than his Master. If they persecuted Him, they would persecute His followers as well (John 15:20).

Although the gift of salvation is free to anyone with enough faith to believe, there are still some minor strings attached. First, let us look at what's included in the package of salvation. The cleansing of all unrighteousness by the blood of Jesus. God no longer remembers your sins. Once justified, you are now the temple of the indwelling Spirit of God. You've received a new heart and have the mind of Christ. The Holy Spirit is your forever Guide throughout your period of sanctification. Hopefully, one day you will stand vindicated before your Father, Almighty God, and the Lord Jesus, completely glorified in your new imperishable body, eagerly awaiting life anew among the family of God in the heavenly kingdom for all eternity.

There is a necessary exchange however, but nothing that God hasn't prepared His child for. The Bible is God's instruction manual and spiritual guide to every believer's productivity. Without a comprehensive understanding of the Word, you are no more effective than a car without fuel. Let me explain. Suppose someone in your family knew that you wanted to be a veterinarian and paid for a full-ride scholarship on your behalf. But throughout that period of required study, your continued absenteeism, stubborn disinterest in study, lack of knowledge and fitness for the profession demonstrated your true incompetence. So, when it came time to graduate, the dean of the university couldn't write your name on a diploma because you failed to achieve the necessary proficiency. Without passing a few tests and mastering the subject, your name may remain on the student roster but never written on a diploma.

Offhand, I can't think of one occupation where you wouldn't be expected to perform in some capacity. Every job requires the use of your mind, mouth, or physicality. Being a Christian requires the use of all three, including your heart, to share the good news of the gospel of Christ. Every ambassador for Jesus Christ must offer Him their unreserved viability. And if necessary, it means walking away from everything and everyone that hinders, constrains the Word of God or their ability to live up to every Command set forth in the Bible. The Christian life is entirely sacrificial, loving, helping, and doing so without regard for recompense.

Then there are the worldly Christians. Those that are more concerned with material goods and the cares of this life rather than a spiritual existence. Most of those Christians have forgotten how to turn the other cheek (Matthew 5:39). They no longer forgive seventy times seven (Matthew 18:22). Many so-called believers disguise themselves among the brotherhood. They are seemingly the same as unwavering Christians, but they have no depth of Scripture, and so they don't live according to the gospel. They are carnal, living life on their own terms, not by the authority and will of God.

It's truly ironic that the very same people we are supposed to love and uphold before our heavenly Father are those we bicker with and seem to take umbrage the most. There is little agreement among the children of God concerning the Word of God. Can two journey together having separate destinations? (Amos 3:3) Church division is caused by deceptive actions and erroneous accounts of biblical Scripture. Too many Christians spend all their time fault-finding over irrelevant matters while the outside world watches and wants no part of what Christians have to offer.

The obvious problem today is the same problem as in Jesus' day. Christians wear the logo but do not personally honor the Word or their commitment to Christ. They may be fooling others, but God knows His children. Far too many Christians begin their pilgrimage with high expectations and great zeal, only to fizzle out at some point along their way to the eternal city. And therein lies the problem. People become weary when they don't receive an immediate pay-off or profit from their effort. This is especially true with Americans. Americans have been brought up to expect their due rewards straightaway. Flattery and honor, trophies for participating, bonuses from employers. But that's not how it works in God's kingdom. Christians lay up their treasures in heaven (Matthew 6:20).

God's chosen people, the Israelites, were thoroughly knowledgeable in the first five books of the Bible, the Jewish Torah. Although they knew the Law of Moses exceptionally well, they were nonetheless rebellious, failing to act in accordance with God's instructions. That's far from the case with Christians in America. We have been spoiled to the point of laziness. Our Bibles are lying around everywhere, and most Christians haven't a clue what's written in them. Why? Very simply because they haven't taken the time to read Scripture. They don't know what God's Word says. Knowledge is power. Take anything you purchase for example. When you bypass the directions, you miss out on the particulars concerning safety, operating procedures, and guarantees. The Bible isn't any different. Therefore, if you haven't made any effort to read the Creator's blueprint, rules, and requirements that guide life's journey, how then can you expect to operate in a manner that is suitable to God and beneficial to your spiritual health and longevity? Furthermore, think of all God's promises you'll forfeit.

Third-world nations can't get enough Bibles. Often whole communities must share a single Bible among many families. I once heard of an underground situation where single pages were torn from a Bible and passed around for the spiritually thirsty citizens who were passionate to learn God's Word. But here in America, the nation supposedly under God's sovereign direction, there are far too many unopened Bibles. That is unless someone remembers to bring a Bible to church on Sunday to show others how devout they are. Jesus had a name for the Pharisees who behaved in the very same way. He called them white-washed tombs. They were sanctimonious hypocrites. Their public appearance was irreproachable, although no more than a staged performance. Inside, they were rotten and stinking.

Therefore, since we are surrounded by so great a cloud of witnesses, let us also lay aside every weight, and sin which clings so closely, and let us run with endurance the race that is set before us (Hebrews 12:1, ESV). Just for the sake of clarity, the cloud of witnesses mentioned in the preceding Scripture are all those beautiful, God-adorning saints documented in the Bible. Each of them ran their race obediently and faithfully without quitting, enduring every hardship until they finished their race. Those were the valiant souls that crossed the finish line, thus proving their loyalty to God and, consequently, their worthiness and suitability for entry into the kingdom of heaven.

What is the message in Hebrews 12:1? First, we must take notice of the two hindrances that will encumber the runner. There is weight, and there is sin. Excess weight is another way of interpreting the many worldly distresses that slow or impede our race. Look in your backpack and see what's there. Worry, shame, guilt, sorrow, stress, et cetera. They all represent unnecessary impediments. Then there is the additional burden of sin. Those are the sins that offend the Lord. Those immoral acts that He forbids. Moreover, there are other sins, somewhat more indistinct. They are various in nature. They might be certain acts that you know should be performed, but you've been deficient in your responsibility to care for them. All those additional worldly cares heaped upon a Christian put the runner at a severe disadvantage. Jesus Said, His burden is light (Matthew 11:30). We are to leave the weight of this world at the feet of Jesus, pick up our cross, and follow Him.

Everyone having received Jesus as Savior and Lord, should be aware of their starting line and objective. It is the first step in the spiritual race to secure the crown of victory in the kingdom of God. However, what is unknown to us, is where we are positioned during the race or what obstacles we might encounter along the way. Or, even more importantly, where our finish line is.

God makes it very clear that each one of us is running our own faith-based race and at our own pace. How other runners run their race has no effect on your race or the position that you hold. Therefore, it must be understood that there is no competition or rivalry among believers. Children of God are not in competition with each other. Nevertheless, it is still a race. The reason this journey is called a race is because there is a Timekeeper involved. The objective is to finish your race before the specified time runs out. And that moment is determined according to the Timekeeper exclusively. Consequently, it is essential to keep a competitive edge. Everyone must understand that their "soul" objective is to reach the finish line, completing the race before time expires.

Suppose the Lord gave you a gift on your twelfth birthday. Upon opening it, you were surprised to see a video of your potential future from beginning to end. Maybe there would be parts of that video you would prefer to do differently. Or suppose God gave you a glimpse of an hourglass that measured your time of life with grains of sand in the top half of the timepiece. How often would you wonder about the number of grains remaining? Would it have any effect on how you utilize the days of your life?

Life is like the morning fog, only around for a little while. Our very existence is a fragile mystery, and each of us must prepare ourselves for the inevitable. Everyone's time will eventually run out. None of us can afford to waste any of those precious moments. We may not have tomorrow. We may not even have the next hour. If any of us knew in advance what the future held, we might very well decide to live our life a whole lot differently. Time is invaluable, and every soul is worth whatever sacrifice must be surrendered to secure a place in heaven for all eternity.

So, besides understanding the importance of eliminating sin and the excess weight of the world and the encumbrances they incur, there is another element just as important: the pathway, or track, upon which a Christian is running. There will be many different avenues along the route to the finish line. Twists, turns, short-cuts leading to dead ends, and many other obstacles and hindrances to delay one's victory. It's almost as though Satan has studied our habits and knows exactly the right signs to post, tantalizing our curiosity, tempting us into taking an alternative route. The devil will do whatever it takes to detour God's children away from success in life, thereby robbing them of the heavenly afterlife that God has promised those that belong to Him. There is only one sure way to paradise. Take the straight narrow road and stay on it the entire distance. Don't step off to the right or the left. That could impede your destination. Don't be misled into taking the wide road that everyone else is on. That may be the scenic path, but it will only lead to sorrow and destruction.

Chapter 2

Religion or Relationship

You may be surprised to know that many believers don't honestly know the difference between being religious and having a relationship with God the heavenly Father, His beloved Son, Jesus, and the Holy Spirit. Many so-called believers today are confused about how church and God are distinct. They are often under the mistaken impression that their involvement with a particular church affiliation fulfills their claim to Christianity. Those are the souls who can't seem to differentiate between the two kingdoms. The earthly kingdom where the flesh dwells and the heavenly kingdom where Christians are citizens. God wants us to take a personal interest in the influential works of the Bible. It is a how-to manual for Christian living. The Holy Spirit communicates with His children while they ruminate over Scripture. Like an onion, there are layers and layers of ever deeper cognition when Christians invest their time in the Word. Only then will faithful Christians begin to recognize the immensity of the Lord's sacrifice on their behalf. And just as importantly, the emphasis and actualization that Jesus is the Master of your soul and Lord of all. And with that understanding, the believer becomes ever increasingly obedient. Works and church programs have their role, but nothing replaces that One-on-one devotion to God while in His presence learning Scripture, quietly meditating on His Word, and speaking praises to Him in heartfelt prayer.

This might be a good time to explain the difference between the manner of churches. In the Christian religion, the church is described as the body of Christ. Therefore, the body of Christ is made up of His believers. Those are the born-again, faithful followers of the Savior Jesus. The Lord Jesus deserves reverent and sincere veneration for the essential and unparalleled love gift He provided for the salvation of sinners. With the next two Scriptures, let me explain the difference between our holy God and a place of worship. *In the beginning was the Word, and the Word was with God, and the Word was God* (John 1:1, NKJV). *And the Word became flesh and dwelt among us, and we beheld His glory as of the only begotten of the Father, full of grace and truth* (John 1:14, NKJV). Both Scriptures refer to Jesus, the Word at the beginning of creation, and the Second Member of the Trinity. After which God's only begotten Son, Jesus, came as a Babe in the Flesh of a Human, God incarnate. The house of God, also commonly referred to as the church, is the building where mortals meet to worship Almighty God. But a church is merely a building where the saints of God congregate to extol the Lord, study Scripture, and celebrate other marked occasions. But first and foremost, as in the Words of Jesus Himself, it's a house of prayer. *And He said to them, "It is written, 'My house shall be called a house of prayer,' but you have made it a 'den of thieves'"* (Matthew 21:13, NKJV).

In the very ancient past, church was referred to as the tent of meeting, where God and man met together in a dedicated place. That union between God and man was completely different than how the church functions today. But never forget, it was the new covenant made manifest by the sacrifice of Jesus upon the cross that allowed God and man to be reconciled in the first place. Upon the death of Jesus, the veil of the Holy of Holies that separated God from sinful man was torn in two from top to bottom. It was the death of Jesus that made harmony possible between the Almighty Creator and mankind.

Whenever or wherever Christians gather in the Name of the Lord, He unites with them. *For where two or three are gathered together in My name, I am there in the midst of them"* (Matthew 18:20, NKJV). All authentic believers are temples of the living God. So, when believers come together, the Holy Spirit is right there among them. The Lord's Day is a time to offer praise and thanksgiving for all God has done for us. We joyfully praise God and honor Him for His grace, His forgiveness, and kind mercy offered new every morning. Each soul has its own reason for glorifying God. This can be done in any number of ways. When believers want to exalt the Lord God Almighty, there are no hard and fast rules. Sincere praises and adoration from the heart are pleasing to God, along with acclamation in song, music, and prayer. Homage to God may also be done by offering the Lord a portion of the prosperity He's blessed us with. This helps greatly advance the kingdom of God in many additional ways.

Other forms of worship are humility, obedience to the Word, testifying of God's goodness, and giving sacrificially to the kingdom of God. When seeking His wisdom, we profess our humility and desire to be led in a proper and advantageous direction day by day. But gathering as a family unto God on the Lord's Day is special. There is an additional benefit when we assemble with like-minded, consecrated Christians. Disciples of Christ can share in one another's joy as well as their sorrow. No one ever feels alone when they are surrounded by the love of God through His many children.

I remember a time long ago when churches were never closed. Back then, appointments with clergy were seldom necessary. The church was a sanctuary, and a seeker knew instinctively that the Lord would be there, and God didn't disappoint. God's divine presence was felt immediately upon opening the church door. But it isn't that way anymore. The church doors are locked tight. They are no longer ordinary, modest little places of worship. Megachurches have edged them out in favor of a more sophisticated and opulent alternative. And of course, those buildings must be secured. Whereas, at one time, a repentant thief might feel led to enter God's house of prayer, eager to amend for his sins. Discarding his filthy rags at the altar, he leaves justified. But times have changed. Now with all the grandeur, a thief might presume that it's far more lucrative to break in and steal than to confess his sins.

Regardless, never let it be said that God wastes any opportunity to interact with the children of earth. He is an ever-present Help in times of trouble. As a matter of fact, He Said just that. *He shall call upon Me, and I will answer him; I will be with him in trouble; I will deliver him and honor him* (Psalm 91:15, NKJV). *Come unto me, all ye that labour and are heavy laden, and I will* give you rest (Matthew 11:28, KJV). If anyone is looking for God, they don't have to find a church to meet with Him. The Lord is sympathetic, and His hand is always extended. God isn't a far-away out in the Cosmos God. He is always near and listening, waiting to hear the faintest whisper calling His Name. The Lord is ever faithful and ready to respond to every sincere prayer of those who are hurting and heavily burdened.

I AM is God's Name. God of the present, here and now. He is your answer. He will meet you right where you are. He is your peace in life's storms. God is your place of refuge at all times. He will be your hiding place in the cleft of the rock when you need a place of safety. The Lord Jesus is a secure Haven for all who are weary. He is an attentive Listener, always ready to commune with you privately. There is nothing or no one better able than Almighty God to change people and situations. It is only when you come into the presents of God and lay your heart at His feet that you will leave forever changed. Jesus is the Altar of love, a love that you've never known before. It is there you can surrender to Jesus and open your heart seeking absolution from Christ for your sins.

The Lord Jesus will cleanse you and remove your old heart burdened with sin, wickedness, and disgrace. Then the Lord will give you a new heart dedicated to the tenets of the kingdom of God. You are then born a new creation in Christ. The following Scripture defines the beginning of God's desired relationship with a repentant sinner. *And I will give you a new heart, and I will put a new spirit in you. I will take out your stony, stubborn heart and give you a tender, responsive heart* (Ezekiel 36:26, NLT).

The faithful apostles of God had only just begun their relationship with Jesus when in no time, He was gone from their midst. Nevertheless, He had entrusted them with bringing the good news into various communities and planting the new religious order, eventually known as the church of God. We have only a small measure of knowledge with respect to the hostility and persecution Jesus' apostles had to endure at the beginning throws of Christianity. It's true that Christ's death on the cross opened the Holy of Holies to new religious freedom, peace, and brotherhood with a gracious offer of eternal Life. But in the initial stages, that new amnesty seemed strangely contradictory to the long-established Law of Moses and altogether reprehensible to the Jews who favored their traditional customs. The effect of the cross may have been instantaneous, but there was a certain period necessary to complete the phase from the old law into the new dispensation of liberty. And serious disputing often surfaced because of the new liberal doctrine. Many times, the disciples were treated poorly or with outright hostility. Other times, the new believers were eager to repent of their sins and be baptized in the Name of the Father, Son, and Holy Ghost.

At first, a small circle of Christians was able to gather in homes, but when the fellowship began to grow exponentially, they were forced to move into larger quarters. Since the apostle Paul was responsible for many of the church plantings, he felt it necessary to occasionally oversee their spiritual direction and proper development. Therefore, thirteen of Paul's epistles were canonized and added to the New Testament.

Keep in mind the early churches were dependent upon spirit-filled, insightful men for divine clarification, understanding, and correction. Those were men like Paul and Barnabas, both influential disciples of Jesus. At other times it was necessary to solve any hostility or fall-out among the different religious sects of the day. Building the early kingdom of God was a serious undertaking. There were times when a difference of opinion would cause a severe clash in ideology. Those same issues are with us still. And still there is no room for ideology in God's doctrine.

On one particular occasion, Barnabas took a young relative named John Mark under his wing, hoping he would be of assistance to them on their missionary journey. Barnabas probably thought it would benefit the young man spiritually, as well as lending the men an extra pair of hands to help with various assignments. Having the opportunity to learn from those seasoned veterans was invaluable. But evidently, the young apprentice hadn't yet acquired the zeal for all the necessary hard work required or wasn't committed enough to responsibly continue in his role. As a result, at one point along the journey, John Mark simply left their company without advance notice or explanation. John Mark's broken fellowship put a hindrance between Paul and Barnabas. On their next missionary journey, Barnabas was willing to give John Mark another chance to prove himself worthy, but Paul was emphatically against the idea. *Now Barnabas was determined to take with them John called Mark. But Paul insisted that they should not take with them the one who had departed from them in Pamphylia, and had not gone with them to the work* (Acts 15:37–38, NKJV).

There are many logical justifications to guard against the frequent preferential treatment of our relatives. When Barnabas insisted on taking John Mark on their next pilgrimage, it caused a serious disagreement between Paul and Barnabas. Paul thought better of it because of the way John Mark had completely betrayed their trust. Paul was adamant and refused to allow the young man to accompany them on their next mission. After an exchange of incompatible views, the two men resolved the situation amicably and went their separate ways. In any event, time and forgiveness have a way of healing old offenses. On one subsequent occasion, John Mark indeed proved himself responsible and worthy, becoming an asset to Paul in later years. And it is commendable to note that not only did John Mark mature in his calling, but he also went on to author the book of Mark in the New Testament.

It's vitally important to be conscious of the impatient motivation in a newborn believer. The early stages of a Christian's walk are critical to an everlasting fellowship with the Savior and Lord. Just as any baby direct from the womb needs milk for nourishment, so does every baby Christian. They are tender and should be nourished in the milk of Scripture. In other words, starting at an elementary level. Later, they will be able to cut their teeth on the meatier or more formal Scripture.

When it comes to immature Christians, regardless of age, there is one important aspect to be cautious of. The jubilation that goes along with conversion is totally vivacious. Their enthusiasm is delightful, and it should never be dampened. However, in their newfound zeal, an undeveloped believer may want to take on a role or responsibility that they aren't yet qualified to handle. This isn't meant to discourage anyone from following God's chosen direction for their life or ministry. But discovering one's aptitude and gifting may take a little time to develop. Allowing a young Christian to go off ill-prepared might possibly bring discouragement and conceivably extinguish their enthusiasm permanently. Spending ample time in the Word and submitting to a subordinate role will ripen their fruit in due season. *Seek the Kingdom of God above all else, and live righteously, and he will give you everything you need* (Matthew 6:33, NLT).

Having a promise like that from God, you can be absolutely one-hundred percent sure that He will deliver! Notice the words used there. Not maybe—He Said He would. Not some things—everything. But that is a qualifying statement. You must do what God expects of you. You must, above all else, seek the kingdom of God. That is in reference to learning about God and understanding God's order of rule through the Scriptures. It's all part of developing a solid relationship with the Lord. You must be obedient and live righteously. Not according to society's standards, but God's standard. And you can rejoice in the knowledge that you will never be on this journey alone. The Lord has given you His Holy Spirit to prosper you along the way. Think of lessons from the Bible in terms of instructional training from the best spiritual Coach possible.

At the time you began your public education, you no doubt started at the rudimentary level, preschool or kindergarten. Before the Covid years, every day, five days a week, you went there to study and learn. You repeated that schedule year after year, growing in knowledge and wisdom. It was an indoctrination in mental and social development. You hammered the books every day, and after years of dedication, you had accumulated a competent understanding of the subject matter. By the time you graduated from high school, your years of academic support had provided you with a wealth of comprehension.

Oh, how very high-minded we are today compared to the historical beginnings of the fundamental church. How foolish to think we can be a part of something we know nothing about. If you are taking your cues from the church or your fellowship, then check everything against Scripture. Too many churches have gotten off course by looking to the world's standards for imagined success. God's facts are indisputable. Unfortunately, one of the primary reasons that many Christians are reluctant to share their faith with non-believers is timidity due to a lack of Scriptural knowledge. In other words, no time spent studying the Bible to learn about your Father's business. Jesus was never at a loss for Words. Whatever the occasion, His answers were scripturally flawless. Had the disciples of Jesus done nothing more than hand out paper leaflets announcing the Messiah's arrival, there wouldn't be a church. It takes face-to-face boldness to confront Satan and those under his demonic influence.

As Christians, we are not only to develop and maintain an ongoing relationship with our God but with the family of Christ. Our responsibility is to snatch unbelievers from the clutches of Satan and add them to the kingdom daily. That may require a few risks. We must have confidence in the Lord's message to save the lost by turning them from darkness to the light of truth. But that isn't a job for the faint-hearted. God wants us to show courage. The Lord provides everything else that the situation might require. Suppose one day you come across someone asking you a serious question about God, heaven, or the Bible. Are you just going to hand them a tract? Every Christian is required to explain the hope within them. The odds are great that God will arrange such a divine encounter just to test your faith.

Any such encounter could be a critical period in the life of a serious seeker. The truth could mean the difference between life and death. It's not for us to know, just to share what we know. Whenever asked, Christians must always be prepared to give solid biblical information. If more wholehearted Christians were better equipped scripturally, they wouldn't stammer or struggle in terror at some of the doubts spewed by infidels. Are you well equipped to be the planter, the waterer, or the reaper? It's the Christian's calling to be prepared for each of those events. *But dedicate your lives to Christ as Lord. Always be ready to defend your confidence in God when anyone asks you to explain it. However, make your defense with gentleness and respect* (1 Peter 3:15, GW).

And then, of course, there are the spoilers. They're the ones who want to argue and frustrate your cause for Christ. They have no idea that you're trying to save their soul. They are either clueless or don't care that their eternal soul is literally hanging in the balance. They could care less what you have to say. They only want to debate the issue. They'll do whatever it takes to keep your message from hitting its target. You may not win the spiritual battle over their soul that day, but nonetheless, they, unfortunately, are the biggest losers. Regardless, never let their rejection of your message be a deterrent. They have not rejected you; they have rejected Christ. But a least you had an opportunity to plant a seed. *And wherever they do not receive you, when you leave that town shake off the dust from your feet as a testimony against them*" (Luke 9:5, RSV).

Every one that is of the age of consent will likely have had several opportunities to make peace with God before death. No Christian standing before the throne of God in heaven will be judged in a manner apart from God's code of ethics. Christians must never forget that God is just. God's standard of justification is based upon His supreme definitive principles of incorruptible equity. *But he who did not know, yet committed things deserving of stripes, shall be beaten with few. For everyone to whom much is given, from him much will be required; and to whom much has been committed, of him they will ask the more* (Luke 12:48, NKJV).

And having said all that, I have this to add. Every Christian should conduct themselves toward others as the preeminent example left to us by Jesus. *But if a person isn't loving and kind, it shows that he doesn't know God—for God is love* (1 John 4:8, TLB). There are limitless ways to show love. Caring, warmth, compassion, friendship, goodwill, and sympathy. Sometimes just listening is love. These are all relationship builders. Every Christian is an ambassador of our Lord Jesus. Christians represent Him and His tenets. Pastors and teachers must repeatedly encourage their congregation to enrich their personal knowledge of the Word of God so they are fully equipped to build spiritual relationships out in the dark world. A Bible in the hands of a sincere Christian is like being at the feet of the Rock of Ages. A Bible in the hands of a mature Christian is a sword and shield well prepared for spiritual warfare if necessary. There is no lack of edification in Scripture. There are no dead-ends or cul-de-sacs in the Bible. The deeper you dig in the Word, the more spiritually prosperous you will become. The church is secondary to the Lord. Seek ye first the kingdom of God, and He will provide all the things you will ever need in this lifetime (Matthew 6:33).

Don't expect your pastor to be able to teach you everything you need to know in one short visit to the church on Sunday morning. Furthermore, every Christian is personally responsible for being familiar with the contents of the Bible. *As for you, the anointing you received from him remains in you, and you do not need anyone to teach you. But as his anointing teaches you about all things and as that anointing is real, not counterfeit—just as it has taught you, remain in him* (1 John 2:27, NIV).

Dust off your Bible and set your mind toward serious learning. The Holy Spirit is your Helper; He will teach you and assist you in the deeper concerns of God. Then, should you need some additional clarification about a particular subject, your pastor would be delighted to expound the doctrine for your understanding. That's what he's there for. He will also be highly impressed that you are cultivating Scriptures on your own time. Furthermore, if he is at a loss to enlighten you on a particular matter, he too will have to do a little additional research for his own personal edification.

One of apostle Paul's duties in the early church was to help qualified church leaders to continue in the faith of Jesus Christ. That is what the apostolic movement was designed to do. As a result of Paul's ministry, mature leaders and elders sprang up far and wide, becoming the continued lifeblood of the church. The same principle applies in our modern churches everywhere. Paul was all business but very charismatic; he knew exactly how to reach the lost and equip believers to carry the mantle of life; thereby sharing the good news with everyone throughout the land.

Among church leaders, the apostle Paul was greatly admired, and popularity is no different in churches today. Believers have their preferences in leadership. A congregation will become very devoted to their pastor and often depend on him for almost everything. Parishioners often run to their pastor for all their prayer concerns, counseling, encouragement, and direction. Sometimes unknowledgeable Christians will even stretch the limits of what is considered spiritual. Then there comes a point where a pastor could become a crutch to such a dependent believer, one who refuses to grow up spiritually and equip themselves in the practical wisdom of the Bible.

Sunday sermons can be another limitation to the immature Christian. If you think that your pastor is capable of teaching you everything that you need to learn from the Bible, think again. That's not even a realistic possibility. No preacher alive has exhausted the layers of wisdom within the pages of the living Word of God. That is like comparing our finite mind to the infinite mind of God. But even if someone went to a church service three times a week for an entire year, it's still only one-hundred and fifty-six lessons. That's a mere drop in the bucket compared to what God wants you to learn. Besides that, the Lord may have specific things that He wants to instill in your life. And those specified details may only be revealed in a private devotion between you and God. Open the

Bread of Life and drink of the Living Water. It will greatly deepen your relationship with the Lord.

Don't stop attending church. And don't stop learning when you exit the church door. Build upon the solid leadership of an evangelical pastor. Study your Bible. You'll be amazed at how the Word can change your life. *Work hard so God can say to you, "Well done." Be a good workman, one who does not need to be ashamed when God examines your work. Know what his Word says and means* (2 Timothy 2:15, TLB).

The bottom line is that if you're a Christian, your entire spiritual dependence should be focused firstly upon your relationship with the Lord. Jesus is our High Priest, and only the Lord knows your heart, your needs, and your fears. He will direct your path and help you conquer any shortcomings that may be holding you back from achieving your spiritual goals. Whatever investment you make in God, He will compound that investment in you. You won't believe how fast the spiritual man in you will develop.

The Divine One wants to spend intimate time with His child. He is your Father. He doesn't always want to address you through a third party. Think of it from any parent's perspective. There are probably occasions when you just want a few precious moments alone with the one you parent. It is no different with God. Offer the Lord the first fruits of your day. *I must work the works of Him who sent Me while it is day; the night is coming when no one can work* (John 9:4, NKJV).

Chapter 3

Reckless Assumption or Fatal Reckoning

When giving a little child instruction, should that youngster then be allowed to demand an explanation from their parent? Not if they've been taught to trust and respect the wisdom and guidance of the guardian overseeing their care. A responsible parent will set up certain parameters wherein a child is expected to grow and function developmentally. Using that same analogy is like comparing the mind of our infinite God to the finite mind of man. The Almighty needn't justify Himself additionally to His creation. I use the word additionally because we've already been given a complete reference guide and instruction manual. It's called the inspired Word of God, customarily referred to as the Holy Bible. Everything we need to know is written therein. God made His principles to live by very clear. The criterion for the circumspect, along with the final consequence for rebellious behavior, has all been put in black and white. The passionate love of the Lord is indelibly written for the well-being of God's beloved creation.

However, there could be times when even the most seasoned Christian may sometimes have difficulty understanding the correct meaning of Scripture and the sovereignty of God. That's why it is imperative to rely on the Holy Ghost. He is every Christian's Helper, Teacher, and Comforter. Everyone who lives is going to experience trials, hardships, and sorrow. Sometimes people invite their own unhappiness. At other times, although no invitation was extended, sorrow showed up at their house anyway.

Oftentimes life can be very unpredictable. Therefore, it is prudent to prepare beforehand, especially when we've been given advance notice to expect the unpredictable. Obviously, it's impossible to avoid every catastrophe, but a state of preparedness is nonetheless comforting. How that might look is dependent on who or what you put your faith in. Is it bars on your windows?

Maybe it's a bunker and a variety of firearms. But then, I suppose it just depends on what it is that you're afraid of.

With few exceptions, much of the pandemonium that has distressed other nations worldwide has eluded America until recently. Other nations all over the world have dealt with recurrent violence and civil disobedience on a somewhat routine basis. But now, throughout our own homeland, there appears to be an abnormal escalation of unusual kinds of sin, violence, and fervid unrest, the likes of which many of us have never seen before. The current intensity of Satan's demonic activity leaves very little doubt as to where this malevolent direction will eventually take us.

Not only does God say man's ways are foolish, but He adds a guaranteed admonishment. *For the wisdom of this world is foolishness to God. As it says in the book of Job, God uses man's own brilliance to trap him; he stumbles over his own "wisdom" and falls* (1 Corinthians 3:19, TLB). This puts me in mind of man's futile attempt to correct the effects of what is commonly referred to as global warming. There is little doubt that global warming can indeed be attributed to mankind's negligent use of God's benevolent resources. But the real undeniable cause isn't named on any government list of dangers to the planet. It's greed! Moreover, the escalating weather conditions and other harsh phenomena are a direct result of man's rebellion against his Creator and Benefactor. God's hand is at work in the drought and fires. He makes use of the tornados, floods, and severe winter storms to get the attention of man. Those events may only seem to be innately coincidental. God uses the little things to confound the wise, even if it's the elements of nature. Judging by the viral pestilence, chaos, lawlessness, and unpredictable atmospheric conditions, it's all too obvious that God's peace and goodwill toward man have waned. Adding to that, it certainly looks as though America may have exhausted her final days of tranquility. If God hasn't already turned His face from our nation, at the rate sin is escalating, it won't be long before He does. If there is anyone foolish enough to argue the point, may heaven help them.

When God determined it was time to move His people from the wilderness toward the Promised Land, they broke camp and closely yielded to the Lord's directives. Their choices were limited. Remain in the desolate wilderness and suffer the consequences or accompany God into their promised paradise. Don't think for one moment that our choice is any different than theirs. It's either go with God or be left behind. It's time to get serious about the redemption of your soul. Can anyone honestly say they would sooner stay behind during the tribulation rather than meet the Lord Jesus in the air when the trumpet sounds?

There is only one thing that stands in the way of this world's reprehensible judgment. It's the faithful saints of God. God's committed church remains obedient in its continued effort to win the lost, liberate the captives, and rescue the dying. Who can say how much time there is left to complete God's work? When the Lord finally decides to remove His shield of protection, there is no other safeguard for the unregenerate people of earth. Those who rejected the Lord Jesus will be subjugated by Satan.

Sadly, even in these dark days of disgrace, most messages from the pulpit today are shallow and entirely without any vertical direction or authoritative council based on Bible passages. As of late, preaching has become distorted, watered down, and in many cases, in direct opposition to the inerrant truth of God. All too often, rather than expounding the in-depth truth and meaning of Scripture, pastors rely on a three-point presentation authored by someone other than God. Their focus is on humor and theological accounts purchased from preprinted publications that instruct pastors in the fine art of keeping their spectators entertained. Rather than infusing the faithful with spiritual strength and vigor, their parishioners leave the church empty and disillusioned. Their heads filled with nothing more than lighthearted anecdotes, substandard principles, and philosophical opinions. God's children hunger for the gospel truth; Words to satisfy their need for spiritual food, the Bread of Life, and a drink of revitalizing Living Water. Not feigned preaching that is void of the power of the Holy Spirit. God expects

His people to be nourished on His invigorating Words of Life, not shallow concepts... *for everyone who lives on milk is unskilled in the word of righteousness, since he is a child. But solid food is for the mature, for those who have their powers of discernment trained by constant practice to distinguish good from evil* (Hebrews 5:13–14, ESV).

Has your preacher been called by God to be the under-shepherd of your church? Or is he just another dime-a-dozen charismatic hireling? Here is a valuable word that every parishioner needs to put into their vocabulary. The word is *hermeneutics*. That is the rightful method of Scripture interpretation. Every Sunday, when you leave the church, you should have learned some meaningful insight from a passage of Scripture that you never knew before. When a preacher is expounding systematically throughout the Bible, it's to help the hearer understand and know how to incorporate that knowledge into daily life. Preachers today could take a lesson from the apostle Paul. *With great confidence and with no hindrance, he proclaimed the kingdom of God and taught about the ultimate authority—the Lord Jesus, God's Anointed, the Liberating King* (Acts 28:31, VOICE). All Christians, new believers as well as seasoned followers, should be continually learning, gaining greater insight, and always delving deeper into the knowledge and character of God.

If you truly want to experience the mighty power of the living God, then He must be emphasized and magnified through His Word. Christians don't go to church to hear about how great the pastor is. We want to hear how great the Lord Jesus is. There is no spiritual benefit or fruit if God's Word isn't being read and carefully explained. If your preacher isn't doing that, then he is not properly shepherding the flock of God. Just preaching morality is pompous and erroneous. In every evangelical church service, the Word of God should be read aloud, and the explanation be clearly expressed. If the Word of God isn't given preeminence and taught thoroughly and properly explained, then it's time to find a pastor that exalts God's Word and venerates the Lord Jesus, the High Priest over the church. After all, worshiping the Savior Jesus is why you went to church in the first place. Therefore, glorifying

God should be the entire focus throughout the service.

Too many souls are dying without a proper understanding of doctrine. Preachers must stop mollycoddling God's congregation and use the specifics of written Scripture, just as Jesus did. It's time for preachers to get down to the Father's business of instruction. The people need to hear how to receive eternal salvation and live spiritually victorious. There's no time to lose; these are the last of the final days. There is nothing pretty about sin and what sin has done in the lives of mankind the world over for centuries. It's more important now than ever before to know what the Word of God says about sin and how the Lord intends to deal with unrepentant sinners, those who habitually practice sin. Preachers need to stop worrying about their popularity, personal prosperity, and headcount on Sunday. It's time to be explicit—not tolerant when dealing with man's abhorrent sin in today's liberal society. Instead of trying to run the church like any other business that passively caters to the public, return to the definitive authority, the Word of the Almighty Father and Lord Jesus. The church belongs to Him, and He Declared it His house of prayer. *And the Spirit said to Philip, "Go over and join this chariot." So Philip ran to him and heard him reading Isaiah the prophet and asked, "Do you understand what you are reading?" And he said, "How can I, unless someone guides me?" And he invited Philip to come up and sit with him* (Acts 8:29–31, ESV). What exactly does that Scripture tell us? The full story in Scripture lets us know that this man was a sinner showing sincere interest in learning the way of salvation. How many people are like that man, thirsty to hear the refreshing truth explained to them in a clear and decisive way? The Holy Spirit wants everyone not only to hear His message but understand how to make personal application of the Word's precise intent. If you don't understand those things, then how can you expect to be sanctified and live a life holy and pleasing to the Lord?

God never does anything without informing His people first. But don't expect a new revelation through some self-appointed prophet. There is no need for God to use a prophet when He has already warned us of the approaching and unalterable climax to our present way of life. The Day of the Lord will come like a thief in the night. There is no need for God to repeat His warning. It's confirmed through His Word (1 Thessalonians 5:2). Therefore, it's our responsibility to be ready. Ready for what? Ready for the return of Jesus, the King of kings.

My friend, we are living very near the last chapters in the Bible. Soon Jesus will return as King to pass judgment on earth and all its remaining inhabitants. That isn't going to be a social call. The Lord is coming to pronounce retribution on the entire world. Take some earnest interest in the future of your soul. Don't let the Lord find you sleeping. There are two passages in the Bible that speak poignantly concerning the sleeping servants of God. The first story can be found in the book of Matthew.

There were ten bridesmaids awaiting to greet the bridegroom on his arrival at the marriage feast. Five of the ladies were smart enough to anticipate the possible late arrival of the groom. Therefore, they filled their lamps fully with oil. Unfortunately, the other five ladies were foolish and far less concerned about the time. And so they neglected to fill their lamps. Sure enough, the bridegroom was delayed, and all the waiting ladies fell asleep.

Then suddenly, they were all awakened by a shout: "Go and welcome the arrival of the bridegroom!" But the lanterns of the five unprepared ladies had burnt out. Then they asked to borrow some oil from those who were prepared. "Sorry," they replied, "we haven't enough to share; go and buy oil for yourselves." While the unprepared bridesmaids went shopping for oil, the bridegroom arrived and invited the prepared ladies to accompany him to the marriage feast. Then the door was shut tight and locked. Sometime later, the other five ladies returned but found that they were forbidden from entering the wedding celebration. They stood outside knocking and calling, asking to enter, but the answer that came forth was, "Go away, you are too late!"

Here is another heedless incident from the book of Mark. It is even more shameful. It was the night of Jesus' arrest. Peter, James, and John accompanied Jesus to the Mount of Olives after the Passover meal. Jesus knew what lay ahead in only a matter of hours, and His heart was in torment. Jesus was immensely sorrowful and asked His disciples to be seated and keep watch while He went to pray privately. Jesus was in such agony that He began to sweat great drops of blood. His extreme physical and mental suffering wasn't entirely self-directed; Jesus was concerned for Peter and the others that He was leaving behind. When Jesus returned to His disciples, He found them sleeping. He then specifically instructed Peter to watch and pray for strength against temptation. Jesus knew the devil was out to destroy Peter if it were possible. Upon returning the second and third time, the result was the same. His closest companions were found soundly sleeping. Jesus Declared, "The spirit is willing, but the flesh is weak." Jesus was trying to caution Peter to be prepared for what was coming next. Peter didn't heed the warning and indeed fell headlong into temptation. The Bible is full of wisdom and strategies to defeat the enemy of our soul. But even all the wisdom of Solomon didn't help him, and it won't help anyone if they don't avail themselves of it.

One final thought on the inattentiveness of Christians. We already know through the Covid-19 experience of 2020–21 that the states were working hard in conjunction with Satan to shut down every church in America. With additional variants on the rise, who's to say the authorities won't try it again in the year 2022 or beyond. The devil is trying harder than ever before to succeed in hindering the work of God. And, if his strategies were to triumph, then where will the people turn? Who will they turn to? Censorship is already out of control, then where will you be? If the government can shut the church doors, it can pull the plug on the inspirational networks just as easily.

Stop depending entirely on others to teach you the Bible. It's time to be self-reliant. Learn for yourself what is written in Scripture! First John 2:27 (ESV) bears repeating. *But the anointing that you received from him abides in you, and you have no need that anyone should teach you. But as his anointing teaches you about everything and is true, and is no lie—just as it has taught you, abide in him.*

Have enough faith in God to open your Bible and ask for the Lord's help. Don't just sit there staring at the Words on the page. Ask God to help you to understand the things that He wants you to know. Those are the prayers He responds to. What does it mean to pray? It simply means having a natural dialogue with God. Being honest about what is on your heart. If you want God to hear your prayers, you must immediately stop any sin that you're involved in. Sin is anything in any form or degree of immorality, evil notions, or expressed conduct that God is against.

The Lord God directs us to the solution of our despair. *if My people who are called by My name will humble themselves, and pray and seek My face, and turn from their wicked ways, then I will hear from heaven, and will forgive their sin and heal their land* (2 Chronicles 7:14, NKJV).

Christians who are familiar with the Bible know the mind of Christ. God's children understand that when they pray in agreement with the Lord's will, He is even more likely to be in favor of their request. But first, there is a little matter of changing certain aspects of our lifestyle. Notice how God uses the word "then." That is the key word that unlocks the door to answered prayer. When God's demands are met, then He will hear from heaven and follow through with His promise to heal our land. Take notice who God is speaking to. Not the unsaved sinners. He is talking to His ambassadors on earth. If His people do as commanded, He will hear from heaven and follow through with His promise. But again, there are conditions that must be met first. If we don't meet the right conditions, then the healing might not come until after the tribulation when the Lord has promised to create a new heaven and new earth. Remember, the Lord always keeps His promises no matter how long it takes.

Hopefully, God's people have truly considered the profound

message in 2nd Chronicles and understand the serious implication of its meaning. It is just as important to see what isn't stated as what has been stated. In other words, if we don't honor God and do according to His request, we won't have our sins forgiven, and America's ills will only worsen. No one can say unequivocally what will happen to our nation in the next few years, but there is still hope for the individual God-seeker. Then maybe the dark days encroaching upon society will force the church to realize and admit it's powerless without knowing the Word of God. My friend, that is the perfect definition of humility. God is still waiting for the day of awakening. He wants to forgive our sins and heal our land. But it seems that we only turn to Him for our personal interests or dire needs. We want God to help us in distress and grant our requests according to our will, not the will of God. We extend our hand to God, but not in sweet adoration or fellowship. We have no shame in asking for handouts, healing, prosperity, et cetera. It's as though God is only recognized to supply whatever yearning desire we request of Him without giving Him the only things He asks for in return for His Son's surrender. Our soul, fidelity, and love.

Every morning the news is filled with someone's tragic death occurring the evening before. What saddens me the most is the needless pain people are suffering at the hand of hate. What little comfort avails the bereaved while tearfully gathered together in prayer vigils, with lit candles, singing the familiar hymn, "Amazing Grace." I don't mean to sound unsympathetic, but what if all that misery might have been avoided altogether? What purpose is served by all the little mementos at the memorial site of the dearly departed after the tragic fact? Just who benefits from the flowers laid at the site of a harrowing loss of life? Can any of those heartbreaking ceremonies assure the mourners of their loved one's entry into heaven? *For God intended that your faith not be established on man's wisdom but by trusting in his almighty power* (1 Corinthians 2:5, TPT). Losing a loved one is bad enough, but the uncertainty of their salvation in Christ is even worse. There is no comfort apart from Christ the Savior. A sound action with regard to seeking

God's amazing grace and protection is to request His help before tragedy strikes. *My help comes from the Lord, Who made heaven and earth. He will not allow your foot to slip; He who watches over you will not slumber* (Psalm 121:2–3, NASB). Whether you know it or not, we are in a war with Satan, a mass murderer. God is our only defense against the wiles of the devil. Prayer is our sword. The Word of God is our shield. Uniting neighbors and the community in prayer to ward off those grim occurrences is the only preventative action that is effective. Of course, we know that death is a component of life, but there is no greater comfort on earth than the assurance of the Lord's salvation. Thereupon, even in the event of an untimely death, knowing that the dearly departed is secure in the presence of their Savior Jesus is especially comforting in those grievous hours. This I know first-hand.

Chapter 4

Embrace the Price of Living Righteously

Unfortunately, most people don't pay a lot of attention to things until they are bothered by them. Take nature for instance. We hardly give rain a thought until it begins to cause a disruption in our daily life. The same can be said for the wind. I live in a town in the high desert of California, where the wind is seldom considered a refreshing breeze. When the wind blows there, it's often tumultuous. It moves the desert sand around from place to place, shredding the spring blooms and ripping the greenery right off the tree limbs, sometimes toppling fully grown trees to the ground. Other areas of the country see the force of nature in distinctly different but amazing ways. The sea crashing over the shoreline for instance. Or the illumination of the night sky with bolts of lightning preceding the terrorizing crack of thunder. Torrents of rain persisting for days on end until the earth can no longer swallow the continued saturation, and the flooding begins. Those are but a few of the gentler forms of a controlled dynamic in our environment. Each one of nature's exhibitions is under God's authority and released or held at bay according to His will. Although I can't say that I look forward to those days when nature shows humanity its superiority, nevertheless, the thing I most respect about those various circumstances is the mighty Holy Spirit commanding all that power. We can only see the visible effects of such an enormous force. Nature gives us but a mere glimpse into the majestic dominance and influence God manifests on this little planet that we occupy. Think about the devastating ramifications should the Almighty decide to release His hand that restricts a force far greater and more destructive than that of any nuclear explosion. But be assured that day is coming.

God made two decisions the world should never forget. Both were catastrophic events of God's judgment upon a lecherous civilization. One in Noah's day and the other in Sodom and

Gomorrah. The termination of those two societies should give everyone a clear understanding of God's control over our lives and the environment in which we live. You can call it climate change if that helps you to feel empowered over the weather conditions. But the reality of such a ridiculous concept is utterly laughable. Nothing in our universe is beyond the control of God. *The wind blows all around us as if it has a will of its own; we feel and hear it, but we do not understand where it has come from or where it will end up. Life in the Spirit is as if it were the wind of God* (John 3:8, VOICE).

God's Spirit on earth is in control of everything that affects all earthly habitation. We may not be able to see God physically, but similarly to the wind, the power and craftsmanship of the prestigious Holy Spirit can be seen and experienced by everyone. Thereby, whenever you witness the beauty and grandeur of nature at work, stop and think about how those same unseen forces are working within the heart of every true Christian. Believers must be content to accept the many mysteries kept hidden while their relationship with God grows deeper and more intimate over time. There are many things earth's children aren't fully capable of understanding from a finite perspective of the flesh, but we must learn to express appropriate gratitude to the Lordship of Jesus for His many graces.

Faith isn't persuaded through one's intellectual understanding, coaxing, or practical participation. Faith only comes to those who are willing to hear and honor the Lord's sovereignty over their life while growing spiritually through the inspired Word of God. If you're a born-again Christian, then that same spiritual power lives within your heart in a modified and controlled capacity. But the same cannot be said for those with a hard or prideful heart. Sadly, they are unable to comprehend the things of God because they refuse to hear the good news.

Now, most of us have learned the universal lesson, nothing in life is free. There will always be a price to pay. Jesus paid the highest price possible when He exchanged His sinless life for the sins of mankind. And in the case of a steadfast Christian, it could cost you everything to follow Jesus. But being a counterfeit Christian will cost you even more.

An interesting story in Exodus of the Old Testament reveals the anguish experienced by the Israelites while they were under the harsh rule of the Egyptians. But when the time was right, God's plan to set the captives free was implemented. The Lord intended to lead His people to the border of an abundant land they could call their own. A possession God described to them as a land flowing with milk and honey.

After God set the Israelites free from Egyptian captivity, they were routed on an eight-day journey through the desert that eventually lasted forty years. Initially, God had a beautiful plan for their inheritance, but when they were faced with a challenge, the nation's leaders choked and persuaded the entire population to fear what lay ahead. They refused to go forward. They had no confidence in God. None. Therefore, God led them back into the wilderness, where they continued wandering in the wasteland year after year for decades. Unfortunately for Israel, they just went from one dismal situation to another. Why? Because of their rebellion. But let me encourage you otherwise. When God is in the plan with you, it's infallible. When following His direction, you can't lose. *What then shall we say to these things? If God is for us, who can be against us?* (Romans 8:31, NKJV)

Every Christian must keep their eyes upon Jesus, thereby avoiding unbelief while determined to confront fear. The few cowardice examples shown by the Moses generation are what kept an entire nation from attaining the promises of God. Hopefully, you are much smarter than the Israelites. But if it seems that you've been traveling in circles and always end up back at the starting line of life, never really advancing forward into a blossoming future, it's time to open your eyes. This Bible Scripture addresses that very situation. *Let them alone: they be blind leaders of the blind. And if the blind lead the blind, both shall fall into the ditch* (Matthew 15:14, KJV).

How ill-advised it was for that entire nation of people to be led astray by ten self-reliant, faithless dissenters. By refusing to place their trust in Almighty God, they decided their own fate. Even after being set free from four hundred years of slavery and witnessing all the miraculous signs and wonders the Lord displayed on their behalf, it still wasn't convincing enough. Not trusting in the mighty arm of the Lord cost them dearly. We should remember if something is worth having, then whatever struggle necessary to attain it or keep possession of it is warranted. *Because narrow is the gate and difficult is the way which leads to life, and there are few who find it* (Matthew 7:14, NKJV). Be determined to be part of God's few and not Satan's many.

Everyone born of the flesh will experience various impediments in life. A good place for believers beginning their journey is knowing who they should depend on to lead them in the right direction. Let's see where that solution takes us. Hopefully, we can get you off the Farris Wheel and move you in a forward and worthwhile direction. Toward a goal post that won't be moved, and your efforts will be advantageous to you and profitable in the lives of others.

To start with, it's important to identify where you feel the most comfortable in the following category of people groups. Honesty here is vitally important. Furthermore, you are the only one other than God who will know the answer. And besides, this isn't a test. It's only to ascertain where you stand according to the conventional framework on spiritual matters.

There are only three categories of people. The first, individuals having no relationship whatsoever with the Savior Jesus. Those souls are referred to as "the lost." Unfortunately, when they take their final breath, and their heart beats its last, they will stand before the throne of Almighty God, known also as the judgment seat of Christ. It is there that they will be expected to enter a plea. Only one question will be asked: "Were you washed in the blood of the Lamb?" If the answer is no, then your odyssey isn't going to be pleasant. Hell is your destination.

You see, death is a misconception. If anyone is under the impression that they can live like the devil now and die in peace, that being the end of it, they are sadly mistaken. God created you with a soul. On earth, your flesh must die to release your soul. It is only your physical remains that are left behind. It is your soul that lives for all eternity in one of two places: heaven or hell. Therefore, if you've been misled into thinking that a mass or rosary prayer will purify your soul and deliver you from purgatory, you're wrong. There is no such halfway house. And furthermore, don't be fooled into thinking that hell will be any different than just another bad trip on LSD. No, hell is far worse and indescribable. It's hell! Hell is an unrelenting lake of fire, tormenting the unregenerate soul day after day for all eternity. *And whosoever was not found written in the book of life was cast into the lake of fire* (Revelation 20:15, KJV).

Incidentally, if that's your fate, you won't be there alone. The beast and false prophets will be there to keep you company, right along with Satan and all the rest of the demons that deceived you. And there is a good chance some of your friends will be there too. And one last mention to the unbelievers. There are no do-overs. This life is the only opportunity there is to receive Christ's salvation. Don't let Satan fool you into thinking you have as many retakes in life as necessary until you finally succeed in earning your passage into heaven. If that's your strategy, you'd better rethink your plan. You were born of sinful flesh, and only the blood of Jesus will alter that condition.

Next, there is the nominal Christian, somewhat pious but mostly sanctimonious in their faith. Their spiritual association is centered mainly around their lifelong church affiliation, rather than their allegiance to the Lord God. Jesus referred to those believers as lukewarm Christians because they are neither hot nor cold. They show very little enthusiasm in their veneration to God. It is sad to think that these wonderful folks wouldn't recognize the presence of Jesus if He walked right up to them. They have all the outward trappings of the biblical definition of a Pharisee. Those Christians will face a type of judgment also, but theirs will be considerably different. Their works will be judged and their labor assessed to determine how their gifts and talents were used to advance the kingdom of God and to what degree. Indeed, there are rewards to be given in heaven, but only for the selfless or benevolent works done during the natural lifetime. But here again, those works must also pass a test. They will be proved by fire. Anything short of pure motives for the kingdom of God will be burned up like wood, hay, or stubble. Any works surviving the purification by fire are then authenticated and will be rewarded.

Last but certainly not least in the kingdom of God are the loyalists. They are the ones that remained faithful to the Lord Jesus in all walks of life and in every circumstance encountered. They love the Lord and recognize His Voice and obey Him with all diligence. *And they said to one another, "Did not our heart burn within us while He talked with us on the road, and while He opened the Scriptures to us?"* (Luke 24:32, NKJV)

This final group of believers understand what it means to be a disciple of the Lord and happily spend their lifetime lending themselves to His service as the Holy Spirit directs. You might identify them as the mailman in your town or your child's athletic director. Perchance it was the nice police officer who delivered your baby or comforted you in some other emergency. Perhaps it was the stranger who came to your aid when you were stranded with a flat tire by the side of the road. Maybe it was the nurse who gave your grandmother such tender care in her last hours. Or the bank teller, or janitor, or fireman, or waitress at the diner or plumber, or the trash collector. Maybe it was the helpful clerk where you purchase goods or do other business. Have I made my point? They are God's faithful warriors. They may hold down regular jobs, but they are always undertaking the Lord's business.

Who will you turn to when suddenly faced with tragedy? Almost all of us will be confronted with painful events during our lifetime. Who will be your advocate when those times occur? If you are a member of God's family, the Lord is sure to provide for you.

Why have I told you this? Because life is fragile, and the tragedy of an unforeseen death can come at any moment. Just as it did to nine innocent shoppers and one security guard—all gunned down at a grocery store on a Saturday afternoon in May of 2022 in Buffalo, New York. All that carnage was motivated and delivered under the evil influence of one devil-oppressed soul with a high-powered rifle in his hands. On the following day, another shooting at a Presbyterian church in Laguna Woods, California. There, one individual was slain, and four others were critically wounded. Once the angel of death receives orders to fetch you, there is no turning back. Your fate is sealed. What is done is done. The Holy Father is the Author of Life and death, but it was the Lamb of God Who purchased salvation for you. It wasn't a pretty sight at the time, but there is no greater gift in all the world than the Body of Jesus, surrendered upon the cross for your redemption. Accept His gift while you still can.

Chapter 5

Building a Life on the Immovable Rock

Whatever sort of building, regardless of its intended purpose, it must have an appropriate foundation laid to exact specifications and depth to support the weight of its edifice. A flimsy structure is the only way to describe how entirely too many Christians have haphazardly constructed their spiritual underpinning. Little or no concern for the prototype, a reckless framework, and a hastily applied coat of paint, and it's done. Is that how your spiritual structure is thrown together? Just looking at the temple of God from the outside, it isn't possible to know its durability to withstand the violent storms of life. The Old Testament uses the fitting term *Cornerstone* to describe Christ. The Life and work of Jesus is the foundational structure that raises the church walls one stone at a time. Each stone is another born-again soul added to the church daily. But it is the Cornerstone that is the single most pivotal and influential element that keeps all the other stones consistent with His integrity and purpose. *So the Lord, the Eternal, has this to say: Eternal One: See here, I am laying in Zion a stone, a tested stone—a cornerstone, chosen and precious—for a firm foundation. Whoever trusts in it will never be disgraced. Justice will be the line by which I lay out its floor plan, and righteousness will be My leveling tool. A hailstorm will pulverize and wash away the fraud and deception behind which people hide, and floodwaters will overrun their hiding place* (Isaiah 28:16–17, VOICE).

The children of God should be easily distinguished by their righteous character. Faithful Christians are holy and completely loyal to the heavenly Father and consistently obedient to the Lord Jesus, the Redeemer of their soul. Jesus will unfailingly keep His allegiance and fidelity to those who are His committed followers. God's children are prepared to live for Him and die for Him if necessary. Faith is the indispensable requisite for a Christian's complete dependence upon God, especially in unpredictable circumstances and unprecedented calamity. Whereas, for everyone else in society who chooses to defy God, they are carelessly underemphasizing their providence.

Not all of today's wretched conditions are in the streets of society. Some of the most dispirited examples are occurring right under our noses in the very churches where we seek solace and refuge within the body of Christ. Would it surprise you to know that the very clergy preaching to you on the Lord's Day may be leading you spiritually astray? Many of this nation's ecclesiastical educators and pastors have lost their footing and fallen face first into compromise. Who would have imagined that the lofty and highly regarded spiritual leaders in this critical dispensation of time would deliberately and subtly delude the infallible standard of Bible doctrine and lead their congregation into moral decay? In fact, it's very likely that you may unknowingly be worshiping next to an infidel. And it is for that very reason that every person born of the Spirit of God must put on the whole armor of God (Ephesians 6:11). Thereby guarding their hearts and minds against the danger of freethinking liberalism that ultimately leads directly into apostasy. *These people honor me only with their words, for their hearts are so very distant from me. They pretend to worship me, but their worship is nothing more than the empty traditions of men"* (Matthew 15:8–9, TPT).

Here is an old saying I learned as a child. The road to hell is paved with good intentions. Maybe you intended to ask Christ to forgive your sins, but you just haven't gotten around to it. Intentions are no better than a basket of empty dreams. There is something else to consider. Don't be deceived into thinking that you have all the time in the world or that all roads lead to paradise. No one has the promise of another tomorrow, and there is only one narrow way into the heavenly kingdom. Jesus is the Door. If you're on any road other than the narrow road, then you are on the road to destruction. Through blind ignorance, Satan has assured the masses that the wide road will accommodate everyone just as effectively as the narrow way. The wide road is leisurely and picturesque. The wide way is enchanting, paved with temptation and many entertaining obstacles to impede your journey.

But it's the road less traveled that leads to heaven. Before you start playing follow the leader, it's imperative to know the character of the one you're following. People have the same herd mentality as sheep. If most people are going in the same direction, then it must be safe to follow along. Right? Wrong! Those people are not thinking for themselves. They have just fallen into mindless behavior by blindly following the crowd. That same conduct reminds me of a certain demonic event that took place in the time of Jesus. Two fierce men that were demon-possessed came out of the tombs to meet the Son of God. *A herd of pigs was feeding in the distance, so the demons begged, "If you cast us out, send us into that herd of pigs. "All right," Jesus told them. "Begone." And they came out of the men and entered the pigs, and the whole herd rushed over a cliff and drowned in the water below* (Matthew 8:30–32, TLB).

Although the details of this story are a bit scant, the point is clearly made. I must emphasize that this is just the sort of thing that demon spirits do well. They raise havoc with everything around them. There is no end to the destruction they will cause. Those demons didn't drown. Only the pigs were lost. Notice that the pigs didn't scatter and go in all different directions. They all followed the same course and met with the same dismal fate.

On the other hand, the narrow way is the most stringent route of the two. And according to what Scripture tells us, few find the narrow pathway that leads to glory and eternal Life in the heavenly kingdom. And it is for that very reason that spending time in the Bible, learning for your own benefit what it says, will undoubtedly be the most profitable time you will ever spend, especially in these last days of depravity. When filling your mind and heart with Scripture, your confidence will be focused entirely upon Almighty God and the Lord Jesus. That is where you will find the knowledge to comprehend these words; greater is He that is in you than He that is in the world (1 John 4:4). Furthermore, if you are standing on the Rock of your salvation, you will be immeasurably stronger spiritually and significantly more competent to oppose this nation's unprincipled leadership. *So shall they fear The name of the Lord from the west, And His glory from the rising of the sun; When the enemy comes in like a flood, The Spirit of the Lord will lift up a standard against him* (Isaiah 59:19, NKJV). Don't be deceived; there will be severe ramifications resulting from the departure of God's fundamental spiritual principles of morality. The harmful restructuring of America's legal system and the inclusion of deleterious laws has invited the wrath of God.

Certain edicts have remained since the beginning of time, and they are applied to everyone alike—just as the goodness of God enriches the just and the unjust the same. The sunshine warms us all. The moon and stars light everyone's way in the night. The Lord's paradigm is firmly in place, and nothing is going to change that fact. God does not controvert His truth. The Sovereign's will and His objectives will be satisfied at the chosen time. The Day of the Lord will come when the fullness of the Gentiles is complete. Will it be a thousand more years or just one more day? *But, beloved, be not ignorant of this one thing, that one day is with the Lord as a thousand years, and a thousand years as one day* (2 Peter 3:8, KJV). The children of God are duty-bound to wait expectantly and watch faithfully for the second advent of the Lord's return. It's important to bring this up now because every day, all over the world, people are dying in their sins. For one reason or another, they fail to believe in the incarnate Savior Christ sent here to atone for the sins of humanity. Eternal damnation is the cost of faithlessness. *And without faith it is impossible to please Him, for the one who comes to God must believe that He exists, and that He proves to be One who rewards those who seek Him* (Hebrews 11:6, NASB). Faithlessness is the same death sentence regardless of ethnicity or generation.

It was that same faithlessness demonstrated by the people in Noah's day that caused their catastrophic demise. Why do you think the ark that God designed was so very large, if only to accommodate eight individuals? Was all that extra room just for the animals? I'd like to believe that it was God's hopeful expectation that at least some of the people would respond to Noah's strange omen. How long was God willing to wait for the people to accept His offer of salvation? One hundred and twenty years. Just as long as it took for Noah to build that massive ark.

The circumstance with the Israelites was much the same. They too refused to enter the Promised Land. Jacob and Caleb were the only ones who offered the people hope and confidence that the Lord would give them Canaan as He promised their forefathers. But the people had no faith in God. Therefore, the Lord returned them to the wilderness until every man who spoke fear instead of faith died. So, what is it going to take to save this generation? How long will God wait on this stiff-neck, hard-hearted generation to accept the compassionate salvation of His beloved Son Jesus? This much I do know. *My brothers and sisters, I do not want you to be in the dark about this mystery—I am going to let you in on the plan so that you will not think too highly of yourselves. A part of Israel has been hardened to the good news until the full number of those outside the Jewish family have entered in* (Romans 11:25, VOICE). Father God is keeping count of every soul saved. The heavenly Father is the only One Who knows when that fulness has been reached.

Tragically and much too often, the Bible is dismissed as being unfashionable. Consequently, certain generations tend to evaluate the Bible by their own standard of ethics. They consider it a Book of too many limitations and out-of-sync rules and restrictions that no longer apply to the advanced society in which they live. Furthermore, as new generations come along, they believe less and less spiritually. Their way of reasoning is corrupt. Their free-thinking ideology is to flow with the current popularity of issues and change according to the demands of certain prevailing ideas and practices. They proclaim, "This is a different era." They are pleased to welcome new customs and trendsetting ideas.

Whether you choose to honor God or not, He is in control

of your very next heartbeat. Who would dare be so arrogant as to imagine that the created beings are the ones in power? Those individuals who think they are liberated from what they perceive to be the strict boundaries of an obsolete way of life are deceiving themselves and are certainly no better off for their rebellion. In fact, they are under the nefarious dominion of Satan. Then there are others who think they know better than God what's in the best interest of whole societies. That is like grasping a concept out of thin air without having any evidence to back it up. Just because you hold a particular viewpoint doesn't necessarily make it true or socially beneficial. Wake up to the harmful effects of wokeness! My friend, those distorted perceptions couldn't be further from reality. When there isn't any factual basis to support society's foolish and rebellious claims, it is nothing more than reverie and totally ill-considered.

Some in society say there is no God. Some in society will go to hell believing that. Actually, there are two gods. So, if anyone is not a born-again child of the Almighty, then that person is a child of the devil by default. Satan is their taskmaster. He holds the key to their leg irons. That's right! Let me repeat. If you're not a born-again child of the heavenly Father, then you are a progeny of Satan, the father of lies and the god of this world.

In the Old Testament, God showed Himself supremely magnificent through powerful signs, wonders, and many other astonishing marvels. Some of the spectacles were so frightening that the people were terrified of Jehovah. Then Jesus came humbly and unobtrusively. His manner was gentle and loving. He healed the sick, fed the hungry, restored the broken, and offered His Life in place of our own. Nevertheless, He was rejected. God has offered all the visible and tangible proof He intends to provide. If the self-willed remain unconvinced, then they are damned, right along with their convictions. But I must ask, what if your stubborn convictions are wrong?

No pestilence known to man will have anywhere near the effect that the deadly scourge of evil will have on America. Those viruses are mere warnings of God's continued admonition. If immorality in America continues unchecked, subversiveness in unimaginable forms will propagate widely. God's plan has always been to protect us from the kind of lawlessness that leads to any such tragic or bitter calamity. We've all heard it said: hindsight is twenty-twenty. Wouldn't it be better to look ahead to a bright future with God than to look back at the destruction and rubble left in the wake of a defiant and out-of-control debacle encouraged by Satan's demons of desolation?

Maybe your Christian walk hasn't been what the Lord Jesus Commands. If that is the circumstance, then I hope something you've read will touch your heart and motivate you to look for the narrow road to salvation. It is the only way to be fully assured of your eternal Life in the kingdom of our dear Lord. Don't hesitate. Claim your identity as a child of God and become co-labors with Jesus in the great commission. Through the power of the Holy Spirit, you will begin developing a far deeper spirituality and see things in ways that escalate a fuller comprehension of the Savior's love for the lost. Every Christian should love their neighbor as themself and pull the lost from Satan's grip into the loving arms of Jesus.

And that brings me to something additionally important for you to consider. Your loved ones. Your child, your husband, wife, mother, father, or anyone with whom you deeply care. Maybe some of those you dearly love are unbelievers or less than faithful to Christ. I'm sure they are wonderful people, and yet, they may have drifted away from the Lord or haven't made Jesus their Savior. So, think of your cherished loved ones having their soul damned for all eternity in the lake of fire, enduring the agony of utter darkness in unyielding torment. Hell is an irredeemable condition of the unredeemed soul. Tortured by the never-ending awareness of guilt. Relentless agony of remorse. Not a single moment of relief from the echoes of despair lamenting throughout the black chamber of damnation. There is no clemency there. Death would be a welcomed release from the ceaseless agony of intense shame. For all eternity, they will lament in miserable torment, anguishing over their callous disregard of the blood of Christ. *And without faith it is impossible to please Him, for the one who comes to God must believe that He exists, and that He proves to be One who rewards those who seek Him* (Hebrews 11:6, NASB).

Turn into the waiting arms of Jesus. Through the wholehearted passion of King David, we learn of the peace that ensues in a personal relationship with the Lord God. In all the world, there are no safer arms to run to than the loving arms of Christ. Furthermore, there is no hiding place where Jesus isn't right there with you. God created you with one intention in mind: the joy of having you with Him in heaven throughout eternity. God's enduring love is truly pure and beyond explanation. As you read the comforting words of King David, think about the kind of love being expressed by the Pursuer Jesus. *It is the most amazing feeling to know how deeply You know me, inside and out; the realization of it is so great that I cannot comprehend it. Can I go anywhere apart from Your Spirit? Is there anywhere I can go to escape Your watchful presence? If I go up into heaven, You are there. If I make my bed in the realm of the dead, You are there* (Psalm 139:6–8, VOICE).

Chapter 6

The Diminished Light of Eternal Life

Today there is a very serious problem among the divergent community of evangelicals. Unfortunately, the entire church system has been in a pathetic decline for the past century. Why do you suppose that so many people are leaving the local churches? To be perfectly frank, the pastors aren't providing church attendees with the sound doctrine that God Commands. In fear of offending, church leaders no longer minister in the way, the truth, and the life.

Many older citizens that have had some church exposure, especially during their youth, recognize Bible inerrancy and reject the empty, fraudulent monologues perpetuated in most churches today. But because elders don't generate the greatest amount of revenue, any criticism from them is laid aside and left unaddressed. Within today's current style of religious application, there is little if any teaching in the church on the various aspects of sin; therefore, it should be no surprise when sin runs amok in an unregenerate society.

The target in today's church market is the childbearing, working-class family that brings in most of the revenue and adds numbers to the membership role. Sometimes the children are used as a magnet to attract adult turnout. And so, the allure demographically is toward a younger generation. By nature, the young families are less mature and more apt to go along with whatever their emotions respond to in an enthusiastic sort of way, but not necessarily in a spiritual direction. A doctrine that would immediately address today's rebellious dissension would be considered offensive and, therefore, utterly disregarded. But I tell you, turning a blind eye to sin happening in the home and within the church is irresponsible. If you think that's nonsense, then read what the apostle Paul wrote to a youthful minister over two millenniums ago. *The time will come when people will not listen to the true teaching. But people will find more and more teachers who please them. They will find teachers who say what they want to hear. People will stop listening to the truth. They will begin to follow the teaching in false stories* (1 Timothy 4:3–4, ERV).

Let there be no misunderstanding; many of today's church leaders are in league with the devil. Their watered-down oration and feel-good pep talks are deceiving the uninformed and thereby aiding Satan in his effort to cause death to as many human beings as possible. What was it that Satan said to Eve in the garden? "You will not surely die." Eve believed that lie, and we are all dead in our sins as a result. If we repeat the biggest error of all time, it's because we refuse to obey God and listen exclusively to a false-hearted windbag behind the pulpit.

It certainly seems that Satan's avant-garde form of marketing is far more palatable than the hard-hitting sermons that would save a soul for all eternity. Once again, I must caution, the church has furnished society with what they are attracted to, not what God knows is good and profitable. Today's lightweight, unsubstantiated double-talk is not what an under-shepherd is called by God to teach. Unfortunately, modern-day pastors must wear many hats, and it seems their business sense takes first priority. Despite that, a true under-shepherd of God's church has but one calling period! That is to oversee the soul's condition, direct the lost, correct the sinner, and instruct the children of God how to walk in newness of Life while advancing to full spiritual maturity.

Woefully, the true foundation of the gospel has been routinely eroded and is now patterned after any other worldly business model that has gained a measure of success and profitability. In a foolhardy attempt to become user-friendly, the modern church is conducting itself with a prevalent attitude that coincides with the base level, secondhand worldly notions of how to elevate the bottom line.

Entertainment is what attracts a better attendance. But that has never been God's standard for a successful church body. This practice of trading the souls of mankind for the short-term profits in this life will bring many to a tragic and unexpected end. *Then He spoke a parable to them, saying: "The ground of a certain rich man yielded plentifully. And he thought within himself, saying, 'What shall I do, since I have no room to store my crops?' So he said, 'I will do this: I will pull down my barns and build greater, and there I will store all my crops and my goods. And I will say to my soul, "Soul, you have many goods laid up for many years; take your ease; eat, drink, and be merry."' But God said to him, 'Fool! This night your soul will be required of you; then whose will those things be which you have provided?'* (Luke 12:16–20, NKJV)

What happens to the sincere people who go looking for truth in today's church? What happens to the many souls seeking comfort in a time of desperation when tragedy has knocked them to their knees? In these dark days, those who are seeking God and the authenticity of Bible doctrine for spiritual comfort and guidance are destined to be thoroughly perplexed by the shallow psychology of ill-equipped clergy that has no substantial biblical doctrine to provide. Therefore, those hurting individuals go away entirely empty and possibly even exploited. Why is that? It may be that the preacher who you have put your faith in has failed God and consequently failed his charge over your soul.

Sunday after Sunday, the frivolous messages from the pulpit are deluded and completely void of the Lord's character, His wrath, or His redemptive power. Man's ways are foolishness to God. We, like sheep, have gone astray. And the worthless charismatic ideology being spewed from the American pulpit won't save those who are lost.

It's bad enough when congregations are being led astray by nominal pastors. But sadder still is the unsuspecting, goodhearted but blind believers who are supporting those dissenters extravagantly. Many church leaders today have been brazenly dishonest, hiding behind their own agenda, power, prestige, and greed. They are what the Bible calls hirelings and not true shepherds of God's flock.

Those kinds of churches put me in remembrance of this Scripture from Proverbs. *Like one who takes away a garment in cold weather, And like vinegar on soda, Is one who sings songs to a heavy heart* (Proverbs 25:20, NKJV).

Adding to that, when many present-day congregations aren't being properly disciplined in the absolute veracity of Scripture, it frequently leads the vulnerable directly into the mouth of wolves hiding among the flock. Why do you think the Lord referred to His chosen ones as sheep? Sheep are helpless. They have no protection against predators. Without a caring shepherd, they are completely defenseless. Today more than ever before in the history of the church, believers need to hear the unadulterated Word of God and know what their obligation is in the vital role as born-again children in the kingdom of heaven. But teachers and church leaders lack proficiency in the knowledge of Scripture. And without the ability to superbly expound God's Word, all believers are weakened and left to their own resources, still markedly ignorant in the knowledge of the Lord's mastery and dominion. Any preacher that doesn't apply himself to the study of Scripture with diligence and self-discipline is powerless behind the pulpit, and the Holy Spirit will be conspicuously and routinely absent.

Christians in name only may attend a Sunday church service now and then, or on special occasions for appearance's sake, or to fill their weekend calendar if there are no other high-spirited events scheduled. Unfortunately, that leaves that same segment of people untaught and spiritually bankrupt when it comes to the Word of God. Sadly, those individuals have no depth in solid doctrine, and that is a most vulnerable position to be in. Hear the agony in David's prayer as he pleads for a desperately needed condition that a mere hireling would be totally unequipped to assuage. *My soul clings to the dust; Revive me according to Your word. I have declared my ways, and You answered me; Teach me Your statutes. Make me understand the way of Your precepts; So shall I meditate on Your wonderful works. My soul melts from heaviness; Strengthen me according to Your word* (Psalm 119:25–28, NKJV).

This modern era of hireling pastors and teachers are fully aware of abusing their position of power by disregarding legitimate doctrine and manipulating Scripture to suit their own demands. They have not only failed God's saints, but they are also toying with God and inviting harsh judgment to themselves. But none of those pastors should be astonished on the day of judgment. In the book of James, he tells us that their sins will be judged the severest (James 3:1).

Worship is the foremost reason to gather on the Lord's Day. Most present-day worship is totally unsatisfactory, self-serving, superficial, and thoroughly vacant of any real heartfelt thanksgiving. There is very little sacrificial reverence or commemoration for what God has graciously done in the lives of those who call themselves Christian. There is only a kind of facsimile of adoration for the Savior Who died for them. And because of all the lawlessness and unorthodox methodology being brought into the modern church, a great many parishioners don't understand the true significance of reverence to a holy God. If the attendee gets a goosebump or two, they are happy just going through the hollow motions of adoration. The sad fact is that most concerts or sporting events generate far more enthusiasm than a formal expression of worship during a Sunday service on the Lord's Day.

This generation of Christians are creatures who demand a comfortable environment in their church setting. They want what they want, not what God wants them to have. When believers arrive at church, they want to be seated comfortably and be suitably entertained, but not for too long. They have their own agenda to keep. They expect the preacher to tell a funny story to put everyone at ease. It keeps the mood light, and the people are likely to return more frequently if the message doesn't touch on sin. Most sermons today are mostly computer-generated, good-natured, and mellow—nothing too profound. Preachers never want to use the Bible to offend anyone or cause their anxiety. In some instances, the preacher prefers to talk about himself and his own accomplishments rather than specifics from the Bible or its main characters. And the unfortunate thing about all that, the Christian community is getting exactly what they've asked for. The Lord has no objection to creature comforts or humor if the parishioners are serious about developing spiritual awareness and living in obedience to the doctrine of God.

Frankly, there is no pleasant way to express this next issue. However, I believe it's crucial to make mention of the troubling condition regarding the sanctity of the church sanctuary on any given Sunday. I admit that I'm old school. But what I've experienced over many decades is an apathetic irreverence for God's house of prayer. Indifference has replaced the impassioned conduct of deep respect for exalting the Name of the Lord God in what should be a sanctified setting on the Lord's Day. Casual trends and shallow devotion have changed the spiritual direction in which Christians interact with God in the holy place Jesus refers to as, His house of prayer. *Jesus said to them, "The Scriptures say, 'My Temple will be called a house of prayer.' But you are changing it into a hiding place for thieves'"* (Matthew 21:13, ERV).

Many young people have nothing to compare their present-day church experience with. But that isn't the case with elders from my era. Quite frankly, the reason I feel the need to discuss the matter openly in this way is because God isn't present in most of the church services today. Why do I say that? Because man has remade God's house into just another informal place for a brief socialization in the community. Until God truly lives in the heart, there will be nothing reverent offered to Almighty God on Sunday. The church atmosphere will be no different than any other place in town where people happen to be gathered throughout the week. And that one aspect alone is totally irreverent and unsuitable for God's house of worship. What was once considered a solemn, holy place of worship to the living God, has become just another multipurpose center.

What am I implying? I'm not implying anything; I'm declaring my frank opinion regardless of whether it's welcomed or controversial. God deserves better than what He's been offered Sunday after Sunday. When anyone enters the house of God, they should be prepared for a distinctive and uncommon rendezvous with the Most Holy Father and High Priest of our confession and Savior of our soul. Leaving the world and everything associated with it outside for that brief period to be spent with God. Once someone walks through the doors of the church, they should experience an atmosphere far contrastive and markedly different from anything temporal. The sanctuary should remain an uncommon place of awe, deliverance, and refuge, respectfully submitting to the sacred and sensitive work of the Holy Spirit.

Long before the time of Jesus, the place where God communed with Moses was referred to as the Tent of Meeting. God's meeting place was highly venerated, and the people showed great humility in God's presence. *Now Moses took a tent and pitched it outside the camp, at a distance from the camp; he called it the tent of meeting. Anyone who wanted to consult the Lord would go to the tent of meeting that was outside the camp. Whenever Moses went out to the tent, all the people would stand up, each one at the door of his tent, and they would watch Moses until he entered the tent. When Moses entered the tent, the pillar of cloud would come down and remain at the entrance to the tent, and the Lord would speak with Moses. As all the people saw the pillar of cloud remaining at the entrance to the tent, they would stand up, then bow in worship, each one at the door of his tent* (Exodus 33:7–10, CSB).

The people showed great reverence for that first humble but consecrated meeting place that joined God and man together. That was the first example of an early church setting. Somewhat later, the fineries were established according to God's exact specifications. I'm not suggesting there should be an ostentatious exhibition demonstrated as in some religious services. Quite the contrary. If you study the days of Jesus, everything about His person and His ministry was exactly the opposite.

What am I saying? That all believers should properly prepare themselves to gather before the Lord's divine presence in humble adoration. Ready the environment in such a way that honors the majesty of God and His expected appearance on the Lord's Day. Church leaders should do everything within their power to set God's house of prayer in order and apart from the system and timetable of the world. We must remember that God is a holy God, and church leaders have a responsibility to make the Lord welcomed in a hallowed environment. Not one that necessitates man's itinerary. Quite honestly, I believe we've become far too detached in God's house of worship. And I'm certainly not suggesting all churches need to correct their rules of religious conduct. But many have lost the solemnity of a holy environment. As I stated earlier, if entering your church is like walking into any other business in town, then maybe it's time to make some serious changes. Think of that individual who hasn't set foot in a church for decades. What is the first impression that you want a new seeker to experience? Hopefully, it's the Shakina glory of God's presence. Firstly, put the likeness of the cross back in the church. Not to be worshiped but remembered. How can anyplace be called a church if it doesn't have the cross that represents the New Testament fellowship that we are a part of today? That is the one symbol everyone understands without a single spoken word. The cross communicates the courage of Jesus, the sacrifice He made for us, and the gift of salvation by His own blood. It's my hope to enlighten and encourage all Christians to examine their church environment and request the necessary improvements when and where necessary.

The church sanctuary should be profoundly unfamiliar to that of any other social setting. God's house is a house of prayer and should reflect that spiritual aura. Young Christians are under the impression that the church and all the rest of it is just another form of Sunday social networking. It's no wonder our nation is in the mess it's in. Half the Christians walking around are spiritually dead, and they don't even realize it. That is precisely why, in many cases, Christians are called out for their hypocrisy. Why should unbelievers be convinced of the love of God when the Life of Christ isn't reflected in the Name by which they call themselves? Many of today's Christians aren't that much different from a society without God. Grievously I say, Christians are the biggest letdown in our culture today. Some half-hearted believers, by their own reluctance, have failed to learn the way, the truth, and the life; therefore, their lives remain spiritually dead. And yet, most of them are under the false impression that they have escaped the fires of hell, and that's all they were interested in to begin with.

If you desire to be a co-laborer in the kingdom of our dear Lord, it's necessary to evangelize the lost. Once you have identified yourself as a Christian, you are expressing to the entire world that you represent the eternal Father and His only begotten Son, Jesus. For all those faithful Christians who are truly born-again, it's imperative that you show yourself as light in the darkened world around you. Only your deep affection for Christ and your assent to Scripture will reflect the Lord's love.

The main objective of every believer should be to capture and release Satan's prisoners. Not by your clever words or philosophy of life. It's the Word of God that brings light into the darkness and life to the dead. Christians are the hands and feet of Jesus. In that respect, faith and obedience to God are tantamount if one's purpose is to serve as a disciple to the Lord. Just claiming to be a follower of Jesus does not guarantee your passage into the kingdom of God. If you want to be admitted, you must obey God's directives and live according to His holy standard.

Older Christians still have much to offer and should never be cast aside. The apostle John wrote four different books in the New Testament. Revelation was written during John's nineties, while exiled on the isle of Patmos. Elders have years of invaluable spiritual experience that should be utilized for the kingdom of God. It takes a concerted effort with many willing servants, young and old, to bring the good news of salvation through Christ to every nation, tribe, and tongue.

Jesus knew His time was short, and the work had to continue long after He gave His Life on the cross. In the very beginning, He told Simon Peter and Andrew, his brother, that He would make them fishers of men. And Jesus truly accomplished that. The Lord's disciples had the amazing experience of being with Him in the flesh. Although nothing on this side of heaven could ever equal that experience, Christians today can claim one unique phenomenon of their very own. Every child of God is the living temple of the Holy Spirit.

Chapter 7

Hear the Lord Speaking

Think about this. When your dad wanted to speak to you, he didn't call the neighbor or your teacher and communicate his message through them. He spoke to you directly. That's the way our heavenly Father wants to commune with His children. There is an interesting experiment that teaches a very serious lesson. Select a few friends to participate in this simple demonstration. Let someone begin by whispering a secret message to anyone in the group. That person will then whisper what they heard to someone else. The procedure is repeated until everyone has been told the secret. Whoever received the message last will then reveal aloud what was told to him. The whole purpose of the experiment is to be made aware of how easily the original message can be misstated or even falsified. Whether through ignorance or deliberate manipulation, the outcome is nevertheless misleading. And, if the subject matter is Scripture, the fallacy in spiritual instruction can be deadly.

That is exactly what was occurring in Jerusalem and throughout Galilee at the time of Jesus' incarnation. For generations, the common people were completely dependent upon the scribes and Pharisees to lead them properly in accordance with the laws of Judaism. But throughout many generations of diminished understanding and casual compliance with God's Commands, the elders devised a series of alternative directives to God's holy mandates. Those rules and regulations were called the traditions of the elders. So, rather than convey the sacred doctrinal truth to the citizens, they misled the people by falsifying the law and encumbered the population with countless nonsensical burdens. The common Jewish citizen had no choice but to rely upon the man-made traditions of their leaders. The ordinary people were led astray and didn't know any better. Unfortunately, this practice led their entire society into deeper darkness and greater confusion. It was just as Jesus Said, when the blind lead the blind, they will both fall into a ditch.

Jesus began His ministry in direct contact with the people. His teaching was error-free and explicit. Nevertheless, most people found the Words of Jesus to be unusually refreshing. His lessons were in simple terms that illuminated the Scriptures and brought understanding to the hearts of ordinary citizens. Wherever Jesus went, He became a Fountain of unfeigned blessing to the many needs of the people. He fed the hungry, healed the sick, and brought hope to the spiritually blind and dejected. At the Master's insistence, no one was ever turned away. *They came at last to the village of Capernaum on the Sea of Galilee; and on the Sabbath Day, Jesus went straight into a synagogue, sat down, and began to teach. The people looked at each other, amazed, because this strange teacher acted as One authorized by God, and what He taught affected them in ways their own scribes' teachings could not* (Mark 1:21–22, VOICE).

Regrettably, Jesus perceived the real motive behind the enormous crowds that followed Him. Their concern wasn't to have their sins forgiven and receive eternal Life. They came to Jesus for healing in their bodies, food to eat, and sometimes release from demonic spirits. Many others were just plain curious. It was at that point in His ministry that Jesus changed directions. The commonality in the masses was their lack of faith, limiting Jesus' effort to save souls. He therefore provided for their physical needs only. As an alternative to His earlier messages of light and Life, Jesus allowed the unpersuadable to remain in their incorrigible condition, thereby providing only for what they desired. But for the benefit of His faithful companions, Jesus taught in parables, whetting the appetites of His curious students so they would ask for further clarification. It's worth noting that out of all the thousands of persons intrigued with Jesus, whether near or far, there may not have been more than seventy souls, besides those of His twelve close associates, that had a burning interest in His Words of Life.

In the distant past, anyone interested in learning about God through the chronicles of Scripture was often held captive to an inexact interpretation from unscrupulous or poorly qualified church leaders. Whether past or present, people typically rely upon the knowledge and accuracy of their church elders to give them factual truth concerning the inerrancy of the Bible. But instead, what most people get from their esteemed religious leaders is ambiguity and prevarication. What was once a high calling and life's work unto God is just another occupation in modern society. Yet, with very isolated exceptions, finding a true Christian shepherd is rare nowadays. But when he is found, the search will be well worth the effort.

Christians are advised against departing from fellowship with like-minded believers. The Lord's Day is especially gratifying when your pastor is knowledgeable and proficient in exegesis. That is the critical interpretation and application of Scripture. But God also wants each of us to learn from Him directly. There is much to be cultivated from the Bible and enjoyed from personal devotion in God's presence. Anyone who fails to utilize cherished time in Scripture is short-changing their own intimate relationship with the Lord. There is a short excerpt from the book of Luke in the New Testament that vividly expresses the Lord's thoughts on this very subject. Jesus and the disciples are staying with their friends, Lazarus and his sisters, Mary and Martha. Martha became frustrated that her sister wasn't helping with the meal preparations. When Martha's irritation reached its limit, she went to Jesus for support. *But Martha was upset about all the work she had to do. So she asked, "Lord, don't you care that my sister has left me to do the work all by myself? Tell her to help me." The Lord answered her, "Martha, Martha! You worry and fuss about a lot of things. There's only one thing you need. Mary has made the right choice, and that one thing will not be taken away from her"* (Luke 10:40–41, GW). The choice that Jesus Spoke of was Mary sitting at the Master's feet as He taught life's lessons to those around Him.

There is no longer any reason or excuse for Christians to remain clueless about Scripture. Bibles are inexpensive and readily available everywhere today. Holy Bibles in their entirety are available on the Internet. Churches often give copies of the New Testament away to anyone who asks. There is no justification for anyone to remain in spiritual darkness. That's Satan's territory. He wants as many souls as possible to remain ignorant of the promises of God. If you are a devoted Christian, then become knowledgeable in your godly heritage. There is only one way to determine the facts from fiction. Learn everything you can about what you claim to profess. Whatever is being taught or preached from the pulpit of your church must be substantiated through the inspired Word of God. Any biblical inaccuracy must be disavowed immediately. Please, don't put your soul at risk over incompetent preaching or teaching that is inconsistent with the exactness and perfection of the Holy Bible.

Prior to the first publication of the Gutenberg Bible in 1450, having a personal copy of a Bible wasn't commonplace. People's spiritual comprehension was held hostage by an elitist system that defended a superior attitude concerning holy Scripture. But all that has changed. Pastors and priests no longer have ascendancy over the gospel. In fact, read what is written in the New Testament. *It is true that I felt I had to write the above about men who would dearly love to lead you astray. Yet I know that the touch of his Spirit never leaves you, and you don't really need a human teacher. You know that his Spirit teaches you about all things, always telling you the truth and never telling you a lie. So, as he has taught you, live continually in him. Yes, now, little children remember to live continually in him. So that if he were suddenly to reveal himself we should still know exactly where we stand, and should not have to shrink away from his presence* (1 John 2:26–28, PHILLIPS).

Calendars are a very common feature in everyone's lives. They are in our homes, on our desks, and in our cellphones. We keep track of everything important on a calendar. And yet, the one date that has eluded everyone for thousands of years is the Day of the Lord's second coming. Although it is the most significant future event, it's rarely mentioned in church. Jesus made sure His companions understood its relevance. The Bible gives us ample warning of the last days. When the tree branch is still tender, and its budding leaves begin to open, we know from experience that summer is approaching (Mark 13:28). This might be a contemporary indication that time is running out, and the end of days is closer than we know. Believers and unbelievers should be preparing for the return of King Jesus. But unfortunately, rather than storing up spiritual assets in heaven, modern society is far more interested in keeping abreast of certain sporting events, concerts, and what material things this life has to offer. Would it surprise you to know that when you have God in your life, He will give you the desires of your heart? (Psalm 37:4)

It's positively incredible how closely generations resemble one another, though separated by thousands of years. The commonality between the ages is evident in the insensitive attitude toward the end times. When Jesus was confronted by religious leaders demanding a sign, the Lord responded with this observation. *In the morning you say, "It will be a stormy day, because the sky is red and there are clouds." You know the meaning of these signs in the sky. But you do not know the meaning of the signs about the time in which we are living. People today are wrong. They have gone away from God. They want a sign. No sign will be given them but the sign of Jonah.' Then Jesus went away and left them* (Matthew 16:3–4, WE).

There is a deep significance to the story of Jonah and his perilous plunge. When Jonah found that he was helplessly confined in the belly of an enormous fish, he repented for his disobedience and cried out to God. God listened to Jonah's plea and Directed the big fish to spew him out safely upon a shoreline. Jonah immediately responded to the Lord's Command and set out for the wicked city of Nineveh. The municipality was so tremendous in size that it took Jonah three days to thoroughly sound the alarm, warning of God's judgment in forty days. When the king heard the Word of God's coming judgment, he took the warning very seriously. He laid his robe aside and covered himself in sackcloth and sat in ashes. He then decreed a fast, forbidding man or beast to eat or drink and that every man and animal should humble themselves in sackcloth. That was a complete expression of humility and submission. He further stipulated that everyone should turn from their evil ways and cry out to God for mercy. God saw their sincerity and relented the destruction of the city.

The purpose in telling you about Nineveh is to explain something you may not have considered before. There are certain parallels of scriptural truth that we should be aware of. Jesus spent three years evangelizing and manifesting His Lordship to the spiritually hopeless, the suffering, and those in physical need. But none of that was enough to convince the religious elders. The chief priests and scribes wanted a miraculous sign in the heavens to prove He was the Son of God. The Pharisees and Sadducees blasphemed the Holy Spirit when they accused Jesus of doing His many wonders through the power of Satan. If His miracles, unfeigned teachings, and inexplicable deeds wouldn't convince them, another sign was entirely useless. Therefore, rather than accommodate their request, Jesus gave the whole world a revelation that would forever amend the passé Old Testament law, giving way to the unfeigned grace and mercy of God in a new and better covenant.

Jesus knew they were impervious to His deity. The religious leaders were hardhearted and determined to maintain their status quo. They saw Jesus as a disruptor of their resourceful arrangement. And so, the Pharisees and Sadducees plotted to kill Him, exploiting the practice of Roman crucifixion. It was Jesus' destiny and longing to consummate His earthly mission, but not before the appointed hour designated by the Father. Therefore, He left the temple's sanctimonious deceivers in their desolate condition. When He Told them they would not see Him again, He meant just that. The unsaved Jews are still waiting for their Messiah, and many still live according to their age-old traditions. Jesus finished the remainder of His earthly ministry by concentrating on His disciples, healing and teaching in the small villages throughout the Galilean countryside while making converts of all who had faith to believe.

We know how the story of Jesus' Life on earth concluded in Jerusalem. He did in fact die on a cross between two thieves as predetermined by God. But the cosmic sign the Pharisees and Sadducees hoped for eluded them entirely, as did the resurrection of Jesus Christ. *Jesus answered, "Evil and sinful people are the ones who want to see a miracle as a sign. But no miracle will be done to prove anything to them. The only sign will be the miracle that happened to the prophet Jonah. Jonah was in the stomach of the big fish for three days and three nights. In the same way, the Son of Man will be in the grave three days and three nights. On the judgment day, you people who live now will be compared with the people from Nineveh, and they will be witnesses who show how guilty you are. Why do I say this? Because when Jonah preached to those people, they changed their lives. And you are listening to someone greater than Jonah, but you refuse to change!* (Matthew 12:39–41, ERV) That is a profound and stunning rebuke to all the hard-hearted unbelievers that day and every day thereafter.

After Jesus was resurrected to Life and awaiting His ascension into heaven, He very discretely revealed Himself to His disciples and a small number of faithful followers. At no time during His remaining days on earth did Jesus disclose Himself to those who refused to receive Him as their Messiah. So, with only a few exceptions, Jesus left the blind and hard-hearted nation of Israel to their own desolation, as it is even today. Jesus spent His last earthly days celebrating His triumphant conquest with those who genuinely loved Him and trusted Him with all purity of soul. So, the greatest of all signs was the resurrection of the Lord Jesus and only witnessed by those in faithful allegiance to Him as their Lord and Savior. In commemoration of Christ's conquest, when Jesus ascended to His heavenly throne, He sent gifts to men and the Holy Spirit to the church. The sign of Jonah pointed directly to the resurrection of Jesus, but the Pharisees gave no consideration to the Lord's dynamic evidence. Let the Words of the Lord be comprehended.

Jesus became Savior by way of His death on the cross. But He didn't fail in His commitment. He accomplished His missionary assignment masterfully. Jesus vanquished death and the grave by means of His resurrection to Life. Jesus reigns supreme over all the earth. In the Old Testament, we learn certain details about various battles. In those days, when a king returned in victory from battle, that king would share the spoils of war with the people of his nation. That is precisely what King Jesus did. At the time when Jesus returned to His rightful home in heaven, He ascended with many captives bound in chains. Jesus was triumphant over death and the grave. He won the keys to hell and obtained the right to the spoils of war. Then, according to tradition, Jesus gave gifts to men to celebrate His mighty victorious battle. If you are wondering what those spoils consisted of, I'm delighted to tell you. All who trust in Jesus and believe His Word and works, are cleansed from sin, reconciled to the Almighty Father, adopted into the family of God, given His Holy Spirit, and upon the death of the flesh, they are transformed and given a glorified body, equipping them for all eternity in the heavenly kingdom of God.

Chapter 8

Freedom Means Accountability

One of the most delightful and prophetic images a parent can witness is when they see their darling toddler attempting to walk around in their shoes. And as flattering as that may be, it's far more important to nourish a little one's desire to walk in the footsteps of the Lord Jesus. Modeling the Life of Christ will lay a firm foundation throughout the child's future. The inception of God's love and faithfulness, when accompanied by the early introduction to the Bible, is paramount in the spiritual life of every child. If the parent doesn't reverence the deity of Christ, why would their child want to?

Everyone on this planet is a creation of Almighty God. He is a Christian's heavenly Father. And, just as any other father, He wants us to emulate His pattern for a superior and fulfilling life. That is a life that follows the high ethical morality of God's beloved Son, Jesus. Just as any other parent builds a physical relationship with their children in the natural, God wants a spiritual relationship with His children, and each to duplicate His code of ethics and integrity. And that's not too much for any parent to ask of their child. A family that has characteristically maintained their good name has every right to expect as much from their children. There is great honor in a good family name. If you are a member of the family of God, you are expected to perpetuate a virtuous reputation and not bring disgrace upon the Name of the Lord.

Many of us have enjoyed recognizing or comparing the similarities and resemblances in the family tree. Certain characteristics may indeed follow us from generation to generation, but not all of them are considered reputable. Most of us know a family member who has led a life of rebellion. Often generational patterns continue within a family and sometimes lead a person entirely in the wrong direction. It is important to identify any such propensity and immediately make whatever correction is necessary for the continued good health of that individual. Otherwise, instability, discord, and grief are sure to accompany that unfortunate soul and those they are close to.

God has given us a wise and foreseeable path to follow. A far better direction than the one we may have unwisely chosen for ourselves. Hopefully, you have already established a developing relationship with the Lord. But, if that relationship has not yet been confirmed, now would be a good time to consider it. The book in your hands is merely intended to be an incentive to embark upon a deeper intimacy and commitment to Christ. Just use this book as a signpost guiding you in the direction of eternal Life. The Holy Bible is the actual model and pattern for living. And whether you give credence to any of those things or disregard them altogether has no bearing on the incomparability of truth according to God's Word. His principles and standard for reconciliation, forgiveness, and righteous living are irreversible and eternal, believe it or not. *God's temple cannot have anything to do with idols, and we are the temple of the living God. As God said, "I will live with them and walk with them; I will be their God and they will be my people"* (2 Corinthians 6:16, TLB).

The preceding Scripture was delivered to God's people over two thousand years ago. And what's so confounding, since then, there hasn't been more than a few generations in succession willing to consistently obey God's instructions. Many faithful Christians do try very hard to follow the golden rule and God's many other Commandments as well. But for some unknown reason, multitudes of mis-appropriately named Christians find it hard to accept the one Commandment that tells us to separate ourselves from unbelievers. Why do you suppose that is? Sin is attractive to the unregenerate human flesh. Sinners have no moral compass and Satan's temptations can be very alluring. It takes a spiritually strong child of God to wholly resist the devil's decoys. Please understand, first and foremost, God Declared everything that He created was very good. That would even include our first parents, Adam and Eve. God, in His infinite wisdom, allowed them to possess their own free will. Thus, permitting them to follow their own inclinations however they chose to. That liberty set apart any appearance of manipulation or exploitation that God might be accused of. And as it turned out, one misleading impulse of Adams became spiritually fatal. So then, the question must be asked. Because God predetermined to give His creation freedom of choice, should we, therefore, hold God responsible for someone's detrimental decision? Never let that be said.

The Creator's design of the human being is unparalleled. His model was complete and without any flaws whatsoever. It was that little thing called choice that imploded the beauty of Adam's life and caused all of humanity to live under the shadow of sin in this fallen world. Although free will is absolutely a magnificent liberty, it can endanger our mortal flesh in a heartbeat. Think about the repercussions following Adam's decision. If Satan could use one person to cause that much damage to so many future generations, then consider how much more devastating when causing whole societies in our own generation to rebel against God. It's not too preposterous to suggest that we may indeed be seeing only the tip of the iceberg right now. But the full intensity and repercussion of such an insurgency would be utterly catastrophic.

The well-being of our very existence is defined by those hundreds of choices we make each moment during our lifetime. Every individual will encompass an enormous number of assorted responses to diverse situations, both pleasant and perilous. Will the decisions you make work out in your favor? God only knows. But His expectation is that we make affirmative choices. Prudence and self-control will go the distance in keeping everyone as safe as possible. Nevertheless, regardless of the outcome, God still allows each of us to live our lives as we so choose. And whatever the consequence of those choices, they are our own responsibility to bear.

Unfortunately, we have people in our society that don't

necessarily have high regard for rules, laws, or even the lives of others. They just do whatever pleases them. They are pawns of Satan. And it doesn't matter to him what walk of life they come from. There is no certain age or skin color to the subversive activities of Satan's offenders. Satan doesn't discriminate. Moms, dads, or children. His instruments can be high-end government officials or someone living on the street. And usually, there is at least one innocent victim for every crime committed. If someone chooses to follow their wanton, radical inclinations, an unjustified assault on society is usually the fruit of their accursed mind. We hear the word evil associated with reprehensible acts upon society, but let us understand where that evil originates. Let's tell it like it is. All the evil in this world is influenced by the diabolical mind of Satan. It is Satan we have to thank for all the carnage perpetrated in the world.

That brings me to this question. Why did you do that? In a conversation I had recently, I asked the question: "Why do you do such a thing?" The response to that question was startling. "That's just the way I've always done it." It wasn't that I disagreed with the answer to the question; it was the superficiality of the response. One that I believe is quite a common impulse in humanity. That was an illuminating moment for me, to be sure. Suppose there was a better way to do something you've always done? Would you be interested in knowing?

Habitual behavior is sometimes compulsive. Because I've always done it that way isn't an introspective explanation. If an individual doesn't take the time to analyze the reason for their behavior, they could easily be jeopardizing their good health and well-being. Habits can be formed without any rhyme or reason. Some habits are awful but harmless, and others may be just plain weird. But when a habit interferes with one's welfare, spiritual growth, or endangers others, then it becomes a worrisome situation. I'm certainly not ridiculing anyone for their harmless idiosyncrasies; I have my own. Nevertheless, let me share this little story I heard many years ago. Hopefully, it will clarify my point.

The farmer's wife was preparing dinner for the family. There by her side was her oldest daughter being very observant of her mother's every move. The girl paid particular attention to how her mother prepared the large roast for the evening meal. Before placing the meat in the roasting pan, she methodically and with precision cut the roast into pieces. Many years later, the grown daughter was teaching her own little daughter how to prepare the family roast for dinner. The girl watched carefully as her mother took the roast and removed certain sections from the large cut of meat. The child being curious, asked her mother, "Mama, why did you cut those pieces off the roast?" Her mother thought for a moment and answered, "I don't know why...except that was the way grandma always did it." Thinking it over, the child's mother gave grandma a call to find out the actual reason why the roast was prepared in that special way. When the grandmother heard the question, she burst out laughing. Her reply was very simple. Her roasting pan wasn't big enough to accommodate the entire portion of the large cut of meat.

That is a lighthearted way of illustrating how foolish it is to acquire habits without being conscious of the kind of influence they may have on your life. For instance, smoking, the overuse of prescription medications, illegal street drugs, the abuse of alcohol, or deadly relationships. Although some things may be legal, not all are healthy, and still others might lead into the clutches of sin. Smoking is an acquired habit. There is no pleasure in someone's first cigarette, so why do people continue with a habit that will eventually harm them? Whether it's street drugs or prescription drugs, the side effects of abuse are deadly. I'm certainly not in favor of any habits that are harmful. However, my main concern is the one habitual habit that will jeopardize your eternal soul. Unbelief. Doubt is the devil's amusement park.

Maybe you've heard it said: you're a long time dead. Well, let's put that into perspective. Of course, we know that this earthly physical life must be discontinued at some point. But the good news for the genuinely born-again person is that life will resume in the blissful heavenly kingdom for all eternity. Unfortunately, for the unsaved, death will not be such a beautiful experience. Permanent separation from the heavenly Father and continued existence in the eternal flames of hell isn't a delightful picture of serenity. In fact, the Bible doesn't go into much vivid detail beyond the picture of intense thirst, outer darkness, wailing, and the gnashing of teeth. But the worst horror was what Jesus experienced briefly upon the cross. Godlessness.

Physical death isn't final. It's probably like walking through one of those magnetic screen doors. Just stepping from one dimension into the other. Eternal Life after death is good enough reason for everyone to examine their spiritual condition while there is time to do so. Make whatever changes are necessary to avoid the torments of hell's inextinguishable reminder of Christ's offer of grace. No one should take damnation lightly. Never test the limits of God.

But there is a side of salvation that may be overlooked by most. It's the here-and-now relationship developing between you and the Savior that is truly remarkable, unique, and very personal. It's as though Jesus becomes your best Friend. It's easy to see why His disciples were so absorbed by Him. The Lord makes everything in this life better and brighter. Jesus adds a special kind of value to the moments you spend together. Learning from such a profound Teacher opens areas of understanding never considered. When the Holy Spirit illuminates things from His perspective, it's awe-inspiring. Jesus just makes living life many times more meaningful. Being a disciple of the Lord Jesus is the most rewarding relationship I have ever experienced.

Chapter 9

Acknowledge Your Need for the Savior

Look at the high cost of perceived success today. How much are you willing to surrender to attain the many things your heart desires? Even the best that earth has to offer is still only temporal. If time doesn't tarnish, corrode, or shatter the things you love, Satan will be there to rob you of their pleasure.

Just consider the divorce rate, feticide, and identity crises happening in the lives of everyday people caught up in the revolution of sin triggered by selfishness and greed. Unfortunately, busy citizens spend most of their lives striving to satisfy their immediate expectations, aspiring to reach personal and professional goals or to satisfy their carnal desires. The noble commitment of parenting has taken a back seat to career and success. People in almost every walk of life are driven to have more possessions, power, prominence, and sometimes even worldly acclaim. The more modern the generation, the greater the effort to obtain far more things than what is necessary for a comfortable and secure lifestyle. You may indeed love all your possessions but remember, at the end of the day, that stuff doesn't need you or love you in return. Furthermore, the intoxicating drain on you physically and emotionally to have and maintain all the possessions you value so highly may wind up costing you more than you ever dreamed. *People who want to be rich bring temptations to themselves. They are caught in a trap. They begin to want many foolish things that will hurt them. These things ruin and destroy people* (1 Timothy 6:9, ERV).

Very few people in this present-day appreciate or are content with living a life of moderation. Universal signs of narcissism are everywhere. Everything we endeavor to achieve is to make an outwardly display. It feeds the ego when we can impress those around us with our implied success. We struggle endlessly to measure up to an unrealistic standard set by the glamorous

Hollywood elite. Gyms, personal trainers, and beauty products have everyone body-conscious. There's no end to dissatisfaction, especially with the outward image. The influence of media fuels every physical fad put in the spotlight for public consumption. The exorbitant amount of money, time, and energy that is spent on personal appearance is mind-boggling. Perfect teeth, Botox injections, nose jobs, face lifts, tummy tucks, implants of all kinds, and many other assorted enhancements, just for starters. What an enormous sacrifice, just to prop up a shallow self-image. And that only addresses the body-conscious.

Then there is the lifestyle. Living in the most affluent neighborhoods where lavish homes and estates highlight one's prosperity. Keeping pace with the affluent means putting the children in only the best private schools. Mingling with just the right group of business associates is vitally important. Another critical consideration is to have the proper social circle of friends. In some instances, the right political connections are essential to perpetuate a fashionable and forward-driven itinerary. Pulling up stakes for just the right career opportunities is a must. And, of course, luxurious cars, vacations, and fine dining all go along with having and presenting an opulent lifestyle. Just considering it all is exhausting.

Today's fast pace and careless manner of living have taken a tremendous toll on all members of the family unit. There are many perverse lifestyles that have morphed out of insensitivity and selfishness. Covenant vows are no more sacred than the paper they are written on. Partners without the benefit of a marriage pledge have gained tremendous popularity in modern society. This enables one's counterpart to be replaced without a big to-do or much financial entanglement. Then in no time, the singles are ready to mingle all over again. Just as soon as the sparkle wears off the old one, it's on to the next conquest. Casual relationships are referred to as a one-night stand for a reason. Neither party is interested in commitment. Their only desire is immediate gratification. And should a pregnancy occur from one of those apathetic relationships, chances are very slim that the baby would be allowed to survive. Bringing a child into the world is a life-long commitment. Therefore, in the event of an unwanted pregnancy, the life of a child is negligible and therefore becomes just another unfortunate but expendable casualty of fornication.

In a broken home or broken relationship, children, through no fault of their own, will be torn in half emotionally. Then the probability is very good that one of their parents will be replaced by a stranger, and the children are usually compelled to embrace those strangers favorably. They might even be considered potential prospects for family consolidation. Those situations may be considered acceptable by today's standards, but God looks upon those circumstances quite differently. The casual indifference to marriage and family creates a persistent and severe malfunction in the home where children are expected to adjust constantly. These are but a few of the unhealthy circumstances that hinder sound emotional development in children. It's no wonder that many young people are angry, depressed, confused, detached, and suicidal.

Who is left to put the children's necessities first? The closed schools for the greater part of the years 2020 and 21 dealt a crushing blow to the development of their academic and social skills. Their teachers were gone, and their friends were relocated to other places. Kids' dreams are dying; many feel secluded and alone. Is it any wonder their hope for a bright future is fading? Far too many undeveloped youths find their early life experience full of stress and very transitory. It's devastating when they've discovered they have nothing with which to anchor them to solid ground. There is no authenticity in their lives. What tangible and lasting things do they have to cling to? What fidelity do they have holding on to them? Everything about their world is a pseudo existence. Many see their lives as disposable, temporary, or entirely worthless. The thought of suicide among teenagers is a serious epidemic. Those committing suicide is beyond tragic. How much dejection are the children of those circumstances able to withstand if they have nothing more important in their life to hold on to other than a cell phone and their disenchanting relationships on social media?

And quite honestly, there isn't a worse feeling than one of hopelessness. But the Bible offers good news. Read the Scripture written by King David in the book of Psalms. *O my soul, why be so gloomy and discouraged? Trust in God! I shall again praise him for his wondrous help; he will make me smile again, for he is my God!* (Psalm 43:5, TLB)

Dysfunction isn't something that just came upon the world since Covid-19. Dysfunction in the family unit has left many deep and lasting scars on far too many past generations, beginning with Abel's murder in Adam's family at some point after being expelled from the Garden of Eden. The Bible tells many stories of personal life and entire nations destroyed because they chose to depart from God's established standard. Nevertheless, there are many more outstanding examples showing the way to avoid those tragic circumstances. The sad truth is, in an advanced society such as ours, we should be able to recognize the hazards and alleviate those pitfalls in our culture. The Word of God has countless wholesome ways of promoting exemplary alternatives to life's complex impediments.

Thanks be to God, most children are resilient and will grow up to power through the rough patches in life. But what trauma have they suffered because of it? They will either become productive citizens or fall through the cracks and be labeled outcasts according to society's standards. And I would be remiss if I failed to mention that those standards are not the standard set for us by God. However, most of society seems to be dissatisfied with God's design for peace and contentment. When will enough be enough? What will it take to satisfy you? If most of your time and vitality is spent chasing false expectations and acquiring material goods, how much quality time will there be left to enjoy those acquisitions or even the simpler pleasures life has to offer? *A greedy person is in a hurry to get rich, but he is ignorant of the loss that is about to overtake him* (Proverbs 28:22, VOICE).

Have no delusions; in the reality of infinite time, this life is but a vapor. What happens at the end of your rat race? Everything you've sacrificed for, everything you've acquired is left to another. Have you made provisions for your eternal future? This lifetime is your only opportunity to do that. *Instead, put up your treasures in heaven where moths do not attack, where rust does not corrode, and where thieves are barred at the door. For where your treasure is, there your heart will be also* (Matthew 6:20–21, VOICE).

For where jealousy and selfish ambition exist, there will be disorder and every vile practice (James 3:16, ESV). The previous Scripture in James says it clearly. Current trends of horrific violence on America's streets have shown us some vivid examples of repulsive and egocentric behavior. Rioting, vandalism, theft, slander, adultery, rape, and murder. Those are only a few among the many atrocious acts that are corrupting this once relatively tranquil nation. Preoccupation with self is the diabolical force behind all the superficial discontentedness we see in the world today. And the constant fixation with things is just another form of misplaced worship. Being under the false impression that having worldly goods makes people happy, then pitifully, those individuals will soon realize that they have been deceived by greed and a fast-fleeting sense of contentment. Chasing after happiness by ill-gotten means will prove illusionary in no time.

Nevertheless, there is a good reason for optimism. Once we realize that we've been in pursuit of the wrong treasures in life, then it's just a matter of adjusting our course and choosing the right objectives. Seeking God and putting into practice the true wisdom of His Word is what delivers people from violent behavior and deliberately inflicting harm upon others. Unrightfully taking things that other people worked hard for will just backfire upon them. *"Woe to you for getting rich by evil means, attempting to live beyond the reach of danger. By the murders you commit, you have shamed your name and forfeited your lives* (Habakkuk 2:9–10, TLB).

Today in America, the city streets are filled with homeless people. For some, it's their chosen path in life. For others, it's the result of some unfortunate incident that resulted from adversity. The situation has become so overwhelming throughout America, the answer has yet to be addressed effectively. Meanwhile, some of the people in tent shelters have very serious physical, emotional, and mental problems that remain unaddressed. These men and women are tragically rejected by society and, in one sense, considered lepers.

But let me share with you a brief story about a real leper and how the Lord Jesus always treated everyone equally, with dignity and respect. Not even the lepers isolated from their community were overlooked by Jesus. *While Jesus was in one of the towns, a man came along who was covered with leprosy. When he saw Jesus, he fell with his face to the ground and begged him, "Lord, if you are willing, you can make me clean." Jesus reached out his hand and touched the man. "I am willing," he said. "Be clean!" And immediately the leprosy left him* (Luke 5:12–14, NIV).

Lepers were contagious and not allowed to be within a certain distance of other persons within a community. The Bible doesn't tell us much in the way of that man's background or situation. But with the seriousness of his condition, he probably hadn't experienced any human contact or physical affection for a considerable length of time. In desperation, this determined man took an unsafe risk by entering society. Somewhere in the midst of the great multitude of people was the one Man the leper was looking for. And when he spied Jesus, he fell at His feet and offered humble reverence before requesting his petition with fervent sincerity and great hope.

Not everyone who sought Jesus for healing needed a touch. There was one occasion when a centurion soldier had such great faith he asked Jesus only to speak the Word, and his servant would be healed (Matthew 8:8). But Jesus knew all too well that the leprous man hadn't been tenderly touched by another human being in a very long time. When Jesus reached out with compassion and touched the man, it was a gesture of empathy and love. Jesus could have just Spoken the Word and declared the man healed, but Jesus has a powerful need to touch us. That man's whole life was changed in that brief encounter with the Son of God. Notice the distinguishing degrees of faith. The centurion had no doubt whatsoever of the healing power of Jesus. The case of the leper was much different. He didn't doubt that Jesus could heal him, but he was uncertain if Jesus would be willing to relieve his suffering. Jesus was quick to affirm His effectual desire to honor the man's heartfelt request.

Unfortunately, almost everybody we associate with today has dealt with or is dealing with some type of unwholesome variance or adversity they are trying to manage. No matter where we live in society, there will be evidence of suffering and affliction. Drugs, violence, death, sickness, disease, and poverty. All of society's insufficiency is caused by turning our back on Jesus and choosing to live in spiritual dearth. But there is no reason to be discouraged. Jesus is waiting to touch all who will come unto Him with a contrite heart. *Then he said, "I am the Lord your God, and I cure your diseases. If you obey me by doing right and by following my laws and teachings, I won't punish you with the diseases I sent on the Egyptians"* (Exodus 15:26, CEV).

Chapter 10

Two-Thousand Years of Warning

Instead of securing the future for the many joys of a heavenly afterlife, the majority of people today are totally sullen and fixated on having their best life now. They are unsure of the future and have lost hope of having a brighter tomorrow. They are living like a hamster running on a wheel that always takes them right back to the starting position. Their efforts to keep pace with their friends, neighbors, and the privileged set, have greatly encumbered any thought of having a tranquil life. Keeping up with whatever happens to be in vogue is a big job. Having all the latest technical gadgets and toys, electric automobiles, eating at the French Laundry, a residence in Napa Valley and leisure holidays is all very gratuitous. But being immersed in all the pleasures of this life just might cause you to become a spiritual pauper. Even today, life and times are much the same as they were in Noah's day. That is, before the flood. In God's opinion—and His is the only one that matters—the entire earth had become ruined by man's corruption and continued violence. In all the earth, there was only one righteous man who God would reveal His plans to. Of all the individuals alive at the time, the Old Testament ark gave refuge to only eight persons and selected creatures. Every other living thing underwent the wrath and judgment of God. *In the days before the flood, people were busy making lives for themselves: they were eating and drinking, marrying and giving in marriage, making plans and having children and growing old, until the day Noah entered the ark. Those people had no idea what was coming; they knew nothing about the floods until the floods were upon them, sweeping them all away. That is how it will be with the coming of the Son of Man. Two men will be plowing a field: one will be taken, and the other will be left in the field. Two women will be somewhere grinding at a mill: one will be taken, and the other will be left at the mill. So keep watch. You don't know when your Lord will come. But you should know this: If the owner of a house had known his house was about to be broken into, he would have stayed up all night, vigilantly. He would have kept watch, and he would have thwarted the thief. So you must be ready because you know the Son of Man will come, but you can't know precisely when* (Matthew 24:38–44, VOICE).

The coming of the Son of Man is the Ark of modern-day. Jesus will suddenly snatch away those who died in Christ and every living soul that comprises the body of His church. Scripture doesn't reveal the day or the hour. Only the Father knows the time. Therefore, every living soul should be hyper-vigilant. Be conscious and receptive to the signs. *You are going to hear the noise of battles close by and the news of battles far away; but do not be troubled. Such things must happen, but they do not mean that the end has come. Countries will fight each other; kingdoms will attack one another. There will be famines and earthquakes everywhere* (Matthew 24:6–7, GNT).

Keep in mind, those Words of Jesus were Spoken over 2000 years ago. Hearing of war suggests fighting between other countries. Battles close by might indicate our own military action. Famines and earthquakes are but additional signs. There has never been a time when suffering due to hunger hasn't been specified somewhere, especially in third-world countries. Certain parts of the planet that were never before disquieted by earthquakes have begun to experience the sudden shaking of the earth. Thanks to copious records of historical events and modern technology, we know exactly where the planet's adversities have taken place. But is there a more contemptible and contrived action than that of war? There have been endless civil and national wars dating all the way back to antiquity. Fighting has been consistent even in modern times. How much nearer do all these indicators bring us to the Day of the Lord? The question then remains: how long or to what extent must sinfulness be suffered before the Good Shepherd raptures His children out of this world? That's the one question that should be on everyone's mind. When Lord? All Christendom is wondering how long before the trumpet sounds and the Lord bids His faithful bride entry into their long-awaited home. That end-time phenomenon is commonly referred to as the rapture. Which war will be the final conflict that will open the door to God's long-awaited objective is yet unknown.

As of this writing, there is a raging battle escalating between the nations of Russia and Ukraine. Many allied nations believe Vladimir Putin has gone beyond the realm of reason. But what anyone else thinks hasn't detoured him from his intended purpose. We may think their war is a world away, but that is certainly not the case anymore. The nations around the globe are our neighbors. The use of sophisticated weaponry has put every living creature on this planet in jeopardy. But I want to share this hypothesis with you concerning the last days. Among the final warning signs is pestilence, which has already afflicted the entire world. Then the clash of nations. There is always a possibility that the conflict between Ukraine and Russia could turn out to be the war to inaugurate the beginning of the end. For the most part, according to the news accounts, travel into and out of Ukraine has been suspended. Consequently, medications, water, food, and other supplies have been interrupted. That is certainly a cause for alarm when millions of people are stranded and have little hope of leaving or life-saving resources arriving. With that many civilians, not counting the soldiers, food, and water is sure to be in short supply, thereby leading to famine. Another of the final signs pointing to the last days is earthquakes. According to Wikipedia, the word earthquake is used to describe any seismic event—whether natural or brought about by humans doing something to cause seismic waves. Actually, the word tremor is also used for non-seismic rumbling. That would be bombs causing the earth to quake. But there is one more hint that we can't overlook, although isolated from the other details. Jesus speaks about the weather. *How terrible it will be in those days for women who are pregnant and for mothers with little babies! Pray to God that these things will not happen in the winter! For the trouble of those days will be far worse than any the world has ever known from the very beginning when God created the world until the present time. Nor will there ever be anything like it again* (Mark 13:17–19, GNT).

Perhaps we don't agree on everything, but maybe we can agree on the depraved condition the world is in. It appears Vladimir Putin has the whole world on notice with the threat of nuclear war upon any intervening nation that crosses the line of demarcation in his estimation. In the early stages of the invasion, we watched the women with young children and babies in tow fleeing Ukraine apart from their husbands, who have been ordered to stay and fight for their country. Schools, hospitals, and maternity wards have suffered some of the most horrific casualties. When Russia invaded Ukraine, in February 2022, the temperatures there had dipped into the twenties.

By way of advanced technology, citizens around the world are able to tune in to the latest carnage deployed on the innocent Ukrainian population. Watching the Russian invasion upon the vulnerable is like tuning into a daily soap opera. It sickens me inside. What can be more heart-wrenching than seeing the lives of so many, including little children, being callously destroyed? The carnage and suffering witnessed are beyond belief in a day of supposed civility. But I must pontificate. Most Americans are greatly distressed over Russia's indiscriminate annihilation of innocuous human beings. Some have referred to this war as a holocaust. It seems as though the voices in protest of the obvious war crimes are becoming louder day by day. But let me stop here and ask. Is our outrage because we have become daily witnesses to such atrocities? It's ironic that witnessing such carnage has shocked the senses of American citizens enough to raise their cries against the barbaric slaughter of innocent Ukrainian victims.

Well then, if a few cameras on the front lines of a blood bath are able to arouse our appalled senses, let's try using those same tactics here in America. Before casting the proverbial stone at others, let's take a realistic look into our own indiscriminate carnage right here in our own country. Let's put cameras into every abortion clinic, thereby documenting each savagely cruel, unethical means of torture every tiny, murdered fetus and infant must endure at the hands of a merciless butcher. Show the severing of limbs and body parts in utero, and let us put that carnage on the daily news. We can observe first-hand how life is vacuumed from the comfort of the warm sanctuary of a mother's womb. Then show the mutilated body of the aborted child. Murder is the planned and premeditated killing of another human being regardless of their stage of viability. Let every horrific procedure be documented for the genocide it truly is. Then maybe, just maybe, those same hearts that break for Ukraine will betray our callous disregard for the incalculable unseen lives also longing and determined to survive. Hopefully, some of the tears being shed for the Ukrainians will fall by the buckets full for the sixty-three million fetus deaths in America by the merciless brutality of abortion. Which incidentally is a polite term for the barbaric act of homicide. You may terminate the flesh of a baby, but you can never quell their eternal soul. God knows how His precious lives were treated. Those tiny little beings fought hard and valiantly, with all their might, to live and not die. Regrettably, the force of destruction they fell to was monstrous and powerfully determined to snuff out their tiny lives. Just like the Russians are doing to the Ukrainians. A murderer is either the butcher or the consenter. Neither has any regard for the flame of life, regardless how faint the flicker. One thing more. Throughout the Bible, the word *conceived* was used to describe the woman's prenatal condition. Fertilization has occurred. At conception, there is a baby on the way. If you are pregnant, there is a child in your womb. The trimester only describes the child's development. The King James version of the Bible expressly uses the phrase "woman with child" (Exodus 21:22). God has prearranged everything. Although an essential part of the baby's protective element, mother and child are two entirely different individuals.

All these recent events may be indications of the long-awaited day of glorification for the saints of God. Lawlessness, murder of all descriptions, war, immorality of unimaginable mannerisms and prolific proportions. In the days of Noah, God was so very grieved at men's wickedness, He repented making man on the earth. *And God saw that the wickedness of man was great in the earth, and that every imagination of the thoughts of his heart was only evil continually* (Genesis 6:5, KJV).

Judgment is indeed coming to the world one day. But let us consider a final thought on the subject of timing. Palm Sunday represents the day Jesus rode into Jerusalem seated upon a donkey's colt. There is great significance regarding that event. The people heralded Jesus as their defender King against the oppressive Roman Empire. But Jesus came to His people as their Messiah and Judge. Unfortunately for the nation of Israel, they refused to recognize Him as either.

April 10th of 2022 was the day that the whole Christian world celebrated Palm Sunday. Is it possible that date represents the beginning of judgment for all of humanity? We must wait and see. However, my point in sharing this is to inform my reader that there are no coincidences in God's world. When the Lord Jesus Spoke concerning His ministry, these were His Words. *"Do not think that I have come to bring peace on the earth; I have not come to bring peace, but a sword of division between belief and unbelief* (Matthew 10:34, AMP). That reminds me of a similar circumstance in the New Testament. When Jesus entered the temple in Jerusalem, He immediately appraised the deplorable disorder. Being as the hour was late, Jesus and His disciples left Jerusalem and returned to Bethany. Along their journey, Jesus noticed a fig tree fully leaved and inviting. But when He approached, there were no figs. Therefore, Jesus cursed the fig tree, and it immediately withered and died. Of course, we now know the condition of the tree represented the fruitless state of the Jewish nation. But the same analogy represents America and the world. On the outside, we may look like authentic Christians celebrating our risen Lord, but we have no genuine fruit to show for it.

When Jesus returned to the temple the following day, He wasted no time cleaning out the degenerate waste. So, there you have it. The possibility of a perfect storm. Pestilence, war, famine, earthquakes, and wintertime—all simultaneous indicators that Jesus cautioned us to watch for. Could this be the culmination of the long-awaited day marking the end time? *We tell you what the Lord said. We who are still alive when the Lord comes, will not go ahead of those who have died. The Lord himself will come down from heaven. There will be a shout, a great angel will speak, and God's loud horn or trumpet will be blown. Then we who are still alive on earth will be caught up together with those who were dead. We will be caught up in the clouds to meet the Lord in the air. And then we will be with the Lord forever!* (1 Thessalonians 4:14–16, WE)

Although we are unable to see things from God's perspective, He is sovereign and has every right to use war for His ultimate purpose if He deems it necessary to do so. Besides the fact that God no longer uses prophets, He is under no obligation to reveal His intentions to His creation anyway. But God has often used war for purposes far beyond man's ability to grasp. Therefore, it's not inappropriate to wonder: is God's hand at work in this? The sovereign nation of Ukraine was completely unprepared to fight a war, but its citizens are determined to defend their right to liberty and prevent occupation by Russia. And it's totally naive to think that America is exempt from war or the fallout from Ukraine's misery and suffering. Ukraine's peaceful citizens didn't invite the invasion of Russia, but fighting for what they believe in has already cost the lives of many on either side of the controversy. And it has become blatantly obvious that President Biden is reluctant to offer President Zelenskyy the maximum assistance of airpower needed to fully defend his nation. However, not providing adequate humanitarian relief for a country under siege by the Russian dictator, Vladimir Putin, is unconscionable. Yes, our government has provided billions of dollars in weaponry, but is that really enough? If my neighbor's house was on fire, would lending him my garden hose be morally and adequately sufficient? The administration in Washington has been around long enough to know first-hand exactly how the Russian dictator operates.

Putin's reputation precedes him. The Russian army besieges the innocent civilians. Targeting their neighborhoods, hospitals, and schools relentlessly until surrender is inevitable. I don't believe that God will overlook America's overt neglect of compassionate intervention to the pleading country and citizens of Ukraine.

But that forces the question. How much blood is the valiant President Zelenskyy willing to spill defending a principle? Enlisting sixty-year-old men into active duty and young Ukrainian boys at the tender age of eighteen is ill-advised. The biblical principle set the standard age for fighting at age twenty for young men and able-bodied for older males. Who will blink first and back down from this grievous confrontation before the N-word isn't just a threat anymore? Another nuclear incident, regardless of how it may occur, could have a lethal effect on the entire world. There is no rationalizing with an unreasonable dictator bent on fulfilling his own objective. When will wisdom prevail?

It's merely speculation on my part, but the subterfuge of a mad man forcing Ukraine to defend herself against the tyranny of a brutal dictator is an atrocity, to say the least. Seeing the television coverage targeting the civilian population and a grey-haired granny learning how to pull the trigger on a rifle to protect the freedom of her grandchildren is absolutely heartbreaking. Thirteen and fourteen-year-old kids arming themselves and learning how to make Molotov cocktails to protect their homes should mortify the very soul of every compassionate human being. Mass graves with tiny limbs protruding is an indescribable sight. We must ask ourselves, what if that was me or my children? Let's admire their patriotism but not romanticize the savage actions necessary in armed combat. The adults must protect the children caught up in war. Never, no matter what it may cost the country, never put young lives at risk in military action. Does anyone really believe that a Russian soldier isn't going to shoot whoever is pointing a gun at him? Let the children live another day. Maybe one of them will use these horrendous experiences to teach others how to live peacefully in a world of differences.

It's necessary to add something concerning Ukraine's defense. There seems to be an operative force more powerful and greatly more intelligent, extending well beyond the assistance offered by any of the allied nations. The hand of God is obviously involved. I would suggest that God has heard the outcry of His people world-over on behalf of Ukraine. It appears the Lord God Almighty has fortified the will, the might, and military power to safeguard the sovereign nation of Ukraine. Adding to Ukraine's defense, I'm convinced that God has somehow perplexed the Russian army. The Old Testament has instances where God used a very similar strategy.

With that in mind, let us remember the brave young lad David that defended God's honor against the Philistine giant named Goliath. One stone is all it took to reign victorious over that imposing enemy. What did David have that the entire Israel army didn't have? David wasn't trusting in his own skill; he knew it would be God changing the events that day. David's faith in God didn't fail him then or ever after that.

Then there was a jaw-dropping event that occurred between the fifth and tenth day of June in 1967, called the Six-Day War, ending with an enormous victory for the solitary forces of Israel. Against overwhelming odds and manpower, the Israeli army took possession of the Golan Heights, the West Bank, including East Jerusalem, the Gaza Strip, and the Sinai Peninsula. Then there was the Yom Kippur War in October of 1973. Again, Israel claimed victory with the support of its sister nation America. But the point here is just this. When God's people come together for a humanitarian cause that the Lord Himself would approve of, there will be justice. *"Listen, Israel! Today you're going to fight a battle against your enemies. Don't be intimidated by them! Don't be afraid! Don't run away! Don't let them terrify you! The Eternal, your True God, has come out here with you, and He'll fight for you against your enemies and save you"* (Deuteronomy 20:3–4, VOICE).

The preceding Scripture could just as easily be the Lord

speaking to any God-fearing nation. That's precisely the message Americans need to hear from God right now. But unfortunately, that won't be God's appraisal of America. Not until America turns from her wicked ways and repents of decades of profuse sacrilege. The preeminent detriment leading to the total collapse of America is the unreserved abandonment of God, followed by pride and unwavering determination to pursue her own proclivity (Isaiah 53:6). Since America is firmly committed to separate from God, she is naked without His covering of protection or His hand of defense. We have no way of knowing how the present war between Ukraine and Russia will be resolved or if military involvement will be forced upon America. Nevertheless, no matter how gruesome and unpleasant circumstances may become, God is still in complete control. The Lord's church must continue steadfast and trust in God's unequaled abilities to influence those matters according to His divine purpose. Remember the prayer of Jesus in the heaviest time of His Life on earth. "Nevertheless, not as I will, but as You will" (Matthew 26:39).

Part 2: Chapter 11

Plant Wisely, Harvest Bountifully

In the book of James, he elaborates on the foremost significance of works within the church body of Christ. *For as the body without the spirit is dead, so faith without works is dead also* (James 2:26, NKJV).

Works are earnest proof of the royal law of love in the very heart of every Christian. What would have happened if, at the very last minute, Jesus looked at that empty cross between the two thieves and said, "Oh no. No way am I going through with that!" Where would we all be if that had happened? The Father would need to make a bigger lake of fire for all of mankind. But our courageous Savior led by example and fulfilled His final responsibility by taking our place and our sins with Him to the cross. *Greater love has no one than this, than to lay down one's life for his friends* (John 15:13, NKJV).

In the church community, service on behalf of others, in or out of the sanctuary, is commonly referred to as works. The Holy Spirit conditions every believer to love with the same passion that Jesus possesses. It is beautiful to see God operating through the gifts and talents of His children. But there is a word of caution here. In the book of Revelation, the Lord Jesus sends a letter to the church at Ephesus through His disciple John. It seems that works became their all and all. Among their many good and moral deeds, they left their first love. *However, I have this against you: The love you had at first is gone. Remember how far you have fallen. Return to me and change the way you think and act, and do what you did at first. I will come to you and take your lamp stand from its place if you don't change* (Revelation 2:4–5, GW).

God's sons and daughters are referred to as salt and light. Nothing tastes quite as good without that little zest that salt adds. Every good deed and every kindness is a little trace of savor, sprinkled here and there like a hint of pleasant flavoring. Without that unpretentious spice, the world would be a rather tasteless and wearisome place. And there is nothing more comforting than a glimmer of light after those dark storms and difficult challenges that often present themselves in our lives. Suffering is a part of life that we all must go through at some point in time. But the operative word is through. With God, there is always light at the end of adversity. Light can illuminate in a variety of ways. It could be a single word spoken by a brother in Christ, a revealing insight from God, or even a smile from a stranger, all at just the right time. With light comes hope for a brighter future.

The body of Christ is comprised of many assorted roles. As in the case of an automobile, many individual parts are required for a car to operate optimally. But the fact is, it's just as important for each part to function as one smooth unit to provide the most favorable operation possible. Yet, God has a much better analogy when it comes to His church. The Lord Describes the church comparably to that of the human body. Each part of the body functions in a different but phenomenal capacity. The arms can't do what the feet do. The hands can't do what the mouth does. Just as the parts of the human body have a particular purpose, everyone in the church has their own gifts and duty to perform. So then, the gifts of the Spirit serve many divergent purposes, but all function and operate in perfect unison according to the will of the Lord. Since all Christians are beholden to God, let them remember what was said in James. Faith without works is dead. Simply stated, works in themselves have no spiritual profit unless they are done for the glory of God. *Then He said to His disciples, "The harvest is plentiful, but the workers are few"* (Matthew 9:37, NKJV).

What is being said in the previous Scripture? Of course, the workers are the servants of God. Are they few due to indifference or a simple case of laziness? Either way, when that happens, people die in their sins, and the whole church body suffers. That is exactly what is grieving the Holy Spirit today. The church, as the body of Christ, has become inapt, lethargic, and negligent in its moral and spiritual responsibility to the Lord God. And when the church fails in its purpose, whole societies suffer, and people wind up in the lake of fire when their physical body dies. That revolting place is hell, and it burns for all eternity.

Here then is a succinct illustration of what deficient labor might look like. Suppose you have decided to grow a small garden in the corner of your property. You are so excited about harvesting freshly cut flowers and big baskets of luscious vegetables. Daily you watched over your little patch of potential blooms. But after several weeks without any signs of growth, you have begun to get discouraged. After all the prayer and faith you've put into the project, and still, nothing has come of it. Your hopes have faded. But where was the work? The soil wasn't tilled or made fertile or watered. How could there be any germination when there weren't any seeds planted? Lacking the necessary labor hinders any kind of germination. The very same principle applies both in the natural and in the spiritual realm. Plan, prepare, and pray that your endeavor will bring forth an abundant harvest. If you intend to produce any kind of crop, natural or spiritual, there must be some labor involved. Be assured, the following Scripture says it all perfectly. Everyone will eventually reap what they have sown, whether the seed is good or bad. *Do not be deceived, God is not mocked; for whatever a man sows, that he will also reap* (Galatians 6:7, NKJV).

The whole point of God incarnate was to show mankind the Door to eternal Life and teach others how to share the good news of the gospel message. Evangelism is a practical and necessary service of sowing the Word into the lives of the lost. Then, at the proper season, there will be a special end-time gathering. No one knows the principle of sowing and reaping better than a farmer. He can't plant soybeans if he wants to harvest corn. And, if he expects to yield a crop next season, he must begin the laborious work well before the expected time of harvest. *"I assure you: Unless a grain of wheat falls to the ground and dies, it remains by itself. But if it dies, it produces a large crop* (John 12:24, HCSB).

How could Scripture portray any clearer the meaning of seed time and harvest? Jesus represented the Seed. His burial was the planting or seedtime. His resurrection represented the harvest to come. The time was Passover, and the unsurpassed Life offered by Jesus was appointed to die on the cross at Calvary for the sins of humanity. To symbolize burial, He was placed in a tomb for three days, awaiting the appointed time to resurrect into everlasting Life. The Son of God was buried upon His death that Good Friday morning. But three days later, on Resurrection Sunday, the harvest yielded from that sole holy Heir of God has amassed millions of saintly sons and daughters all over the world. Therefore, you must agree, the death of Jesus brings forth new Life to whosoever will repent of their sins. Truly an indisputable portrayal of seed time and harvest. *Most assuredly, I say to you, unless a grain of wheat falls into the ground and dies, it remains alone; but if it dies, it produces much grain* (John 12:24, NKJV).

Let's pause here for just a moment and think about what is being said in this next Scripture. *For they sow the wind, and they shall reap the whirlwind. The standing grain has no heads, it shall yield no meal if it were to yield, aliens would devour it* (Hosea 8:7, RSV).

It's only obvious that work is the practical function of labor in some capacity while inactivity is worthless lethargy. Inaction is also a type of seed sown. Any seed will produce a crop according to its kind. What crops are produced is entirely up to the sower. A lazy sower will have an empty barn. But keep this in mind. As any farmer will tell you, reaping isn't necessarily spontaneous. There are occasions when planting may begin in the late fall, but the crops will not be harvested until late the following spring. The seed may indeed germinate in the autumn, but the cold earth prevents any continued growth. Thereby, the sprout remains dormant until the winter season has passed, and the ground once again receives its warmth from the sun. Humans may not always encounter immediate results from their deeds. Be assured, there will be a reckoning in heaven, good or bad. *He who plants and he who waters are one, and each will receive his wages according to his labor* (1

Corinthians 3:8, ESV).

Although God is gracious to forgive us our sins, He keeps a very close record of any evil exploits for which there has been no repentance or supplication for forgiveness. And one thing more. Although man's sins can be forgiven, retribution may still be required to satisfy judgment. And you can be confident in knowing that God's data will never be lost or corrupted.

There is no measure of time behind the indistinct veil that separates the kingdom of heaven from our natural reality. The sun and moon are for the benefit of man. Everything done on earth, past or present, is all about judgment, redemption, and eternal Life. Every time I think of that passage of Scripture that speaks of sowing and reaping, I wonder: why would anyone sow to their eternal damnation? It's especially troubling when the judgment of God has been clearly described in the Bible. And redemption has been made freely available by faith to all who would believe. Why would someone even consider gambling with their allotted time in this life? There is only one way to heaven, and that is through the sacrifice Jesus made on the cross. He paid sins debt with His own blood, thereby redeeming the sinner's life from eternal death.

Are you among the chosen of God? His elect? Those are the individuals who God ordained and gave over to Christ's care before the foundation of the world was laid. Their names are written in the Lamb's Book of Life. They are the Lord's church. The real church! His bride. These persons are the body of believers that Jesus will give rise to prior to the time of tribulation. Will you be among the faithful servants that Jesus calls home? Physical death is assured to everyone in some manner and point in their existence prior to the rapture of the church. That is why the wisest servants of the Lord are diligently listening for the Voice of their loving Master. *For the Lord himself will descend from heaven with a cry of command, with the voice of an archangel, and with the sound of the trumpet of God. And the dead in Christ will rise first. Then we who are alive, who are left, will be caught up together with them in the clouds to meet the Lord in the air, and so we will always be with the Lord* (Thessalonians 4:16–17, ESV).

Life in the eternal kingdom of God is granted only through the Son of Almighty God. There is a great risk to those who postpone or delay in receiving the gracious gift of eternal Life offered by the Savior Jesus. Please understand: the rapture is a long-awaited mystery. All living individuals not called up to heaven by the Lord Jesus will remain earthbound throughout the seven-and-one-half years of anguish during the period of tribulation. *For then shall be great tribulation, such as was not since the beginning of the world to this time, no, nor ever shall be* (Matthew 24:21, KJV).

The Lord God is more than willing to extend His grace to all who are repentant of their sins. Many Christians have fallen short of the glory of God (Romans 3:23). That means lacking in the responsibility and high calling to obedience and duty to our Savior and Master, Christ Jesus. Nevertheless, the Almighty is a good Father to all His children and most desirous to forgive whenever they come to Him humbly and repent for the sins committed against the Word of the Lord. But, as for the unregenerate, who can say when God's patience will come to an end. For any sinner living in outright rebellion against God, it is quite a different matter altogether. I can hardly imagine anyone desiring to spend eternity in hell. Nevertheless, insurrection against the Lord leaves God with no other choice but to judge that sinner harshly. Repent or perish. Keep this in mind. Sudden death isn't announced beforehand.

And just to make this one point clear, the Lord doesn't judge any person unjustly, nor does He send anyone to hell; they go voluntarily! Every word spoken and every action sown in this lifetime will be reaped, either on earth or at the throne of judgment. God's verdict is just and in strict conformity to His righteous standard, not the shoddy standards observed by mankind.

Many of the teachings of Jesus were taught by illustration, as an object lesson, both in Word and deed. Everywhere He went, He healed, cast out demons, restored value to the lives of the outcasts, and gave hope to the hopeless. Jesus raised the dead, restored sight to the blind, and fed all who were hungry. Jesus forgave the sinners and Commanded them to sin no more. His message was that of peace, forgiveness, and love. Now remarkably, our Lord's labor continues through His faithful followers, wherever they may be in the world. And like Peter said, "…but such as I have, I give you" (Acts 3:6). And that same desire is in every Christian's heart that submits to the authority and direction of the Holy Spirit.

Perhaps you feel that you have nothing or little to contribute other than your own experience. Then that is the perfect seed to plant in the life of an unbeliever or one in doubt. Even speaking such an earnest personal message, you've shared your heartfelt love with a neighbor. Who can say what they needed just then? Maybe at that very moment, it was God's love or His willingness to forgive. Maybe the pivotal moment was receiving Christ with an invitation. Never waste an opportunity to do your part for the kingdom. The Holy Spirit will give you the wisdom and courage you need to pull down every stronghold. After that, it's entirely up to the beneficiary of your labored investment. Hopefully, God will soften their heart, and they will joyously accept the Lord's invitation to come to Him.

Chapter 12

If the Truth Is Told

Do you remember being asked when you were a child what you wanted to be when you grew up? Well then, now that you are all grown up, how do you want your final chapter of life to read? What will be that one essential characteristic of your life you hope to emphasize? Strangely enough, the one glaringly fatal and commonly overlooked necessity by most is their eternal salvation in Christ Jesus. Once you're gone, leaving your loved ones to wonder about your fate is a haunting question. Absolute assurance of your salvation in Christ is the only true comfort you can leave them with.

A spirit-filled, discerning child of God is powerfully equipped to evade the various deceptions this dark world tries to advance. But unfortunately, in view of the many amoral disparities in today's society, confusion about truth is understandable. Therefore, regarding veracity, it's only reasonable to ask: what is truth? Pontius Pilate facetiously asked Jesus the same question (John 18:38). However, Pilate wasn't interested in accurate information; he was being flippant. If you're asking the same question, hopefully, it is with a sincere heart. Here is an earnest truth. Human goodness cannot placate deliverance from God's judgment. Humans are sinful by their very nature. The salvation offered by Christ is the only alternative to eternal damnation. It must be granted from the Lord Jesus while you are still physically alive. It's paramount to understand and acknowledge that Jesus Christ is the only means by which anyone can be rescued from God's judgment and the punishment of hell's eternal flames. All genuine and faithful disciples of Jesus not only believe in Him, but they follow the teachings of their Master and generously share His truth with others as I am doing with you.

Truth is the inerrant Word of God. In other words, faultless. And when a Christian speaks the words of their Father and Lord, it must be with a special level of proficiency and distinction with regard to their Master's sovereign Lordship. All sincerity, honesty, integrity, and commitment to the faith are essential and must be reflected in the person's time-honored deportment. Hypocrisy is claiming those qualities wrongly. A hypocrite does not exhibit any of the spiritual virtues necessary to promote righteous living. Frankly, truth is an unfamiliar attribute throughout all of today's society.

Take a look at some of the men Jesus chose to be His disciples three years before His death on the cross. Then ask yourself: which one of the disciples does your lifestyle characterize the most? There are several to choose from. Peter was the most impulsive and boastful. It is thought, Peter was the disciple who cut off the soldier's ear when Jesus was arrested. Then it was Peter who later denied even knowing Jesus in a regrettable, faint-hearted act for which he was soon forgiven. Peter's fall from grace was the about-face that led him to humbly honor the cross of Christ for the remainder of his life.

John was brash and arrogant in the beginning, but in time seemed to be fulfilled simply by remaining quietly in the background. It was John who laid his head upon Jesus' chest at their last Passover supper. It was John, the solitary disciple who witnessed his Master's death by Roman crucifixion. When Jesus looked upon His mother from the cross, it was John who was given the honor of caring for her thereafter.

Thomas, or Didymus, (the twin) as he was known by his fellow disciples, had a reputation for being the pessimist among the group. Because of his lack of faith, Thomas was dubbed "Doubting Thomas," a nickname he undoubtedly earned. And although that may have been true, there was another side of Thomas for which he doesn't receive much credit. Thomas loved Jesus deeply. When Jesus wouldn't be discouraged from returning to Judea, where His very Life was in great jeopardy, Thomas was altogether prepared to go with his Master and even die alongside Him if necessary.

And then there is Judas Iscariot, the betrayer, portraying himself as a faithful follower of the Son of God. He didn't look any different than the other disciples, but that is what made him especially dangerous. He not only compromised his own integrity by selling Jesus out for thirty pieces of silver, he took the arresting soldiers right to his Friend and identified the Person of Jesus with a kiss of betrayal.

Paul wasn't one of the original twelve. He was an insurrectionist and fiercely fought against the new church movement of Jesus that was disrupting Jewish tradition. Paul was a Pharisee and the son of a Pharisee. He had no sympathy for anyone contravening the law and long-established traditions of the prominent Jewish elders. But there came that day when he was literally knocked off his high horse by Jesus Himself. Soon after Paul's conversion, he retreated to Arabia for a period of about three years. Did he have a wilderness experience similar to that of Jesus? That period of time is unrevealed. What we do know is that Paul returned in the power and spirit of a man on a mission for God. Over the length of Paul's ministry, he contributed many letters to various churches and fellow Christians. Those letters were then compiled into thirteen books of the New Testament, called the epistles.

Just looking at outside appearances, the men Jesus selected to change the world morally and spiritually didn't have a great deal of panache. But each of those men had exactly the heart that Jesus was looking for. That is, with the exception of Judas Iscariot. That old saying, you can't judge a book by its cover, precisely represents the apostles that Jesus appointed to oversee the planting of His church.

Now here we are, thousands of years later, and Jesus is still hand-selecting members for His church. We will one day become the Bride of Christ if we remain trustworthy and loyal to the justification of His righteousness. *Let us rejoice and shout for joy! Let us give Him glory and honor, for the marriage of the Lamb has come at last and His bride, the redeemed has prepared herself." She has been permitted to dress in fine linen, dazzling white and clean—for the fine linen signifies the righteous acts of the saints, the ethical conduct, personal integrity, moral courage, and godly character of believers* (Revelation 19:7–8, AMP).

Ideally, each new convert will have some of the same attributes that Jesus saw in the men He chose to be His disciples. We know that Jesus didn't choose Peter for his cowardice or his bombastic attitude. Even though Peter's good intentions always seemed to get him into hot water, it was Peter who was appointed to be the reconciler by which the Jewish nation would hear the gospel preached. Three times Jesus asked Peter if He was loved by him. And three times Jesus told Peter to feed His sheep. And Peter did.

John was among the three closest companions of the twelve disciples, and although he always remained near to Jesus, upon his spiritual maturity, it became his nature to remain out of the spotlight. He followed Jesus closely but quietly. John had a profound love for the Master and wasn't afraid to express his feelings. At the last supper, Jesus and His disciples were gathered together for the Passover meal. That is when John laid his head upon the chest of Jesus. He could actually hear the beating heart of God incarnate. John was a careful listener. He would later receive the Words of the risen Lord Telling him what to write in the book of Revelation. John is the revelator of the great unknown.

Not much is known about Thomas. Rather than depending on spiritual insight, Thomas comprehended his impressions in the expected or most logical reasoning of events, thereby earning his nickname. It's true that he usually saw things from a negative point of view, but, to his credit, Thomas wasn't going to swallow just any old notion, hook, line, and sinker. Thomas may have been overly cautious, but at the same time, not the least bit afraid to state his opinion honestly. Thomas was not a hypocrite. And true to his nature, he refused to believe the story of Jesus' resurrection unless he could physically see and touch the wounds in his Master's Flesh. Jesus wasn't offended by Thomas' impertinence but nonetheless gave him a gentle rebuke for lacking in faith to believe. Seeing things through physical eyes isn't faith.

And then there was the amazing transformation of Saul—the man called Paul. He hated what Christ was doing and did everything within his means to destroy the works of Jesus. But then, the encounter he had with the Lord Jesus changed everything. He went from being a destroyer to a builder for the kingdom of God. He devoted his entire life and all of his influence to speaking the living Word whenever and wherever he was given the opportunity. Nothing short of his own death would dissuade Paul from preaching the good news of the gospel. Through every hardship and danger, the mighty apostle truly demonstrated what it meant to him to be a slave in love with his Savior Lord and Master, King Jesus.

We may sometimes think of ourselves as Moses did, unqualified to be an ambassador for Christ. And true humility is seen as a virtue in the eyes of God. But it's not our credentials Jesus is interested in. Jesus has an altogether different criteria. The Master of the soul is looking for a willing vessel with a pliable heart. King David's plea is an excellent example. *Create in me a clean heart, O God; and renew a right spirit within me* (Psalm 51:10, KJV).

With the exclusion of Judas Iscariot, every chosen apostle had an exceptional talent and ability that Jesus discerned fitting for the work they would eventually undertake. It was those very same flaws that, in the end, would become their strong points. Hopefully, we can identify with their weaknesses and emulate their strengths.

The Bible explains that a faithful Christian is the salt and light of the earth. The light mentioned is the Holy Spirit of Christ in every born-again believer. He offers safety and illumination on a sheltered path that leads the child of God in all righteousness. Here is an example of how salt can affect the unregenerate.

Let's just suppose one day, you, a Christian, happen to cross paths with your neighbor. And you know that the man is someone who is obstinately unrepentant, utterly exhibiting no signs of shame for his sins. You, of course, recognize his poverty of spirit and cordially offer him a cheerful greeting. Maybe you feel the necessity to offer something additional and share a gentle Word of Scripture with him, illuminating his need for the Savior Jesus. The light you shared exposed him to the truth and the nature of sin and the destruction it leads to. Along with presenting those exact truths, you've cast light upon the darkness surrounding him. Furthermore, the salt you sprinkled into his life may one day season his desire to turn from his current pattern of living and go in the opposite direction. Jesus loved us enough to die for us. Christians must express that same quality of love to the unregenerate souls in their realm of influence. Those opportunities are all around. They come, and they go. Don't let a dying soul pass you by without sowing a few words of life for them to consider. And what better way to enlighten someone's spirit than to let them know they are loved. Sharing the gospel is the very basis of love to begin with. Remember these words. *God did not send his Son into the world to condemn its people. He sent him to save them!* (John 3:17, CEV)

Chapter 13

The Facts of the Matter

Before proceeding any further, I must emphasize the fundamental truth of Scripture regarding redemption and the Lord's legitimate evidence of His one-time vindication of sin. It seems that for want of tradition, some men never learn, and others never stop conniving. And for that reason alone, I assert that if anyone, man of the cloth, woman, or priest, damns you or curses you with anathema for questioning their ideology or for not fully complying with their orthodoxy or any other man-made ritual, that religion is fraudulent beyond question. Guard your heart against all such deceptions by learning for yourself what the Word of God says.

God, knowing that it was impossible in the weakness of flesh, to meet the high standard of law set by the Almighty, a new covenant with a better promise was then dedicated and confirmed. Thereby, uniting both Jew and Gentile believers into the body of Christ through His death on the cross. Jesus is the Head of the body and Lord of all to the glory of God the Father. Jesus came to release His people from the burdensome laws of Moses and the incompetence of temporal guides and foolish rabbinical traditions. Such persons are not true shepherds of the Lord's sheep; they are hirelings. Beware of wolves in sheep's clothing. Scripture affirms that any proponent of another gospel is under the control of Satan. Every lawless and self-aggrandizing religion is in cahoots with the father of lies and a danger to society.

In the New Testament, Jesus vehemently denounced the traditions of the scribes and Pharisees who made an ostentatious show of piety while distorting the Law of Moses. He exposed them for imposing heavy burdens on the people in the name of theology while teaching men falsely. The Lord Jesus confronted their separatism and emphatically Condemned their hypocrisy on every occasion, referring to them and their historical convention with this statement. Hear the Word of the Lord as He Expresses His great distress over the injudicious leaders of His nation. *Woe to you, teachers of the law and Pharisees, you hypocrites! You are like a grave that has been whitewashed. You look beautiful on the outside, but on the inside you are full of moldering bones and decaying rot. You appear, at first blush, to be righteous, selfless, and pure; but on the inside you are polluted, sunk in hypocrisy and confusion and lawlessness* (Matthew 23:27–28, VOICE).

Those who die to self spiritually are raised to Life with Christ spiritually. *Jesus was given to die for our sins. And he was raised from death to make us right with God* (Romans 4:25, ICB). That is what is meant by justification. And justification is by faith alone, in Christ alone! There is no other way by which mankind can receive redemption for their soul. If you are being told there are additional measures through which to be reconciled to God the Father, then you are being misled. And that includes receiving the sacraments on your death bed. The bread and wine won't wash away your mortal sins. A sincere confession to God, asking for His mercy and to be washed in the cleansing blood of Jesus, is your only hope of salvation. Don't risk the possibility of damnation due to wrong information. It's impossible to retain the absolute purity of Bible doctrine if it is mixed with any kind of works, religious travesty, or pagan rituals. Any belief system that distorts the written Word, exchanges facts for fiction, adds conditions to justification, or removes holy writ, requires payment of money for unbiblical religious services, or any other unauthorized practice not found in the Bible is outright heresy. All of which are intended to mislead an unsuspecting servant of Jesus. That type of controlling power over faith and worship is extremely dangerous and should be avoided at the cost of your soul. Those institutions of dissent are no more faithful to the risen Christ than the Pharisees who plotted to kill Jesus.

Heaped upon the many unholy and illogical traditions held within the Catholic religion is a particularly heinous overburden.

It is truly an inefficacious fraudulent pipe-dream referred to as purgatory. This is a completely fabricated and treacherous charade exploiting the forlorn. There is no after-death redemption. Purifying the soul after death is a preposterous lie. When someone dies, their eternal fate is sealed. There is no amount of money or prayers that will change the predetermination of one's soul after death. Only the unscrupulous lies of religious sects will tell you otherwise in order to bind the bereaved with cords of false hope. Run for your eternal lives. As lovingly as I know how to tell you, there is no such reprieve! Life in Christ is only offered to the living, and He is the only hope of glory there is.

The Almighty Father raised Jesus from the dead to validate His Son's absolute piety and righteousness, extolling Jesus Christ's sole sovereign Lordship. No other person alive is permitted by God to judge any man's heart, let alone damn another's soul. Those matters are entirely in the hands of Almighty God. And that includes the forgiveness of sin or absolution of any kind. King Jesus is the only confirmed holy High Priest and Lord over the church of God. And He alone makes intercession to the Father on behalf of God's living children.

The Words of Jesus make the way of salvation clearly understood and effortless. Jesus used straightforward language like, "Follow Me, believe in Me, have faith in God. Come all who are weary, I will give you rest." His simplistic style of communication was brief and concise, so even the uneducated could believe and accept the uncomplicated truth and be set free from sin. The Master's only expectation is faithful obedience to the gospel of God.

Almighty God Commanded that humanity's debt had to be recompensed. There was a debt owed, and the price of that debt was determined by God the Father. No lifeblood of bulls, goats, or sheep could atone for the sins of mankind indefinitely. Jesus compensated the full price for our redemption with His own Body. His death settled the account permanently, thereby satisfying once and for all eternity the Father's demand for a blood sacrifice.

Continued reenactments of transubstantiation in Catholic rituals are to assert that the Savior's death on the cross at Calvary was less than incomparable. But then, that explains the necessity of the crucifix. Unfortunately for parishioners, giving the impression the Eucharistic elements are converted into Christ's body and blood through transubstantiation is outright heresy. Any departure or pretense contrary to the inerrant Word of God is a diabolical farce, thereby completely discrediting the Roman Catholic religion for disgracing that uniquely special occasion. Without a doubt, the feigned ritual is clearly an abstract look into the satanic activity of Satan disguising himself as an angel of light. How can any true Christian misunderstand the Lord's Declaration? **"It is finished."**

Genuine Christians refer to this religious memorial as the Lord's table. The emblems of bread and wine represent the day Jesus atoned for the sins of humanity with His death on the cross. *God's bread is the man who comes from heaven and gives life to the world* (John 6:33, GW). Jesus is the Bread of Life. Believers partake of the body of Christ symbolically by faith. He often blessed and broke bread to feed those who were physically hungry. The day Jesus was nailed to the cross to die in our place, He bequeathed the Bread of Life to the Father in exchange for the spiritually dead. ... *and when He had given thanks, He broke it and said, Take, eat; this is My body which is broken for you; do this in remembrance of Me"* (1 Corinthians 11:24, NKJV).

Jesus is clarifying the adversity and affliction He will soon suffer, causing His Lifespan to be abruptly broken. His statement had nothing whatsoever to do with His bones (John 19:36).

The breaking symbolizes the suffering endured by Jesus, the emphasis is on the brutality He was willing to endure for the love and salvation of many. Jesus Commanded His believers to remember Him each time they partook of the Lord's table. Thereby remaining ever mindful of the sacrifice He made during that uncommon Passover. Although the bread and cup are profoundly significant, they are only symbolic in nature. Consecration sets a special significance upon something. It does not alter its composition. The bread is still bread, and the wine is still wine. Do not be misled by perverted and untrue claims that they are anything other than that. There is no reality in that claim. There is no authenticity to transubstantiation. It's a deception. Maybe that's why Catholic parishioners aren't allowed to drink of the cup. Child of God, don't be taken in by false assertions, open your eyes, test the spirits. *My dear friends, many false prophets are in the world now. So do not believe every spirit. But test the spirits to see if they are from God* (1 John 4:1, ICB).

When Jesus changed water into wine, there was no question that it was anything other than a miracle. *The man in charge of the feast tasted the water that was now turned into wine. He did not know where it came from, but the servants who drew the water knew. When the man had tasted it, he called the man who was being married. He said, 'Other people give the good wine at the beginning of the feast. When people have had all they want, then they give the wine which is not so good. But you have kept the good wine until now'* (John 2:9-10, WE). Any such emulation, regardless of how many times the lie is emphasized, it's still nothing more than a sacrilegious travesty. Let there be no misunderstanding. The miracle offered at the wedding was exceptional and distinctive. And the wedding guests tasted the verifiable proof.

At Jesus' last Passover commemoration, the Lord enacted a new enduring observance. *After they had finished dinner, He took the cup and in the same way said, "This cup is the new covenant, executed in My blood. Keep doing this; and whenever you drink it, you and all who come after will have a vivid reminder of Me"* (1 Corinthians 11:25, VOICE).

There were twelve ordinary men at the table with Jesus during His last night. The one who was a traitor, Judas Iscariot, was commanded to leave and go about the business he was intent on. The remaining disciples were still unmemorable regular guys from various walks of life. Their only claim to fame during that period was their association with Jesus. They hadn't been filled with the Holy Spirit at that time, and although they loved their Master greatly, their faith was still very shallow. So, when that trust was put to the test, their belief in Jesus' teaching wavered noticeably. And yet, Jesus invited His disciples to drink from the very same cup that predetermined His promise of the new covenant. If you're forbidden from partaking of the cup in your church, then arrange to do it privately in your own home. The emblems can be any small piece of bread or bite of cracker and a small amount of liquid. It is the attitude with which you engage your heart when you consume the bread and wine that consecrates their expressed significance. Jesus looks upon your heart. If you're a born-again believer, then partake of the Lord's table in a worthy manner. When you engage in this solemn right, examine yourself, your deeds, and your obedience to Christ the Lord. If you find that there is something you need to be forgiven for, that's the time. The Lord Commands this remembrance be done in a worthy manner and that His sacrifice for the Life He surrendered on your behalf not be forgotten. Think back to that day and remember Him. The Lord's table is a pensive opportunity to reflect upon what it cost the Son of man. It's all in how the heart expresses solemn gratitude for the gift of God's salvation.

Fifty days after the Passover came Pentecost. Just for a moment, stop and consider this great supernatural phenomenon. God the Father did away with the middleman when He filled every believer with the Holy Spirit. Every born-again child of God is His living temple. Believers communicate with the Lord directly, eliminating the need for any man to act contemporaneously in the role of Christ or speak on His behalf. *You heard and believed the message of truth, the Good News that he has saved you. In him you were sealed with the Holy Spirit whom he promised. This Holy Spirit is the guarantee that we will receive our inheritance. We have this guarantee until we are set free to belong to him. God receives praise and glory for this* (Ephesians 1:13–14, GW). It is here that I want to emphasize the important words in the previous Scripture. The words, believed, sealed, and guaranteed are your covenant promises from God. Your name was written in the *Lamb's Book of Life* before the foundation of the world. When you are washed in the cleansing blood of Jesus, He becomes your Savior. That is what seals you for all eternity to Christ Jesus. The indwelling of the Holy Spirit is Christ's Collateral living in your heart. He is your unequivocal guarantee of sanctification until the day of your glorification. Thereby, nothing or no one can separate you from the mighty hand of the Lord Jesus. Again, let me emphasize. There is nothing at all powerful enough to separate your soul from the mighty hand of God.

Receiving your redemption through the atonement of Jesus means liberty to you without charge, entirely unshackled; no further reckoning is warranted or required. Any attempt to affirm otherwise is an unhallowed observance that profanes the Lord of hosts. There is no other supplement, effort, merit, rite, sacrament, ceremony, or observance compulsory to retain the phenomenal gift of salvation. Do you truly think that Jesus would die for your salvation and then continue to solicit remuneration from you so you could retain possession of it? Do you really believe that Jesus offers His body and blood afresh every Sunday? That only serves to deny the complete fulfillment of the Lord's oblation. Furthermore, Jesus was never a victim! *No one takes my life from me. I give my life of my own free will. I have the authority to give my life, and I have the authority to take my life back again. This is what my Father ordered me to do"* (John 10:18, GW).

Just moments from death on the cross and with His last breath, Jesus cried out, "It is finished." His Words told us that His assignment was accomplished. The temple veil was torn into two pieces. God and redeemed man would never again have to be separated by sin. There was nothing more to do. God has promised, by faith alone, you will receive redemption. Candidly acknowledging your sin to the Lord Jesus is repentance in its entirety. Just believe and receive what is written in the sacred text of the Bible. *"God is not a human who lies or a mortal who changes his mind. When he says something, he will do it; when he makes a promise, he will fulfill it* (Numbers 23:19, CJB).

Faith is having complete confidence that Jesus' death on the cross paid for your sins unconditionally. Man's sin debt to the heavenly Father has been satisfied utterly. No other emissary can replicate the incomparable gift offered by the Savior Jesus. There are no additional conditions or requirements for a sinner's deliverance from condemnation. No baptism, or any number of prayers, repetitive chants, bowing, rituals, or reenactments in any form, can reproduce the Savior's deliverance from God's wrath. What was done is final. In Jesus' own Words, "It is finished." There are no do-overs! There are no repeat performances! No other man, priest, or religion can free you from your mortal sins and grant life everlasting. Anyone daring to suggest co-equality with the Lord Jesus is a disreputable liar.

Only the holy blood of Christ could atone for the sins of the world. Jesus alone is the way, the truth, and the Life everlasting. There is no other Name under heaven and no way other than faith alone by which man can be saved. Don't cheapen the sacrifice of Jesus by believing in token symbols, fables, or allegories. Jesus has no equal. God needs no council. Heresy is simply another type of unbelief that will lead you astray and damn your soul. Jesus Said, His sheep hear His Voice, and another they will not follow. It's a Christian's responsibility to know what the Word teaches and do accordingly. But to acquire that knowledge, you must become devoted to the study of Scripture.

Every deception or fabrication coming from duplicitous denominations is designed for control and intended for the purpose of keeping the gullible in bondage with manmade traditions and unspiritual laws that are perilously corrupt and totally unauthorized by holy Scripture. No human flesh, living or dead, has ever come close to the preeminence of Jesus, the Second Person of the Trinity, our Savior Lord and King. And that would include His birth mother, Mary. She wasn't there when the Lord Spoke the world into existence, and He didn't need her counsel or instruction during His earthly ministry. Praying to Mary, the deceased human mother of Jesus, is detestable to God and strictly forbidden by the Lord (Deuteronomy 18:11). And since the subject is corrupt theology, worship is something principally set apart for God and God alone. Taking part in a religious ceremony that includes any images, graven or otherwise, is afoul of God's absolute Command. *Do not make gods for yourselves. Do not set up for yourselves something to look like a god or a holy object. Do not set up something cut from stone in your land to bow down to. For I am the Lord your God. Keep My Days of Rest and honor My holy place. I am the Lord* (Leviticus 26:1–2, NLV). A crucifix, in or out of church is nevertheless a graven image. The Catholic denomination displays just such an example of the kind of likeness God is referring to. Reverencing any type of idol, icon, or image is most emphatically forbidden by God. The Holy Bible instructs Christians to faithfully remember the day of the cross, but they do not disregard the written Commandment or demean the likeness of Jesus. Unseemly defiance of the Lord's Commandment not only degrades the true glory and likeness of God, it discredits the Catholic religion. In addition, to suggest co-equality to Christ or adulate another's image in the church Jesus Christ died to give birth to, is a transgression against divine law. An empty cross needs no explanation. It is the absolute evidence of the Lord's victory over sin and the grave. There is no other symbol in all the world that gives recognition to Christ any clearer than an empty cross. Regrettably, by extolling the crucifix and portraits of Mary and Joseph, the Catholic religion ingloriously dishonors the Holy Father of Christ and the majesty of the Lord Jesus, the High Priest over the church body. Obedient, faithful Christians walk by faith, not by sight. Only the resplendent Persons of the Trinity are worthy of unequaled veneration to the exclusion of everyone and everything else.

Please don't allow yourself to be taken in by unsubstantiated church nonsense. Discover the truth for yourself. Everything needed to explain away any confusion is in the Holy Bible. The virgin Mary was the human vessel appointed by God to bring

His little Lamb into existence. But she was nothing apart from that. Although highly favored of God, Mary was a flesh and blood human being, the same as any other woman. And respectfully, just for the record, giving birth to additional children, precludes Mary's continued virginity. And, in the most emphatic terms, she was never a co-equal or co-redeemer with Christ, the Savior of the world. Mary's contribution to humanity was to give birth to God's Son. Her responsibility was to love and nurture Him and then disengage, thereby allowing Him to fulfill His destiny.

Chapter 14

The Incomparable Jesus

Allow me to offer some documentation for you to consider. The Almighty Father has an exact timetable for every detail concerning His creation. And Jesus was very observant of the exactness of His Father's instructions. The book of John gives us a picture of how discreetly Jesus' ministry was inaugurated. Jesus' cousin, John the Baptist, was baptizing in the Jordan River. Although John had never laid eyes on Jesus prior to that day, God told him how Jesus would be recognized. Then in the distance, John saw Jesus coming to be baptized, as were many other men. But John knew this Man approaching was nothing like any other man. John looked upon Him and declared, "Behold, the Lamb of God."

Although the preplanning and incarnation of the Savior Jesus was predestined from the foundation of the world, there were still certain protocols mandated by God the Father. Not even the Son of God was given a free pass. Although Jesus was quite unlike any other Man, He was nevertheless still under the authority of God the Father. Therefore, Jesus needed to fulfill the necessary ritual of baptism proclaimed by John the Baptist. And even though Jesus was sinless and had nothing to repent, He was required to fulfill Scripture by publicly submitting to immersion before beginning His earthly mission.

The baptism of Jesus was the most revealing and stunning display of the Trinity in all of the Bible. *When He had been baptized, Jesus came up immediately from the water; and behold, the heavens were opened to Him, and He saw the Spirit of God descending like a dove and alighting upon Him. And suddenly a voice came from heaven, saying, "This is My beloved Son, in whom I am well pleased"* (Matthew 3:16–17, NKJV). At no other time in history was the Lord Jesus so acclaimed as He was at that moment in time. A simultaneous endorsement of the Father and validation of the Holy Spirit imparted upon the Son of God in front of John the Baptist and the community of witnesses. That manifestly illustrated beyond any shadow of a doubt that the living God is three distinct Persons always working in unison with One Another. There was never a better example of the Trinity.

That was the very moment in history when the Carpenter, Who seemed as ordinary as any other villager, received His Holy orders from God the Father. That day the Son of God became Israel's Messiah and before long, Savior of the world. From the very first moment the heavenly Father Called Jesus into His mission field, He was under the complete authority of Almighty God. Jesus was no longer a common Carpenter from Nazareth. Jesus was stepping out of the shadows and about to fulfill His long-awaited destiny as Israel's Messiah and sacrificial Christ to the Jew and Gentile world. It was here that old things had passed away, and all things became new (2 Corinthians 5:17).

After being baptized, Jesus was willingly led by the Spirit into the wilderness. And while there, He fasted forty days and forty nights. Contemplate that for just a moment. He was obeying the instructions of His Father God. He was consenting to go without any nourishment for well over five and a half weeks in a remote wasteland somewhere in Judea. Again, imagine the unswerving determination it took for Jesus to go without any sustenance whatsoever, well into a second month. It was an arduous test of will. I don't think the word famished would adequately describe the debilitated condition of Jesus' Body at the climax of those forty days. But for the purpose of this factual story, we are going to concentrate on Jesus' mental condition by observing the powerful mind of Christ.

Satan hoped that Jesus, in His emaciated condition, would be overwhelmed by weakness and easily persuaded to capitulate to his suggestions. The devil tried using the same tactics that proved effective on Eve in the Garden of Eden. Deceit, pride of life, and lust of the eyes still remains the downfall of all humanity.

After spending forty days and nights with the ministering angels, Jesus was Spiritually ready to take on the nemesis of Almighty God. His sword was sharpened, and that growl heard in the inhospitable backcountry wasn't Jesus' stomach; it was the roar of the mighty Lion of Judah that echoed Scripture throughout the region.

The first temptation that Satan initiated had to do with the physical need for nourishment. Would Jesus weaken and turn stones into bread to relieve the hunger gnawing at His emaciated belly? Hear the effectual Words of Jesus. *But he answered, "It is written, 'One does not live by bread alone, but by every word that comes from the mouth of God'"* (Matthew 4:4, NRSV). Then Jesus and Satan went up together upon a high mountain where Jesus could view all the nations of the world. It was there the devil offered Jesus great power and enormous wealth if He would worship at the feet of Satan. *Jesus said to the devil, "Get behind Me, Satan! For it is written, 'You must worship the Lord your God. You must obey Him only'"* (Luke 4:8, NLV). The final test of Jesus is when Satan took Him to the highest point of the Temple in the city of Jerusalem. The devil wanted Jesus to throw Himself down from the lofty pinnacle. For the third time, Satan was hoping that Jesus would rely upon His preternatural powers. But should Jesus rely upon divine assistance, it would ultimately disqualify Him as man's Savior. *But Jesus answered, "The scripture says, 'Do not put the Lord your God to the test'"* (Luke 4:12, GNT).

The things we need to learn from that exchange between Jesus and Satan are both graphic and revealing. But more importantly, it is meant to be an example to believers on how to resist the enemy of their soul. Satan made three failed attempts to sabotage Jesus from achieving His earthly goal. In each of the three instances, the devil made a clever and deceitful offer that would have easily circumvented the cross altogether. Jesus could have abused His power and turned stones into bread. But ultimately, Satan had nothing to offer Jesus that would justify betraying His heavenly Father or risk the forfeiture of His passion. Jesus had a very sound perspective on Who He was and why He came. He had nothing to prove to Satan. His only objective was to substantiate His suitability and do the will of the One Who sent Him. And as unappealing as the accursed cross was, that would be the only path of justification that would set the sinners of the world free. There was no need to argue over substance, affluence, or obstacles. Jesus just drew His sword and sliced and diced Satan, demonstrating to God the Father He was well worthy of all the authority given to Him.

Upon returning to Galilee, Jesus and His first followers were invited guests at a wedding in Cana. Mary, the mother of Jesus, was also there. When the wedding party ran out of wine, Mary told Jesus about the situation. *Jesus said to her, "Woman, what does your concern have to do with Me? My hour has not yet come"* (John 2:4, NKJV). I realize that there are a great many possible preconceptions one might read into that brief exchange. But first, it's important to note that Jesus met their need graciously by providing an abundant vintage of the highest quality as His gift to the couple in celebration of their marriage. However, my focus is not on the first miracle of water into wine but on the incisive response Jesus gave to Mary.

That significant moment between Mary and her Son Jesus was a pivotal point in their relationship. Without hesitation, Jesus confirmed the emergence of His unadorned but foreordained Deity. The fullness of time had arrived. The Son of God needed to establish new rudiments analogous to His legitimate supremacy. Jesus did this by decisively but tenderly emphasizing to Mary that His transcendence had now eclipsed their brief intimate relationship. Jesus was by no means being disrespectful by using the term woman when speaking to His mother. "Woman" was the gentlest way Jesus could let His mother know that His time was at hand, thus, reminding her of His divine nature and destiny and her fallible humanity. Their lives would now take independent directions. The Baby Boy birthed from her womb had now become the great Man the angel Gabriel had recounted to her thirty years earlier. *He shall be great, and shall be called the Son of the Highest: and the Lord God shall give unto him the throne of his father David: And he shall reign over the house of Jacob for ever; and of his kingdom there shall be no end* (Luke 1:32–33, KJV). *The holy Child you give birth to will be called the Son of God* (Luke 1:35, NLV).

I am like every other believer under the Lord's mandate to show love. And I know of no better way to express that love than to expose Satan's empire of deception by using the light of truth to shine into the dark, secret places of Satan's domain. We must be aware of Satan's feigned tactics. He was even able to use Peter in an effort to dissuade Jesus from going to the cross. Jesus immediately revealed Satan's cloak of deception and resolutely rebuked him (Matthew 16:23). Satan can disguise himself as an angel of light. In other words, Satan can appear to be one thing while being the antithesis of that very thing. The apostle Paul describes it perfectly. *Does this mean that I do not love you? God knows it doesn't, but I am determined to maintain this boast, so as to cut the ground from under the feet of those who profess to be God's messengers on the same terms as I am. God's messengers? They are counterfeits of the real thing, dishonest practitioners, "God's messengers" only by their own appointment. Nor do their tactics surprise me when I consider how Satan himself masquerades as an angel of light. It is only to be expected that his agents shall have the appearance of ministers of righteousness—but they will get their desserts one day* (2 Corinthians 11:13–15, Phillips).

There is no individual in this modern church age that has more influence upon his dedicated followers than the Pope of the Roman Catholic church. Who better to represent the doctrine of antichrist than this renowned and respected voice for progressivism? Catholicism is an all-embracing, all-inclusive elitist faith that adheres to its own traditions and preferences rather than the Lord's holy inspired Word of the living God. Don't take my word for it. If you are a sincere seeker of the undeniable truth, please, read the Bible. Learn the truth for yourself directly from God. Don't be led astray by all their toxic ostentatiousness. *"Woe to you, Pharisees, and you religious leaders! You are like beautiful mausoleums—full of dead*

men's bones, and of foulness and corruption. You try to look like saintly
men, but underneath those pious robes of yours are hearts besmirched
with every sort of hypocrisy and sin (Matthew 23:27–28, TLB).

As the future progresses, the days will grow ever darker, and there
will be a great many more opportunities to fall away from Christ,
your first love. Standing strong in the presence of evil is imperative.
Do not be deceived by any mortal. The devil hides among those
we would least suspect. Learn the sacred text and remain faithful
and obedient to God's Word throughout the remainder of your
days on earth. If you've been reborn by the blood of Christ, give
your life over to Jesus exclusively. Only then will your Savior, the
Benefactor of your salvation, truly be your Master and Lord. It's
then that the Holy Spirit will begin transforming your heart into
a vessel equipped for good works. Only a true branch of the Holy
Vine will develop the good fruit of righteousness and faithfully
confess the Lord Jesus before men.

Chapter 15

Will Your Sin Be Judged or Forgiven?

There may be millions of people walking around spiritually dead and aren't even aware of it. Unfortunately, in the body of Christ today, there are many adults among the Christian community who choose to remain childlike in spirit. If their understanding of Scripture remains dangerously shallow, and they no longer have a vested interest in the spiritual things associated with God and His righteousness, it could very well be that they were never truly born-again in the first place. The signs are usually very clear that something is amiss when a believer no longer reads their Bible regularly, avoids their Christian brothers and sisters, and skips church frequently. The signs are unquestionably obvious when a member of the family of Christ returns to their former friends and prior bad habits. Too many so-called Christians are under the erroneous impression that because they repeated a quick prayer at the church altar one Sunday, they have permanently escaped the flames of hell and established a permanent reservation in God's kingdom. Be that as it may, sanctification is a daily progression and if their passionate appetite for God has departed and obedience to His Word no longer takes precedence in their lives, their spiritual growth has come to a screeching halt as well. A fruit inspector is one of the most powerful resources in the Christian brotherhood. *Yes, the way to identify a tree or a person is by the kind of fruit produced* (Matthew 7:20, TLB).

Nightfall doesn't descend upon the earth all at once. The close of day fades gently into dusk before complete darkness begins to sweep entirely across the land. The subtle tactics used by Satan are somewhat similar. At first, his ways are indistinct, seemingly benign, and frequently titillating. But, be warned! Any proposal you accept from the devil will only lead to one lethal end, just as it happened with Eve in the garden. Rebellion or back-sliding is much the same. It slowly leads a Christian with weak faith back into the bosom of their former friends, lifestyle, and familiar propensity to sin.

One little twist of the truth is all it took to depose our first parents. They promptly fell from eternal Life into the fallen world where sin and Satan abide. And what was the first thing Adam and Eve did when caught? They tried to hide. The same as many others who have done foolishly. It may not always be the first taste of sin or the first step in defiance that becomes the problem. It's those subsequent steps that will take them to a place they didn't see coming. Dependence, disease, prison, and possibly death. And should they survive, the shame and guilt attached to the fall are shattering. That is exactly why pragmatic groups called anonymous are there to assist. The sinner never wants their wrongful behavior exposed. It's human nature to hide from guilt.

Once gripped in the web of spuriousness, the fight for redemption is futile without the help of the Holy Spirit. Only a fool would think he is able to escape the devil's grip in his own strength. Adam and Eve foolishly thought if they could sew enough leaves together, God wouldn't be able to detect their hiding place among the trees in the garden. Is that you? Is there some reason that you are trying to hide from God? Let's be real. There is no possible way to hide from God. Although the Lord considers any immoral act, depraved vice, or perverse transgression a fall from grace, the Lord is quick to forgive all sincere repentance regardless of the magnitude of sin. But then, that sinner must immediately cease any further connection with the immorality that oppressed him. And here is the logic. *"When an evil spirit comes out of a person, it goes through dry places looking for a place to rest. But it doesn't find any. Then it says, 'I'll go back to the home I left.' When it arrives, it finds the house unoccupied, swept clean, and in order. Then it goes and brings along seven other spirits more evil than itself. They enter and take up permanent residence there. In the end the condition of that person is worse than it was before. That is what will happen to the evil people of this day"* (Matthew 12:43–45, GW).

Without the sincere acknowledgment of sin, there can be no amnesty. Perhaps someone just can't stand the thought of having to take any responsibility for their actions. Maybe it's because they simply can't face the pain that they have inflicted on others. Then this old saying comes to mind. If you can't pay the fine, don't do the crime. But that seems to be an unlikely deterrent. Unless sin is terminated immediately, it most assuredly will lead from action to addiction. Whether you smoke, inject, snort, drink, gamble, or ogle, if your shame doesn't convict you, fear of discovery will keep you in that deep hole that you've dug for yourself. The flesh is never going to be satisfied with only a little sin. One small taste of sin leads to another and another until you are trapped in a network of lies and shame by the very thing you once thought brought you pleasure.

Sins are innumerable. Let's look at two of them from the historical accounts of the New Testament. The Lord Jesus hand-picked twelve men that He chose to disciple. They were His students and constant companions for three years. They did everything together and became very close. Jesus intended to build His church upon the teaching He would instill in these men. They watched Jesus emphasize compassion and describe righteousness. The disciples learned that Jesus was especially keen on the importance of being steadfast in the face of provocation and adversity.

Jesus didn't just talk about love. He illustrated love. From the outward appearance, the men chosen by Jesus all looked very much alike. But one of those men had an evil heart and would betray his Master for a few silver coins. Judas Iscariot was a wolf in sheep's clothing. He appeared just as the other men, but his heart wasn't entirely dedicated to the Lord. While the other disciples were learning about love, mercy, and charity, Judas was covetous. His greed led him to do something that he couldn't forgive himself for. *That is when one of the Twelve, the one named Judas Iscariot, went to the cabal of high priests and said, "What will you give me if I hand him over to you?" They settled on thirty silver pieces. He began looking for just the right moment to hand him over* (Matthew 26:14–16, MSG).

Judas then led a group of Roman soldiers to the Garden of Gethsemane, where he identified Jesus by giving Him a duplicitous kiss. Jesus was abruptly and fraudulently arrested and taken to the governor's palace. When Judas became aware of the brutality Jesus was enduring at the hands of the merciless soldiers, he immediately tried to reverse the egregious action he brought upon the innocent, gentle Son of God. *Then Judas, His betrayer, seeing that He had been condemned, was remorseful and brought back the thirty pieces of silver to the chief priests and elders, saying, "I have sinned by betraying innocent blood…"* (Matthew 27:3–4, KJV) *Then he threw down the pieces of silver in the temple and departed and went and hanged himself* (Matthew 27:5, KJV).

I can't say I know of anybody who has ever come to the defense of Judas Iscariot, but there is something that shouldn't be overlooked. Judas appeared regretful for the part he played in Jesus' arrest. He knew Jesus was an innocent Man. Once he realized that Jesus was being condemned fraudulently without guilt, he tried to give the money back, hoping it would put an end to his horrendous mistake. Commendable? Well, maybe, but by then, it was too late, and the entire world knows the eventual outcome of his betrayal. Was Judas repentant for his actions? I believe the answer must be *no*. Judas obviously never offered his soul to Jesus. Like many others, Judas remained on the fringes of Christianity, only to reap the benefits that went along with his association with Jesus and the other disciples. Furthermore, when examining the Scriptures about Judas Iscariot, nothing written about him was positive. Being sorry for an offense is a far cry from repentance. To repent is to recognize sin and seek the Lord's forgiveness and turn from sin's destructive nature. Thus, repentance is a two-part process. If Judas Iscariot was fully surrendered to Jesus as his Lord and Savior, he would have acknowledged his shameful deception and repented. Why was death preferable to admitting the truth? As appalling as his action was, it still would have been a forgivable offense. Judas Iscariot preferred to hang himself rather than face what he had done. This was a man who sat at the feet of Jesus for three years, and yet, he was entirely unregenerate in spirit. That is a treacherous individual. Don't you be that kind of person. Either be for Jesus or against Him, but don't cloak yourself in a shady pretense as some do today.

Although the Scriptures don't elaborate, I'm reasonably sure that Judas was baptized by John the Baptist. Possibly during the very same time that Jesus was baptized. That brings up another good point. Unless you are willing to repent of your sins and crucify your flesh daily by living according to the Word of God, you won't be saved simply by submersion in water. Let that be a cautionary warning to everyone. And never lose sight of the fact that if Jesus is your Savior, He is also your Master and Lord.

Then we come to Simon, the disciple referred to as Peter. In fact, Peter was part of an inner circle of companions that went everywhere with Jesus. There was never any doubt to what extent Peter loved Jesus. His deep affection was authentic. But at times, Peter's arrogance revealed his raw immaturity. He wanted to be what he professed to be, but his strength of character was still underdeveloped. Peter was quick-tempered, intense, and passionate, but he lacked wisdom and composure. Jesus warned Peter that Satan desired to sift him like wheat (Luke 22:31). And in fact, that sifting led to Peter's denial of the Lord three times. Not long after, while standing in the face of fear, Peter's backbone was sorely tested.

After enjoying the Passover meal, the disciples accompanied Jesus to the Garden of Gethsemane, where Jesus frequently went to pray. That night, Jesus cautioned His three closest companions to watch and pray, but instead, they fell asleep. So, when the soldiers descended upon Jesus, it took the sleeping men by surprise. There was an entire brigade of angry soldiers led by their torchbearer Judas Iscariot, just to arrest one gentle, guiltless, unarmed Man. The clammer and shouting were terrifying to witness. There was no reckoning with those men-in-arms. It is mentioned that one of Jesus' disciples drew his sword and cut off the ear of one of the king's soldiers. That man was believed to be Peter. Jesus identified Himself immediately to assure the soldiers that they had the One Who they came to arrest and that His disciples should be allowed to depart safely. Consequently, the three companions of Jesus, along with the others, all fled the scene in fear of arrest, leaving the Lord to fend for Himself.

Soon after, the chain of events continued in the governor's palace, where Jesus was taken. Peter had followed surreptitiously to see what was going to happen to the Lord. Soon Peter was recognized as a companion of the Man arrested. Peter denied the accusation. Then twice more, a finger was pointed at Peter. But both times, the loyal companion of Jesus vehemently denied ever even knowing the Man.

At the very moment Peter spoke those words, he heard the cock crow twice (Mark 14:72). That same instant was the danger Jesus warned him of. Peter lifted his eyes and looked directly into the battered and bloody face of the Lord beholding him. Peter read the grieved look on the face of his Master. It was a haunting image that pierced Peter's heart. He saw with his own eyes how badly he had hurt the Lord he was so deeply devoted to. For many days after, the heartbroken disciple grappled with his shame, reliving the betrayal of his Master. Peter was thoroughly crushed and guilt-ridden. Denying the Christ was a mistake he had to live with for a while longer. In the intervening time, that experience became a defining moment and turning point in Peter's life.

There is no shame in being afraid, but for a Christian to deny ever having a relationship with Jesus could have dire consequences. That heresy could be spiritually fatal. Jesus Said, if anyone denies Him before men, He will deny him before the heavenly Father (Matthew 10:33). That is one boundary you never want to cross. It is a Christian's continued relationship and growth in the spirit that assures eternal Life. The Savior Jesus died for your salvation. As momentous as that moment of awakening was in your life, it was only the beginning. Sanctification is a continuous process. Jesus is your Lord. Obey Him and remember to worship His Holy Spirit, thereby glorifying the heavenly Father unremittingly. *So, I can guarantee that people will be forgiven for any sin or cursing. However, cursing the Spirit will not be forgiven. Whoever speaks a word against the Son of Man will be forgiven. But whoever speaks against the Holy Spirit will not be forgiven in this world or the next* (Matthew 12:31–32, GW).

We all make mistakes, but it's important to let go of your pride before it brings you to destruction. The hand-picked men chosen by Jesus were zealous followers. He was their Spiritual Leader, Adviser, and Instructor in the new way. Jesus carefully taught by demonstration. Three years was a short period of time to teach the disciples everything they needed to know to carry on after the Lord's ascension. Nevertheless, with diligent observance to the power and authority of the Holy Spirit, the disciples succeeded in planting the church and instructing others to build upon the foundation that Jesus laid. As a result of their individual accomplishments, we have an account of their effort and a clear example of the fortitude it took to overcome the many personal hardships in the midst of great adversity they dealt with continually. And in spite of the fact that Judas Iscariot and Peter were constant companions of the Lord Jesus, temptation and dissent were something that the two men would have to suffer through on their own. Each of those men learned their lesson the hard way. Judas took the wrong path. Don't let that be said of you. Peter was humbled by his experience and consequently forgiven.

Have you ever done something awful and then wondered or asked yourself: why did I do that? Where did that thought or idea come from? What in the world was I thinking? Well, Satan may be partly responsible, but in all reality, you are the final authority over each of your own actions. You may not be able to avoid every thought that comes to mind, but you don't have to entertain the unhealthy ones. Furthermore, a strong Christian knows the warning signs and will competently obstruct the devil's agenda.

In the Garden of Eden, Eve was quite content with her life until she began to entertain the distorted thought suggested to her by Satan. In the beginning, she was strong in her convictions, but shortly after Satan's lying council, she began to imagine what it would be like to be wise like her Creator. Eve chose to disobey God and ate from the forbidden tree and offered the fruit to Adam, and he also ate, defying God's Commandment. They immediately fell from the Father's grace. And we know the rest of the story because we are living in the world our first parents chose for us to inherit. So, here is the simplified fact. Whether your thoughts are good or bad, your reaction to those thoughts will give rise to their unalterable conclusion.

Christians do not live according to the same standards of this world. Christians have a much higher calling. Christians answer to a greater authority. Here is the proof. *For though we live in the world, we do not wage war as the world does. The weapons we fight with are not the weapons of the world. On the contrary, they have divine power to demolish strongholds. We demolish arguments and every pretension that sets itself up against the knowledge of God, and we take captive every thought to make it obedient to Christ. And we will be ready to punish every act of disobedience, once your obedience is complete* (2 Corinthians 10:3–6, NIV).

If anyone has confessed Christ Jesus as their Savior and Lord, they are added to the vast number of God's family that comprise the body of Christ. God the Father will reward those who diligently seek Him. Those in the faith have a deep, unending assurance in the Supreme Being and Creator. Christians throughout their various communities must be far more than just a flock of sheep under a sanctimonious label. Following Jesus may very well cost the believers conditions and circumstances yet unspecified. It cost Christ Jesus everything. And it cost His disciples and the apostle Paul dearly as well. Every Christian should be prepared to offer the Lord Jesus no less than what the saints before us suffered to advance the kingdom.

Many of us started with Christ as a collection of rag-tag misfits. Nevertheless, whoever believes the Savior is the Son of God and He died on the cross for our sins, must remain forever faithful and obedient to Christ, the Living Word of God. Perfection is a daily process. You may be asking the question: then what happens? The whole process of perfecting believers is to make them suitable to enter the kingdom of heaven when their work on earth is finished. Whether bond or free, all must die leaving the corrupt flesh behind. With One Rare exception. Jesus' Flesh was incorruptible, therefore, His tomb was empty. Everyone's spirit lives eternally, somewhere. Preferably heaven.

Part 3: Chapter 16

Peril, Risk, or Refuge

Regardless of how you may see things presently, there is a day approaching when progressivism will turn intolerant and violent toward Christians. Then the day may follow when lawbreakers will think they're doing the world a favor by taking your life for preaching Christian doctrine or declaring that Jesus is Lord to the glory of God the Father. At present, no one in the homeland has been beheaded for spreading the gospel. That can't be said for Christians in certain other countries. Therefore, Christians in America must be aware, since the southern borders of our homeland are wide open, purportedly welcoming all who desire to come; friend or foe. That could very well allow for those who loathe Jesus-loving Christians to be the target of hate by the Islamic Jehad. Christians everywhere are considered enemies to nations that deify dead men and idols with glass eyes that cannot see, mouths that cannot speak. Idols are men's false gods that have no heart and cannot love.

For Christians, it is not only our right and great pleasure to proclaim Christ, but it is our strict obligation to do so whatever the cost. In the second chapter of the book of Revelation, Jesus gives the very first church planted by the apostle Paul a stern warning. It seems clear to the Lord Jesus that the church at Ephesus had lost its first love. That distinctly meant their love and passion for God had cooled. But in that same chapter, to their credit, Jesus praised their hatred for the deeds of the Nicolaitans. *Yet you have this to your credit, that you hate the works and corrupt teachings of the Nicolaitans that mislead and delude the people, which I also hate* (Revelation 2:6, AMP). The Nicolaitans were a sect trying to pass themselves off as Christians but patently were not. These illogical religions exist today. They are faction groups, nonconformists that refer to themselves as Christians, but they are frauds. Some nontrinitarians teach there is but one god without distinction of persons. Others believe their solitary god manifests himself in the role of son and spirit. Be careful. Any person or religion that denies the Holy Trinity, God in three distinct Persons is most assuredly Satan's ally, and not Christian. Any person or group that deviates from the gospel is not Christian. Anyone teaching variance or the slightest alteration to sacred text is a worker of iniquity. Any teaching that opposes the Lordship of Jesus Christ in any way, is, without question, an antichrist!

True and faithful Christians are the sons and daughters of the Ancient of Days, the great I AM. He is the Self-Existent One, the Eternal, Yahweh our covenant Father. His Name is Lord, the Light of the world. He reigns as the only supreme Ruler over everything, including His faithful followers. Believers do not question His Word, death, resurrection, or His Lordship. For now, the Lord Jesus sits at the right hand of the Father's throne awaiting the fulfillment of souls. *I can guarantee this truth: Until the earth and the heavens disappear, neither a period nor a comma will disappear from the Scriptures before everything has come true* (Matthew 5:18, GW).

Upon the inauguration of the New Testament, the temple or dwelling place of the Holy Spirit is in the heart of every believer. He is the ultimate Power on earth. If the Lord's Spirit isn't living in your heart, you do not have the privilege of calling yourself a Christian. God owns and manages the farmland, His children, a holy priesthood, are the laborers in the field. But there's coming a day when the Lord of mercy and salvation will advance upon earth in wrath and conquer the world of sin, just as in the days of Noah. On that day, when everything seems very normal, Jesus will retrieve His church in readiness of earth's tribulation. After the suffering, the Lord of lords and the King of kings will no longer be denied His exalted place in the world that rejected Him.

Hopefully, I've laid a firm enough foundation for the incoming that I intend to build upon. Let's take a good hard look at the generation that we are now a part of. Regrettably I say, there has never been another time in American history when its citizens have felt so lost and betrayed. Parents are especially bewildered and losing hope of their children ever having a wholesome and financially secure future. Nothing touches the heart faster than corruption aimed at our children. And that is exactly who Satan is targeting. Indoctrinating his evil and treacherous woke agenda at America's most vulnerable.

For countless generations, the United States of America has been the preeminent example of love, personal prosperity, Christian charity, freedom, security, affluence, and strength, all contingent on a compliant relationship honoring Almighty God. And in so doing, the Lord God has greatly blessed this nation in many other ways we know not of. Christians today, more than ever before, have the responsibility to uphold and safeguard the Lord's unvarnished truth. True believers must stand in unity, resolute in the cause of Christ. Just like when Jesus defended His Father's honor in the temple when He witnessed the people peddling their merchandise and livestock in His house of prayer. But at present, the Lord's church is declining rapidly, contributing to the obvious reason that America's vitality and reputation are on the downgrade.

When Jesus sent seventy of His followers into the communities to do the ministry of the kingdom, He referred to a problem that is comparable to a similar detriment in the modern church. There are many souls ready to be reaped, but too few laborers are willing to do the work of harvesting. In America, there are too many born-again children of God that have walked away from upholding their responsibility to the Lord Jesus, their Savior. Scores of the redeemed have completely abandoned their Christian fellowship. That seems to be a pattern in some modern societies. There came a time late in the Lord's ministry when many of His followers were no longer interested in continuing with Him and left Jesus indefinitely. At that, Jesus asked His twelve disciples if they too would abandon Him. Everyone reading this should take particular notice of Peter's answer to Jesus. *Peter replied, "Master, to whom would we go? You have the words of real life, eternal life. We've already committed ourselves, confident that you are the Holy One of God"* (John

6:68–69, MSG). If Jesus asked that question of you today, what would your response to Him be?

Just look around. How much has America changed in the last decade? How much in the last few months? To those of us that still recite the pledge of allegiance, I would ask this question. Do you really believe that America is still one nation under God? Take a close look at our leaders. Government is under the authority of God. Do any of our leaders exhibit the will or the characteristics of the Lord Jesus? Oh, they use the right words, but their actions and laws are far from God's will. Do any of this nation's current leaders have the proper decorum or prudence to govern America? Let me take you back to a shameful demonstration of impertinence on February 4th, 2020. At the conclusion of Donald Trump's State of the Union address, Nancy Pelosi, Speaker of the House, in an undignified protest, brazenly stood before the entire chamber and televised audience and began to methodically tear up the president's speech. Well, it saddens me to say that the Biden-Harris administration has not just symbolically, but emphatically done the very same thing with the moral mandates of God in America. I would be remiss if I didn't use the strongest possible language to condemn any administration that implements new laws that flagrantly malign the Word of God and His divine moral structure. The usurping of God's authority by President Biden is particularly heinous, especially after taking an oath unto God to value and protect American citizens and never under any circumstances mislead or misdirect them. Moreover, no matter how often the subversive citizens in society demand deviant change to the legal system, they will never be satisfied. Sin is insatiable. There will always be more and more perversions to accommodate. There is no scarcity or end to sin short of death and damnation. People everywhere should know that the Lord God does not play games when it comes to the corrupt behavior of His creation. What we don't know is how much sin the world is able to bare before God decides it's time to fulfill the remaining Scriptures in the New Testament.

There were many instances in the New Testament when Jesus confronted the very issue of heresy. On one such occasion, Jesus was especially enraged with the scribes and Pharisees regarding their sanctimonious posturing, fraudulent guidance, unsuitable hypocritical conduct, and abuse of authority. Jerusalem's religious leaders were distorting the laws and imposing fabricated and unnecessary burdens on the average citizen. Then as today, it's the incidental people in society who have the enormous financial tax burden on their shoulders, which, by the way, includes the bloated salaries and inflated government pensions of the servants on the hill.

Information is a useful tool, especially in the hand of the godly. No matter how appealing the new liberal laws might appear, they are not in the best interest of the American citizens. The majority of individuals who are ill-informed aren't stupid. It's simply a lack of interest. *The mind of the prudent always acquires knowledge, And the ear of the wise always seeks knowledge* (Proverbs 18:15, AMP). Many Christians want to avoid politics altogether. But it's every Christian's responsibility to stand up for the same principles that their Lord teaches and Commands. At times, getting at the truth of the matter may require a little bit of assertiveness. Once you've uncovered the facts, then you are accountable for how you address them.

The government is trying to lure its citizenry by dangling a tantalizing morsel of perverted bait, but that hook has a fate worse than death attached. We mustn't fall for the same skillful cunning that snared Eve in the Garden of Eden. That one misstep led to the severe sentence of God and the entire fall of mankind. Don't think for one minute that America is beyond decimation at God's judgment. In one decree, the Lord terminated every living thing that wasn't aboard Noah's ark. When God chose to judge Sodom and Gomorrah, there were only four persons redeemed before both cities were incinerated.

America is among the few remaining politically free nations

in the entire world. That's because, for now at least, we are still a democracy. Until recently, the voting citizens in America have used common sense and good judgment. How we choose our government is no different than how we choose anything else. Christians particularly discern what is in our own best interest and that of our loved ones. Don't we as parents scrutinize any person who will be in charge of our little ones in our absence? Whether nannies or teachers in daycare or primary or high school, we want to know their qualifications. We want them to have spiritual values similar to our own. We want to know how they are influencing our children. When we have to make those difficult decisions concerning our aged parents, we must choose senior care facilities wisely on their behalf. Well then, how is it any different with who we vote into office? The stakes are even greater there. We should care all the more. Big brother makes the rules of law. And government overreach is becoming commonplace even here in America. Everything from pronouns to gender is now being decided by the bureaucrats. Incidentally, it's your vote or empty ballot that puts and keeps the illogical public servants in office. Stop and think for just one moment. Do you honestly feel that your public servant has your best interest and that of your child at heart?

Most countries worldwide are faced with challenging stages of growth that require varying degrees of adjustment. But today in America, there is a defiant and rebellious youth that grievously opposes so many of the current norms that have always been the bedrock of tradition, maintaining America's solid civil and ethical culture. Then the issue becomes how to resolve those conflicts amicably and without jeopardy to current safeguards, and that requires wise and far-sighted leadership. It must be acknowledged that certain prospective changes will determine either a positive or a negative shape and scope to the future development of our society. Only a weak and inept administration would permit profane changes to America's long-standing ethical and right-minded constitutional law. Pandering to this nation's resentful protesters is like racketeering. Attempts to appease those factions are entirely misguided and a prescription for disaster. If this country continues in that direction, America will be no more fortified than a sandcastle on the beach. *Everyone rejoices when the lovers of God flourish, but the people groan when the wicked rise to power* (Proverbs 29:2, TPT).

There is no longer any question. Apostasy is sweeping throughout America at a fever pitch. To some, the liberal changes perhaps appear refreshing, but the progressive undercurrents are far from moral and most assuredly lethal. If allowed to continue unchecked, the wicked upheaval will soon be entirely unrestrained. When the full force hits, the shockwave will take everyone by surprise and be utterly devastating. Once virtue and wholesomeness are laid waste, the temporal, bestial, and carnal desires of the flesh will proliferate out of control. Then the reckless invitation extended to Satan and his seducing spirits will precipitate unimaginable chaos escalating to greater and greater pandemonium throughout the entire landscape of our nation. The citizens of America must have a realistic understanding and clear perspective of what lies ahead when renouncing the moral high ground previously established by our forefathers. America once stood for God, virtue, principles, and an elevated sense of honor and moral conduct. Regrettably, the former days when God's glory was greatly exalted in America are stored away in the annals of history. And for that very reason alone, America's light has waned, and her zenith departed. Instead of authority and power, America has become progressively weaker, less independent, and more emaciated by the day, thus exposing her frailty to the entire world.

There is a host of nefarious spirits and contemptible conditions at play even now in the unseen spiritual realm. Imagine what will happen if this enemy is no longer restrained by God. Left unrestricted, those noxious principalities will gladly inundate their revolting influence and iniquitous power upon this nation's weak leadership with the kind of repulsion never seen in America. It's time to discern the obvious warning signs. The unconventional storms of life have already begun descending across the entire country. These conditions aren't going to go away. Disorder will continue to get catastrophically worse, possibly even to the point of God's wrath and greater retribution. As a matter of fact, history plainly reveals that wickedness increases rapidly, especially when a society no longer prioritizes moral and civil obedience. Americans should expect no shortage of sorrow birthed from this nation's sinful precedent. Unless God gives us the same reprieve that He gave to Nineveh, we may be subject to the same repercussion suffered by Sodom and Gomorrah. We all need to recognize the perversion that brought the Lord's dreadful wrath down upon the wayward inhabitants of their day. *When the wicked are in power, lawlessness abounds. But the patient lovers of God will one day watch in triumph as their stronghold topples!* (Proverbs 29:16, TPT) No one can play with fire and not be burnt. Every sinner will have to answer to God for their contribution to evil.

Under most normal conditions, Christians are to obey the laws of the land unless they contradict the holy Word of God. The children of God are not obligated to comply with any of the government's deviant enactments that are contrary to Scripture. The first and ultimate authority over all Life is God Almighty. Either obey the authority of the Lord or face the consequences. *Then Peter and the other apostles answered and said, We ought to obey God rather than men* (Acts 5:29, KJV).

Everyone who sincerely trusts in the Lord has constructed their lives upon the Rock, His firm foundation. The Almighty's powerful underpinning will never be shaken. When the violent storms try to batter their structure, the children of God will be unmoved. All others will be in big trouble when all that shaking starts. Let the Old and New Testaments instruct and equally contribute to your spiritual balance throughout life. And because you have placed your faith in the Lord, all discernment and wisdom will be given to you in those days, but only if you continue steadfastly obedient in His will. *Lord, who may go and find refuge and shelter in your tabernacle up on your holy hill? Anyone who leads a blameless life and is truly sincere. Anyone who refuses to slander others, does not listen to gossip, never harms his neighbor, speaks out against sin, criticizes those committing it, commends the faithful followers of the Lord, keeps a promise even if it ruins him, does not crush his debtors with high interest rates, and refuses to testify against the innocent despite the bribes offered him—such a man shall stand firm forever* (Psalm 15:1–5, TLB).

Chapter 17

The Lamentable Sinking of America

If you happen to be a plant lover or gardener, you have learned to identify the needs of a plant by what is exposed above ground. It is the same with people or entire societies. Take a good look around the place where you live. The health of a community is communicated by an alternative language. Boarded-up shops and businesses closed, burned-out dwellings, trees and grass dead or dying, trash littering the streets and graffiti defacing exteriors and tent cities springing up everywhere. The modern term for such deplorable conditions is blight. But that is just the diagnosis; the initial condition is caused by something much more endemic, spiritual decay.

Neighborhoods and individuals may be good at hiding it for a time, but eventually, their lifestyle paints a rather dismal picture revealing to the world their sad and unbecoming circumstances. This plague on society has grown at a pervasive rate. Those once-rare conditions are now commonplace in almost every community in America. The agent is Satan, and the condition is infectious. Please believe me when I say it's not my intention to expose the pain associated with anyone's misfortune. My only purpose is to offer a restorative armament when dealing with any sort of personal decline or life's other dreadful and grievous situations. If the malady is like any other wound that has become inflamed or severely infected due to an invasion of germs or bacteria, it is necessary to clean the lesion before healing is allowed to occur. Other times the damage may be so severe that the infection must be cut away before restorative health can begin to take place. In either case, continued neglect of any such symptoms or existing disorder will most assuredly lead to an incurable condition or fatal circumstance.

In the springtime many years ago, I was inspired to start a

small garden of about six various pepper plants. I bought quality starts from a well-known producer, bags of the proper soil builder to nourish the prepared plot. Everything looked good for about a week, and then the plants took a sudden turn. It wasn't the soil, drought, or lack of sun. They just stopped developing and grew lethargic looking. I had no idea what the problem was until I dug up the first plant. It was all too obvious. There were dozens of voracious grubs feasting on the tender roots of each little struggling pepper. The plants couldn't sustain a proper amount of water or nutrients because they lacked an adequate root system. Once the problem was discovered, the cure wasn't far away. I learned about this indiscernible garden beast called Nematodes that love feasting on fat juicy grubs. That was the answer. In no time, the pepper plants perked up and produced a nice crop of choice peppers that season. Here is the moral of that story. If you want to cure any injurious situation, whether it's a plant or a person, you must first discover what caused the condition initially. Only then can the problem be rectified. Using the garden analogy, we must look at every one individually. There is no such thing as a universal cure. One fix for everyone will never remedy the dilemma. The only way to eradicate blight is to treat it one patient at a time. It might take a lot longer to establish a cure throughout, but the healing effects will far outlast a blanket approach.

That is just one issue plaguing America. You may be shocked at my next opinion, but it is the soundest truth that can be imputed to this obvious infirmity. Satan is at the heart of America's biggest problem. He is just like that little grub in the garden. If left alone, he, along with the rest of the fallen angels, will continue gorging upon this nation's spiritual roots until they have utterly despoiled what made America extraordinary. If you're already a child of God, then guard your heart well and monitor its condition frequently. If you are new to God's kingdom, Satan will come along and try to eat away at your tender spiritual roots as they are being developed. Watch closely over your heart; it can become easily contaminated. Remember Eve? God provided her with the perfect environment, the perfect mate, and the perfect diet. Nothing could have been any more perfect. Then Satan disguised himself as an innocuous garden snake, provoking her into a conversation. Satan is a prevaricator of truth. Warning number one. Never confer with the Lord's nemesis. He is the enemy of your soul! His objective is to kill you. Warning number two. Satan will sometimes disguise himself as an angel of light in order to deceive you and entice you to covet, just as he did Eve.

Whether we are willing to admit it or not, the face of America has drastically changed. I'm not referring to literal faces. I'm characterizing the unwholesome, panoramic image of our deteriorating nation. The scourge of immorality is festering like a boil. The core of that boil is sin. The ungodliness in America is a systemic impediment that is preventing any healthy development anywhere in life. America went from being a healthy Christian nation that reverenced and faithfully served God to a rebellious and defiant nation, creating and upholding laws entirely contrary to God's will. America was once a thriving and bountiful country, but her malady has brought shame upon her. All due to a prolific little seed called sin. Look what it has opened the door to. Spiritual dearth, of course. But that's just for starters. It's everything that grows as a result of sin that will run amok. Open a fresh ear of corn and see what developed from only that one kernel. This is a serious demonic situation. There's a significant health crisis in America. Crime is rampant. The younger generation is being brainwashed. Goods and services, if available, have skyrocketed. Many people can't afford the price of certain foods or medicine, let alone the price of gas. Baby formula, critical in the feeding of American infants, is elusive. What will be the next vital shortage? There are more jobs than bodies to fill them. And might I even dare to suggest that America might be on the verge of a hot war. And why? All because of liberal progressivism.

To say that America is in a repressive free-fall is inadequate at the very least. The radical decisions being made by the current government system are guiding this nation into anarchy. Far too many Americans, especially young voters, are impulsive and too often thoughtless when it comes to making critical changes to our complex system of governmental regulations and laws. It's all too apparent, the majority of voters throughout our nation haven't given much sincere consideration to the wisdom and character needed of those persons representing the interests of America. Many public servants are so completely polarized by their own self-interest, they refuse to be nonpartisan. Some of the elected leaders in America are downright wishy-washy. Still others are anti-Semitic, hostile toward the Lord's progenitors, the Jews. The biggest incongruity of all is when elected officials of diverse religions such as Islam, negatively influence laws contrary to those of our rich Christian heritage. Muslims follow the teaching of the Qur'an, which is in great variance to the Holy Bible. Moreover, Islam and Christianity have two unambiguously different gods. When it comes to the truth of Scripture, God does not allow for any latitude whatsoever! Christians strictly follow God's inspired Scripture. Islam is a oneness religion. thereby rejecting the most important tenet in the Christian doctrine, the Triune Godhead. Muslims worship Allah. Islam is a complete distortion of the Christian doctrine. Their grievous departure from inerrancy wrongly legitimizes the Muslim's claim of any brotherhood to the Christian community. *If anyone unites with our confession that Jesus is God's own Son, then God truly lives in that person and that person lives in God* (1 John 4:15, VOICE).

Although Christians live in a world of many faiths, Almighty God, the heavenly Father, imposes limits on His children's association with sinners, those who remain outside the Christian faith. Christians have dual citizenship. Children under the authority of Jesus live in this world, but they are spiritual citizens of the kingdom of heaven. God Commands His children to avoid being unequally yoked with unbelievers. It is the same constraint that God gave the nation of Israel when they crossed over into Canaan, the Promised Land. *Can two people walk together without agreeing on the direction?* (Amos 3:3, NLT)

Obviously, many irresponsible Christians fail to honor God's authority, often taking their spiritual role in society with pronounced indifference. Could that be the reason why America has done a complete 360 degree change in direction? It's clearly not a change for the better.

By appointing perverted deviants to key cabinet positions, this nation's Head of State is leading America's fall from grace right into a cesspool. This sacrilege is strictly for the purpose of indulging demagogues in a misguided attempt to restore harmony among the liberals and conciliate the unruly. All the subtle tactics of government policy come directly from Satan's playbook in an attempt to normalize an individual's aberrant lifestyle. Regardless, a blind man could see the true attestation of America's absolute moral and liberal corruption. Every effort to legitimize immoral behavior, habits, or perversion is a deliberate transgression against the Lord's divine law and a hostile act against Almighty God.

But just when you think it can't get any worse, it does. When the President of the United States appoints a candidate to a lifetime seat on the Supreme Court based on gender and skin color, without regard to merit or qualifications befitting the appointment, it's nothing short of incompetent lunacy. It's all too obvious, the actual reason behind his choice was the candidate's far-left liberal ideology. For instance. During questioning, Ketanji Brown Jackson, the black female candidate for the highest court of judicial law, refused to characterize the attributes of a woman. Nevertheless, Justice Jackson received her appointment to the Supreme Court. Beware when governmental officials begin perverting the moral course of justice with liberal reform.

Once again, the president has weighed in on the side of God's adversary. Endorsing egregious policies that legally support and encourage transgenderism is one of the same sins that God warns against. Let God be the Voice of reason in the matter of the transgender. What is God's considered opinion? His is the only incontrovertible truth and should settle any dispute once and for all. *"He who is emasculated by crushing or mutilation shall not enter the assembly of the Lord"* (Deuteronomy 23:1, NKJV). *A woman shall not wear a man's clothing, nor shall a man put on a woman's clothing; for whoever does these things is utterly repulsive to the Lord your God* (Deuteronomy 22:5, AMP). This administration is leading America into some dark uncharted waters, for which there may be no escape. No matter how society tries to normalize these many sexual deviancies, they are lecherous, pernicious perversions. Men and women can try altering their minds and appearance—even mutilate their body parts—but the one thing that's hardwired and unalterable is their DNA.

Sadly, anyone who has lost touch with their true identity can refer to their alter-ego or gender in any nonbinary term they wish to choose. Society may go along with its charade, but God will not. Every creation is a beautiful work of art, and to mock God is a sin. And God will not be mocked. No one wants to discuss these issues in terms of sin, but sin is what God says it is. This is just what Satan has waited for. This is his invitation to go after your little children with the same flagrant, unrighteous perversions and evil allurements that his other victims were ambushed with. What's occurring in American society dates directly back to Sodom and Gomorrah. In the early 1980s, a massive death toll occurred within the homosexual population as a result of the AIDS virus. Now the Monkeypox virus is on the rise in that same population. Although sin should be exposed for the harm it effectuates, God is gracious and forgiving. The Lord Jesus doesn't want anyone to perish. That's why God incarnate came. God Himself came as a Man to save the lost, the sinner, the ignorant. He gave His own Life that we could live more abundantly and live everlastingly. God loves His creation and wants to offer immediate forgiveness for anyone who will ask to be forgiven and turn from their sins. Every Christian was once a sinner and needed to be washed from their unholy flesh and irreverent manner of living. The churches all over the world are full of transformed sinners that turned from their darkened lifestyles to the marvelous Light of Christ. Not one of us has reached perfection. We are all in various stages of sanctification.

The powerful blood of Jesus will cleanse the dirtiest of sinners. But salvation is a day-by-day challenge. A child of God must learn the word "no," and, if necessary, speak that word every day to Satan. That is how Jesus defeated Satan in the wilderness. Yet, if sinners choose to wallow in blatant, deviant immorality, that is their choice. Never mind that President Biden has championed all LGBTQIA+ lifestyles, God decrees otherwise. Such practices are perverse and therefore forbidden. Partaking of the previously mentioned is indecorous fruit and an absolute death sentence. *Don't you know that the unjust will not inherit God's kingdom? Don't be deceived! Neither immoral people, nor idolaters, nor adulterers, nor practicing homosexuals of whichever sort, nor thieves, nor greedy people, nor drunkards, nor abusive talkers, nor robbers will inherit God's kingdom* (1 Corinthians 6:9–10, NTE). The children and youth of this nation should never be subjected to these forms of sinful indoctrination. Truly this is just another one of Satan's fiendish influences that Christians need to be aware of so that they can shelter their children from these abnormal perversions and sinful behaviors. Nevertheless, God is gracious and will never force His will on anyone who is defiantly stubborn.

Many of America's sacred rights are quickly vanishing and being replaced by the corrupt ideals of evil legislators and unprincipled people that bring dishonor upon the sovereign God of this nation. The power-hungry president has not only reneged on his campaign promises but refashioned himself into an unremarkable autocrat. And if he persists in having his own way, it won't be long before the Constitution of the United States of America will not be worth the parchment paper it's written on. Do you recall the day of Joe Biden's inauguration? He swore an oath to God before the entire world. And the sovereign Ruler of Creation heard that oath from heaven. Here are those words spoken by the President-elect Joe Biden. "…I do solemnly swear that I will faithfully execute the Office of President of the United States, (and) will to the best of my ability, preserve, protect and defend the Constitution of the

United States, so help me God." Was Joe Biden really asking God to help him preside over his newly elected office? Looking back at the trail of destruction over these many months in the White House, I think not. The speech he delivered to the nation on 9-1-2022 was by far the most dissentient ever uttered from the mouth of any American president. Heaven help us.

Although the spirit of America is changing, Christians are confident in this one thing. God is the same today as He was yesterday and will be tomorrow (Hebrews 13:8). Despite the possibility that the majority of United States citizens have unashamedly betrayed God, He remains faithful, consistent, and forever benevolent! The collaborative heart of America has become progressively hardened against the Lord, and most people no longer uphold Jesus as Lord or want Him ruling over their affairs. The precipitating evidence of enmity against Jesus is seen in most sectors of state and local jurisdictions. America has systematically and progressively removed God from the schools, courthouses, even some churches, and congress. But most emphatically, out of the White House, sending impropriety careening out of control. Murder in the womb is on the rise, and Gavin Newsome, the governor of California is leading the ignoble charge. Thievery and armed robbery have no bounds, and neither does the United States border. And since Americans have brazenly slammed the door in God's face, the future of our nation is now in great jeopardy.

Most Americans, including a vast number of Christians who are unfamiliar with the Old Testament, couldn't see God's hand at work through a Washington outsider like Donald Trump in the 2016 election. Critics didn't agree with God's decision to place a brash and unorthodox businessman in the White House. So, after Donald Trump's first term in office, he was replaced by the people's choice. In a nationally defiant move to separate from God and forfeit all the good that was in the nation's long-range best interest, voters decided that Joe Biden was the perfect man for the job. And on that point, they were right. The entire world watched as the newly elected president put his hand on the Holy Bible and promised to uphold the Constitution.

Yet, as soon as the ink was dry on the official document, he began doing the exact opposite. In no time, the newly elected president had begun to dismantle every positive advantage and security measure that our nation was sure to benefit from.

Anyone who reads the book of Hosea in the Old Testament Scriptures will learn how God dealt with Israel's betrayal when they decided that they no longer needed Him. That situation caused me to wonder: has God responded to America's foolishness and betrayal in the same way God dealt with the nation Israel? Like America, Israel had become proud in her own strength and decided to abdicate the goodness of God for the finite abilities of an earthly king. Could it be that the Lord accommodated the desire of the American people similarly to the chastening of Israel? *Israel has rejected what is good; an enemy will pursue him. They have installed kings, but not through me. They have appointed leaders, but without my approval...*(Hosea 8:3–4a, CSB)

America indeed deserves the Lord's chastisement for breaking her covenant with God and making a spectacle of our sins by grandstanding with a callous disregard for our vulgar depravity. Regrettably, the inconvenient truth is that America deserves Joe Biden. If indeed he is a judgment from God, then what's done is done, and now, we're all in this predicament together. May God help us to recognize our foolish ways.

Now I must add something that is even more important. The Lord tells His disciples to despise all kinds of sin, but we are to pray for those who walk in the dark and commit those sins. Furthermore, God tells us to pray for those who are in authority over us so that we may live peaceable lives. Also, to pray for those who despitefully use us. A Christian's responsibility is to be obedient. God will deal with the previously mentioned in His own way and in His own time. If you are a faithful Christian and want to do what pleases the heavenly Father, then take your kingdom responsibility seriously and do the work of a slave unto the Lord Jesus. He is sure to take care of all the other inconsistencies.

Chapter 18

Lies, Fearmongering, and Ineptitude

Of all the embarrassments endured by American citizens since Joe Biden took office, his first term Address to the Union has to top the list. For America's highest-ranking official to stand before the world and fabricate all his defunct accomplishments in his first year as president was repulsive and degrading. Every one of Joe Biden's policies has had an adverse effect on the hard-working citizens he presides over. And it seems as though he isn't done yet. President Biden is trying to pull the wool over the public's eyes with his conspicuous propaganda. And the news media and left-wing democrats are in shameful cahoots with his loathsome charade. Now in the shadow of Covid-19, Delta, and the Omicron viruses, we realize that the president's widespread overkill was the most menacing inefficacy behind his mishandling of the viruses. A great many people died needlessly as a result of careless and extreme misjudgment. When people stop thinking for themselves and listen mindlessly to concocted rhetoric, they're being brainwashed. If the majority of our population refuses to open their eyes, America will unwisely continue to suffer whatever foolishness their government prescribes to them, gladly accepting whatever breadcrumbs are tossed in their direction. Isn't that just another example of being blind and lost?

A further life-changing impediment to a wholesome America is believing the equivocators on certain news channels and social media. Without taking the time to check the facts, many people have had to learn some ugly truths and painful lessons the hard way. The devil doesn't have a better instrument of destruction in all its atrocious forms than media. What was once meant for good has been turned into a dangerous and dishonest tool of perilousness by twisting truth, spewing vile biases, and censorship. Many television anchors and columnists, once considered noble and objective, are consistently and deliberately deceiving the American public with nefarious disinformation or less than accurate accounting of the actual truth. Unfortunately, all of this imbecilic twaddle is a predictable impetus to the encroaching new era of absurdity.

But this is a time when we should be standing up for the rights our American forefathers provided us. Truth, justness, and liberty. We must turn to God for help, not the government. You've seen what the president has done with your trust. He is forcing the working-class citizens and their children into a hand to mouth existence. Sadly, this is a dangerous time. And there is little doubt, trouble is brewing. Now you might be asking yourself, "What kind of trouble?" The answer to that is quite simple: be prepared for anything and everything. Nothing is as it once was. The Lord will protect those who have a personal relationship with Him. He is ever-present and willing to defend His own in a time of trouble. But to the unsaved, don't gamble with your soul and where you will spend eternity, should an unforeseen event terminate your life unexpectedly. With the defunding of police and the enormous influx of criminal aliens, every street corner, grocery store, and church in America is unsafe. No one can hide from the evil forces of sin. *"Human being, you are living among a rebellious people. They have eyes that can see, but they don't take notice; and they have ears that can hear, but they don't pay attention; because they are a rebellious people* (Ezekiel 12:2, CJB).

Just who are the rebellious people spoken about in the preceding Scripture? Well, let's examine that issue a bit closer by looking at how your life might be affected by an intransigent tyrant. Too many government leaders see through a distorted lens of ascendency when implementing stringent laws, but personally disregard those same basic rules. The open border is putting every American's health and wellbeing in jeopardy. Not to mention the additional tax burden to care for millions of additional illegal migrants. America's economy is already on the verge of collapse, and the ineffective handling of the Russia-Ukraine crisis is going to put even a greater burden on the tax bearers of America. On our own home front, there is a lack of social connectedness whereby certain members of the community feel they aren't obligated to honor the existing moral structure and bylaws. Instead of bad guys being handcuffed, it's our police force that has their hands tied. The justice system is a confirmed kangaroo court. Throughout the commonwealth of America, there is a frightening escalation of civil unrest resulting in the brutalization and inhumane assaults upon the elderly, women, and children. These savage offenders are without conscience. Even the men and women of law enforcement are themselves targeted. The victims receive no justice, and the perpetrators go unpunished and often liberated. The homeless population is an unimpeded epidemic. Groups of organized thieves are plundering merchandise from selected stores resulting in enormous economic loss and senseless property damage. We are already seeing demonstrations, riots, strikes, and unlawful assemblies. Everything is inflated, including medical insurance, pharmaceuticals and utilities, while most paychecks are getting smaller in relation to everyday expenses. I'm relatively certain that no one just struggling to survive would find even a single reason to dispute these assertions.

"*The little foxes are ruining the vineyards. Catch them, for the grapes are all in blossom*" (Song of Solomon 2:15, TLB). It's apparent that a small minority in society has nothing better to do with their time than attempt to change how this entire nation utilizes the common English language. They see this as public-spiritedness, using their influence as a major contribution to humanity by exposing invented injustice and discrimination to certain categories of people. The current use of those pesky pronouns and the like must be ostracized for their damaging impact on nonbinary or any other self-identified individual. Rather than change the way the entire nation communicates with one another, maybe a more practical approach would be to offer compassionate counseling in response to anyone who may be easily offended by a distinctive pronoun. Transgender males encroaching upon ladies' rooms and competing in girls' and women's sports may not be considered a crime under current law, but it is nonetheless lamentable. And furthermore, it's all just a fraudulent eccentricity!

But all this is only a smoke screen testing the temperature of the water. If the American people consent to any of this poppycock nonsense, chances are they will blindly and willingly submit to anything. And that would include global warming and the Green New Deal. During the early weeks of Russia's invasion of Ukraine, while President Biden's right hand was supplying munitions to President Zelenskyy, his left hand was busy buying oil from President Putin. A lot of sense that made. But when has the Biden administration made any sense? Instead of depending on America's own resources for fossil fuel, President Biden is now purchasing our needed oil from other nations. If global warming is as serious as all that, what sense does it make to buy fossil fuel from other countries? So, then it's okay to contribute to the world's pollution if it's done vicariously? I suspect those kinds of underhanded deals are common bathroom practices in most authoritarian governments. You wash my hands, and I'll wash yours.

This liberal madness will no doubt continue until an all-encompassing sanitation has cleansed the United States of everything they see wrong. Or until voters wise up and begin to examine closely their choice of leadership. Currently, everyone in America is expected to show a Covid vaccination card and have a real ID for admittance on airplanes, in Federal buildings, and various other areas for the public's protection. It's not a laughing matter when I say this world is positioning itself for the mark of the beast; "six, six, six" is just around the corner. But keep in mind that America isn't alone in her suffering. There is squalid pandemonium spreading worldwide. Nations that were once considered tranquil and passive are now sharply divided internally. America is completely splintered into pieces as well. But the complex problem is no longer simply a political separation or a disconnect of ideals. No, the digression of clever, analytical planning goes much deeper than that. It's quite evident that many global authorities are changing the direction of their governmental focus, thereby turning a hostile fist toward their own citizenry.

In any event, be assured, a house or nation divided against itself cannot stand. Canada's Prime Minister, Justin Trudeau, is a perfect example of government overreach in the trucker controversy. In an effort to minimize the Covid virus, China has enforced a lengthy quarantine, forcing its citizens to remain in their homes. Soon, freedom and liberty enjoyed by many sovereign nations will no longer exist in any form. In no time, civil liberty will be history. As a high school student, I recall seeing pictures of people in communist China. Every person looked exactly like the person they were standing next to. It wasn't even possible to tell a man from a woman. They were all wearing the same kind of grey uniform. The vision of those images remained seared in my mind for all these years. It was a pathetic illustration of humanity. That could be how future generations will see American citizens.

Chapter 19

The Trojan Horse

There is a new direction on the horizon for America, and it is reminiscent of Israel's progressive evolution into slavery by the Egyptians. They were treated well by Pharoah in the beginning, but by the end of their captivity, they were crying out to God. Ever since God thrust Lucifer out of heaven, the fallen angel has continuously tried to usurp the authority of the Almighty. In the wilderness, Satan failed to entice the Son of man, but in the Garden of Eden, Satan convinced Eve she could be equal in power and authority to God. Satan's fingerprints are all over the disintegration of America. The devil never has to change his bait. Power hooks them every time. Let me remind you of this old saying: "absolute power corrupts absolutely." Therefore, be careful what you wish for. It might just be a diabolical figment of your imagination.

At the quarterly meeting of the Business Roundtable in March of 2022, President Joe Biden made the following statement in reference to establishing a global government. "There's going to be a new world order out there, and we've got to lead it. And we've got to unite the rest of the free world in doing it." The globalization of a one-world government will replace autonomy, and the word choice will be gone from our vocabulary for good. Don't kid yourself. Socialism is just a candy-coated term and the first step toward a godless communistic government. Absolute dominance will be brandished about at the hand of the power-driven despots. Those are the administrators who will occupy the highest seats in government authority. At the exclusivity of all others, only the wealthiest in society during a so-called socialistic age will remain relatively unaffected. Those having superior privilege and entitlement to life's advantages will be able to procure at a premium, choice sought-after concessions that are well out of reach for any average citizen. Electric automobiles for example. The following statement is just that sort of disunity. During the

French revolution, Queen Marie-Antoinette was told the people were starving; they had no bread to eat. When hearing that, she is quoted as saying, "Then let them eat cake." That is a prime example of the lack of empathy between the haves and the have-nots. A socialistic government is a wicked stepmother. Every adult and child will be regulated in accordance with the way government authorities deem suitable. Control may start out very innocuous, but it will definitely intensify by degrees. Oppression in the strictest sense will be enforced to an inordinate extreme. Just pay attention to how the Chinese government rules over its citizens.

Please don't be deluded into thinking that the unrest in America has suddenly come upon this nation, or that it is merely the result of a presidential election. None of the chaos has occurred overnight. Just what is the cause of all this anarchy in our nation? In spiritual terms, it's called apostasy. Unfortunately, that term may be unknown to most American citizens. Especially those born well after the sixties. *Apostasy* is a biblical term that describes what happens to a society when its citizens begin turning their back on God and take an opposite and fatal course. Providence will appraise our direction in time.

If you read the Genesis account of Adam's disloyalty to God in the Garden of Eden, it will clearly show man's unmindful breach of God's Commandment. Scripture doesn't explain the reason he chose to be disloyal to his Father and God, only that he chose to disregard God's warning and put his trust in another. Regardless, Adam's betrayal of God was a death sentence. Adam and Eve were immediately removed from God's presence and evicted from the Garden of Eden. Although it was Satan that tempted Eve to sin, Adam was without any justifiable excuse. Even though the first couple failed miserably, God's mercy for them prevailed, and although they had to endure the consequence of their decision, God still didn't cast them away entirely. He simply removed them from their perfect habitation to the world they chose for themselves. Then, by God's mercy, they were able to begin life anew, but it was in the fallen world. A world without the Light of righteousness.

And that dreadful decision brought us to where we are today.

From that day to the time of the New Testament and the era in which we are now living, God continues Speaking to us through His majestic creation and written Word. Adam and Eve were privileged to converse with their Creator face to face. Modern society has the blessed use of the Holy Bible, and the Holy Spirit lives in those who have surrendered themselves to Christ in the Christian faith. The children of God must always be learning, discerning, and following the sage advice from Scripture to avoid Satan's seductive allure.

God's divine rules are for man's benefit. Adam was cautioned about the danger of eating the forbidden fruit, but he just brushed off the warning, never suspecting the danger misleading him would come from the beautiful hand of his very own wife. See how cunning Satan is. Adam let his guard down. He was warned by God to watch. When God tells us to watch, nothing should be taken for granted. There was a similar event in the New Testament when Peter was cautioned by Jesus to watch and pray. But there again, Peter failed to follow the Command of the Lord. What remains dispiriting is the incredulity that persists throughout the entire world even today. It will always be the devaluing of God's warning that will expose the peripheral Christian and unbeliever to unrevealed hazards and treacherous conditions.

But let's look briefly over our shoulder to the ancient past and get a glimpse of the importance of understanding and obeying. And the perfect example to illustrate attentive obedience is Jesus, the Son of God. ...*I do nothing of Myself. I say these things as My Father has taught Me. He that sent Me is with Me. The Father has not left Me alone. I always do what He wants Me to do"* (John 8:28b–29, NLV).

Regardless of what period of time a person may be living, a follower of Jesus must have a separate distinction from those they share the physical world with. Jesus describes the children of God as a field of wheat among the tares (Matthew 13:30). A fruit-bearing child of God is like a tree growing in well-nourished soil, increasing in size and stature until it reaches its full measure of excellence and bears good fruit throughout life. While representing the Lord's spiritual light in the world, a wholesome Christian must maintain a sound practice of moral obedience while continuing the great commission in love and loyalty. It matters not what condition the world might morph into, God remains in control, and His truth has no variables. When the devoted and diligent followers of Jesus are Word wise, they are appropriately suited in the protective covering of God's armor and have God's assurance that they will flourish in strength and prosperity along their journey. *And we know that to them that love God all things work together for good, even to them that are called according to his purpose* (Romans 8:28, ASV).

Some people discover their direction early in life and stay right on course from beginning to end. Then there are those unfortunate individuals who spend their entire lives trying to find a little happiness, but they never quite secure any real gratification from their many pursuits. Regrettably, untold numbers of that lost and misguided group never seem to find the slightest, honest-to-goodness satisfaction in life. They just seem to go through the empty motions of living. There are two clear-cut directions in life: the path of righteousness or the path leading to destruction. I don't want that to happen to you or to those you love. The following represents two brief examples of someone's wayward course of action.

Abraham fathered two sons. Ishmael, the eldest, was a product of Sarah's impatient and failed attempt to become a mother. Not wanting to wait for the child promised to her by God, she devised her own plan. Ishmael became Abraham's first-born illegitimate son by Hagar, Sarah's Egyptian bondwoman. Sarah did eventually conceive many years later, giving birth to Abraham's second son, obedient Isaac. But many years of great strain upon the family climaxed when Sarah saw Ishmael taunting his younger brother. As a result of that incident, Sarah insisted both he and his mother Hagar be permanently banished from the family. Regrettably, but with God's approval, Abraham honored Sarah's demand.

In time, Abraham's youngest son Isaac fathered his own two sons, Esau and Jacob. Esau, the first-born son, was undisciplined and took the turbulent path in life. He was careless and unconcerned about significant family matters. As a result, Esau traded his birthright to his younger brother for a bowl of stew and even married outside the family lineage.

Eventually Isaac came to be very old and blind. Realizing his time of departure was near,

Isaac wanted to bestow the prayer and family blessing upon his first-born son, Esau. Isaac knew nothing about the earlier trade between brothers or of the deception between his wife Rebecca and youngest son. Jacob's mother contrived a plan to trick her husband into giving Jacob the blessing instead of Esau. That deception was morally wrong and tore the family completely apart. Esau would have killed Jacob if Rebecca hadn't sent her youngest son away for his own safety. Sadly, Jacob and his mother never saw each other again.

As stated in chapter 1 verse 4 of Ephesians, God's elect are the children of promise—those chosen before the foundation of the world. But until that search leads the wayward and lost to be reconciled with God through His Son Jesus, tranquility, protection, and contentedness may be elusive. But once found, Christians treasure their birthright and dutifully follow after righteousness. By means of Jesus, children of the Almighty have the totality of Christ's richness. Anyone can have great wealth and substance acquired from earth's resources, but those things in and of themselves won't yield the slightest bit of actual or lasting gratification. All things considered, material possessions are usually deceptive and have very little enduring value. Only in the love of God will someone have true peace in their spirit and genuine harmony with their fellow man, no matter what their circumstance.

Where do God-seekers find peace, security, and joy in a world of decadence? *Everything we could ever need for life and godliness has already been deposited in us by his divine power. For all this was lavished upon us through the rich experience of knowing him who has called us by name and invited us to come to him through a glorious manifestation of his goodness. As a result of this, he has given you magnificent promises that are beyond all price, so that through the power of these tremendous promises we can experience partnership with the divine nature, by which you have escaped the corrupt desires that are of the world* (1 Peter 1:3–4, TPT).

Still, no one chases after God. It's more precisely the opposite. God seeks after His chosen one, much in the same way a smitten suitor would pursue the affections of a special young lady.

Although God specializes in diversity, all human beings enter life swaddled in a corrupt body of flesh. Each living soul may be distinguishable from all others outwardly, but it's the heart that identifies the character of a person. By nature, most people take after Adam and Eve's erroneous example by ignoring God's instructions, choosing to control their own destiny. Others try to duck any personal responsibility for their immoral acts by placing blame elsewhere. Then there are those who practice outright rebellion, trying to put as much distance between them and God as possible, just as Jonah did. It simply proves God's point. People want to enjoy the Lord's benefits; they just don't want God telling them what to do. Most people have no interest in the Lord's principled standards and high moral ways. They would rather decide for themselves what is right or wrong, even if it means wallowing in their own fabricated stench and indecency. *So, get rid of all the filth and evil in your lives, and humbly accept the word God has planted in your hearts, for it has the power to save your souls* (James 1:21, NLT).

Think of the Word like a grain of wheat that remains dormant until God Himself appoints the precise time it should be watered. The purpose for this might amaze you, but it is a supremely glorious method that God will use for His very own practical purpose, inevitably giving everyone the same opportunity to receive the Lord's gift of salvation. The best way to explain this hypothesis is to offer a simple illustration from various kinds of soil. Everyone gets the same seed, but the soil is what is most important to the survival of every seed. Consider the various soil conditions as though they were a characterization of your very own heart. *"Listen! A farmer went to plant seed. Some seeds were planted along the road, and birds came and devoured them. Other seeds were planted on rocky ground, where there wasn't much soil. The plants sprouted quickly because the soil wasn't deep. When the sun came up, they were scorched. They didn't have any roots, so they withered. Other seeds were planted among thornbushes. The thornbushes grew up and choked them, and they didn't produce anything. But other seeds were planted on good ground, sprouted, and produced thirty, sixty, or one hundred times as much as was planted"* (Mark 4:3–8, GW).

To say it another way, when the Word germinates and springs forth vigorously to life, it must be immediately incentivized to begin its maturation. Therefore, specific activities are then necessary for its resilient, long-lasting growth. If the tender spirit is properly nurtured, it will continue to thrive and eventually develop into a mature Christian. On the other hand, if the spiritual seed is neglected, it may very well remain dormant for many years or die altogether. It's the sovereign will of God Who gives the seed potential for Life in the kingdom, but the fruit is matured solely in the heart of the possessor.

God's assurances are conveyed through Scripture. However, it must be understood that His Word is unequivocal, and His organic rhythms of spiritual Life are perfectly timed. Although the Lord has the power and ability to make all things feasible, the Lord never crosses His stated boundaries. God's Word faithfully decrees that freedom to choose our own direction is paramount. Let's look at it from something in the natural world.

Imagine for a moment that our God is a towering, majestic Sequoia. According to nature, this amazing tree only reproduces after its seeds are released from their woody cones. One of the aids that impact the reproduction cycle of the tree is fire. Fire will travel up through the tree limbs and dry out some of the mature cones. Then the dried cones will eventually drop to the ground and release their seeds where they have fallen. But other cones may remain attached to their limb, thereby releasing those seeds to the flurry of the wind. Soon after the Sequoia's seeds are well dispersed, there must be favorable soil conditions and ample protection for them to survive and therefore flourish. The ground must be fertile and have sufficient sunshine and moisture. So then, in correlation, God is the Tree of Life. Your flesh is the cone. And the Holy Spirit's fire is what will open your heart to birth your spirit. Then it's time to find good ground in which to grow and develop that little seedling. Search out a biblically established evangelical church. Associate yourself with a body of believers that will help you cultivate your newborn spirit in the way, the truth, and the life. A church having the mind of Christ and a shepherd who loves his sheep and is devoted to the spiritual health of his flock and well able to teach the tenets of God according to precise doctrine. These steps edify the ravenous soul and bring glory to the Lord Jesus, adding to the Church one living stone at a time.

If however, the unbelievers search for God is perfunctory, their hunt could last for years without any success, even though the answer was within them the entire time. Without a doubt, fervency and desire is the key that unlocks a heart's passion for God. Only those diligent seekers whose enthusiasm burns intensely will discover that secret place and learn the Lord's purpose for their life. They are the ones that continue down the well-worn pathway formerly labored by Jesus and all His diligent disciples. They are the ones who will joyfully fulfill their God-given destiny. They are the ones that vow, "Your will be done, on earth as it is in heaven" (Matthew 6:10).

There is nothing more repugnant to Almighty God than a lackadaisical half-hearted Christian. Is that you? Has your observance of Christ become routine? Has your worship in song become commonplace? Are you happily receiving God's best for your life but ignoring proper reverence and gratitude for all the goodness He's bestowed upon you and your family? Keep this in mind. If your gestures of exaltation aren't tributes from the heart, then they will mean absolutely nothing to God. Words are merely vocalized sounds the mouth makes. Heartfelt praise in the most exemplary way possible has a tangible influence when done suitably and reverently to the glory of God.

In accordance with Scripture, every legitimate child of God should always undertake these three attributes seriously. The first two, worship and obedience, are central to discipleship and must be offered to God with all sincerity and allegiance. It's wonderful if you are adept at Scripture memorization, but the more advantageous work is to be in compliance with the various directives that you've learned from the Bible. The third is building the kingdom population through evangelizing the lost. You don't have to be a theologian to tell someone about Christ. Just share what you know or what you have personally experienced and leave the rest to the Holy Spirit.

Every child of the Almighty is expected to deepen their relationship with the Lord through His inspired Word. That is the only source capable of building a strong spiritual character. Character is the virtue of the inner self. It is the principled excellence that avoids the easy path and always takes the high road. Sound character consistently does the noble and unimpeachable thing, even when no one else would ever know the difference. No one except God.

Far too many ho-hum Christians waffle between kingdom living and life in accordance with the values of the secular world. If you are a child of Almighty God, then you must always exhibit an unquestionable reputation, especially because you are living among a society that is indifferent or hostile to the ways of God. From the moment of spiritual birth to the saint's homegoing, it's imperative for every devout Christian to remain consecrated to

God throughout the entirety of their life. There is no excuse for disreputable conduct. Christians are known as the light in the world so the lost can find their way to God. When light illuminates, the gross darkness diminishes. But when the oil runs out of the lamp, the flame will begin to dwindle and eventually die. Let's say it another way. If the anointing from the Holy Spirit begins to dry up, your light will grow dimmer and dimmer until it is snuffed out completely. It's rather like taking a hot glowing coal from the flames and setting it aside for a time. Soon the fire's intense embers will begin to diminish until there is no remaining fire.

Let me offer a graphic example of infidelity to the Holy One. Samuel the prophet was sent by God to anoint a man named Saul to be commander over Israel. At some point after Saul's coronation, and even though he was given many great victories in battle, God took away his kingship. Rather than trusting and obeying God, Saul preferred his own counsel. On one occasion, instead of waiting on the nation's consecrated priest to officiate a ritual sacrifice, Saul impertinently took it upon himself to perform the role of priest. God was greatly displeased with Saul's insolence. On another occasion, Saul dismissed the Law of Moses, allowing his hungry soldiers to openly violate a serious dietary precept by eating meat and blood together. Lastly, Saul was given very explicit instructions from God on how to conduct a battle against an enemy nation the Lord wanted to annihilate. Absolutely everything was set for destruction. God put a complete ban against seizing anything associated with the Amalekite nation. Saul's army was to obliterate every man, woman, and child, including the infants, cattle, sheep, camels, and donkeys. By the Commandment of the Sovereign Lord, the wicked nation in its entirety was to be exterminated. But Saul had other ideas. He ignored God's Commandment by making an exception with the king of the Amalekites. Saul preserved the life of King Agag and took him captive. In addition to that defiance, Saul determined to take some of the choicest plunder, including the Amalekites' superior sheep and cattle.

After many betrayals by King Saul, God sent the prophet

Samuel to confront the nation's leader concerning his disobedience. Surprisingly, before Samuel was able to catch up with Saul, he had already built a monument to himself in honor of his victory over the Amalekites. What was worse, he used their profane plunder as a sacrifice to Almighty God. When Samuel finally came face to face with Saul, Saul lied to Samuel, stating that he had followed God's orders exactly. But then Samuel heard the bleating of the sheep and the lowing of the oxen. When Samuel challenged Saul, he blamed his soldiers for preserving the livestock. Saul dismissed any personal responsibility for refusing to obey God's rules. Here is how Samuel responded to Saul's excuse. *"Has the Lord as great a delight in burnt offerings and sacrifices As in obedience to the voice of the Lord? Behold, to obey is better than sacrifice, And to heed is better than the fat of rams* (1 Samuel 15:22, AMP).

Then Samuel demanded that King Agag be brought to him immediately. Samuel finished Saul's failed assignment by cutting down the king of the Amalekites in the presence of God. Saul's pride blinded him to the fact that God had permanently deposed his leadership position on the very same day he disobeyed God regarding the destruction of the Amalekite nation. The Lord's anointing and favor were then consigned to a young shepherd boy named David. And in the fullness of time, He would replace Saul and become the long-standing and beloved king of God's people and a man after God's own heart.

Finally, righteousness comes down to the simplest form of faithful obedience. The most common and well-regarded are the Ten Commandments, originally written by the finger of God on Mount Sinai and given to Moses to instruct God's people. Those strict Commands were written to institute righteousness among the Israelites. However, before we dismiss the original Commandments, I would suggest that you consider them not as rules but as a lifestyle. Although, since Christ's death on the cross at Calvary, there was a new inclusive covenant established that embraces the old law perfectly. It is a comprehensive Commandment given by the Lord Jesus. The first, love the Lord your God with all your heart, with all your soul, and with all your mind and strength. The second, love your neighbor as yourself (Mathew 22:37–39). Those two Commandments fully unite the law and the love of God. *He has made it clear to you, mortal man, what is good and what the Lord is requiring from you—to act with justice, to treasure the Lord's gracious love, and to walk humbly in the company of your God* (Micah 6–8, ISV).

Chapter 20

You Are Naked, Exposed, and Vulnerable

The Bible tells us of certain preeminent civilizations annihilated for their subversiveness. Not much more than a byword remains of those megacities, with few notable exceptions. Jerusalem and God's people, the Jews, are among the most prominent exclusions. In practically every case, those nations that strayed from the grace of God and His purposes were reduced to mere parables. All currently existing nations should consider this an eminent warning for the future. Beware. It's very unwise to treat the Sovereign Lord contemptuously. And as far as America is concerned, the Lord's patience could very well run out at any given moment. The Lord emphatically stated His intention to judge His church first. I believe that we have already begun to see hints of God's great displeasure with His elect. If God's judgment isn't immediate, then it's possible that the initial onslaught of judgment upon our nation will seem like just another calamity or extreme weather pattern. But soon, those events will begin to escalate and become all too obvious that God's wrath is impending. At that point, peace and safety will be a far distant memory. *The coming of the lawless one is according to the working of Satan, with all power, signs, and lying wonders, and with all unrighteous deception among those who perish, because they did not receive the love of the truth, that they might be saved. And for this reason God will send them strong delusion, that they should believe the lie, that they all may be condemned who did not believe the truth but had pleasure in unrighteousness* (2 Thessalonians 2:9–12, NKJV). Once again and more emphatically this time. Abide in holy Scripture, and the peace of God, which surpasses all human understanding, will be with you, no matter what it is you may be facing.

But here is where the rubber meets the road. The wrath of God is not something that people are prepared to deal with. It isn't addressed in church or in Bible studies. Most of the time, the only characteristic projected of God is His immeasurable love, which is beyond question. But there is so much more to discover about God. There is so much that we fail to understand about Him. Without that knowledge, we cannot know how to react in these treacherous and fluid times. I remember thinking as I began writing this book, what will I say that differs from every other book of its kind out there? How will the contents of this book make a positive difference in the life of that special someone who has chosen to invest their money and time? The answer to that question is clearly *the truth*. I am offering truth. Not my truth, but the Lord's truth. The truth is not always something people are anxious to hear, especially in this period of progressive unrest. Nevertheless, the truth is restorative in every respect. And the unassailable foundation laid by Christ Jesus is truth, and His framework plumb, strong, and therefore imperishable. *Lady Wisdom has built her house; she has supported it with seven pillars (*Proverbs 9:1, VOICE). We will be looking into some of those pillars a little later.

Christ is the absolute necessity when constructing a firm foundation for any structure. Then there are certain pillars that add additional strength and support to the erected framework built upon the foundation of Christ. These pillars are to assist the believer in the fundamentals of righteousness. They also aid in the fortification of your spiritual fortress. They are mighty barricades that confirm your testimony, encourage your conviction in the power of the Lord Jesus, and fortify the temple of God throughout a Christian's lifetime. They serve many additional purposes besides. They help to shape moral character and integrity while serving the Lord God in a complete and undefiled capacity. These stalwarts have no equal when it comes to the task of holding up and maintaining many more consecutive generations of Christ's followers, even for another thousand years if it were necessary. God has already established an indisputable and indestructible foundation for Christian living. His Word has supported many past generations for thousands of years, and it's every bit as dependable and inextinguishable today as when it was first established. No matter how mankind tries to desecrate God's biblical principles, the Chief Cornerstone and underpinning of the church will never be moved. Think about that in terms of steadfastness in uncertain times yet uncharted.

Suppose for a moment that you had in mind to build your future dwelling place and make it your permanent home. A home that would serve you and your progeny for many years well into the future. Every detail must be carefully considered before beginning the project. Cost, location, and design: all must be approved by you initially. You have even considered the possibility of future renovations or expansions that might become necessary. You've thought of everything. Then, of course you would want to use only the very best laborers and materials in the construction of your future dwelling place. This would be a good strategy for a well-built and securely established habitation for what lies ahead. But regardless of the planning and construction, it is still only temporal. Those same strategies would be a sensible and realistic approach to acquiring your eternal home in heaven.

But on the other hand, I'm no longer persuaded that today's modern society is interested in permanent arrangements of any kind, particularly heaven. Everyone seems to be in a continuous flow from one thing or place to another. Whatever the cause, people are continuously on the move, clearly showing discontentedness. Culture today dictates a more disposable or short-range interest, especially when it comes to their possessions and, unfortunately, their relationships. There appears to be no immediate need for any kind of future stability. Nowadays, the newest or latest anything has a very short expiration date. We tire easily. We get bored with things, fashion in general, the cars we drive, our cell phones, and sometimes even our careers. Life is fast-paced, and the rat race to stay on the fast track will not only create early burnout but many other dissatisfactions as well. But the good news superior to all that insignificant earthly depravity is this. God does not change with the seasons as we humans do. *Because I am the Eternal One, I never change;* (Malachi 3:6, VOICE)

God is the solid Rock on which America built its foundation. Irrespective of the direction a person decides to go in life, their basic understanding of right and wrong is intrinsic. But much too often, the evolution of subsequent generations is too quick and by far too willing to exchange their moral foundation for one with far greater liberal ideologies. But regardless of any amoral condition the world might undergo, a Christian's responsibility is to remain steadfastly fixed to the Lord. For that reason, their voice represented by their vote must always affirm their commitment to God and His righteousness.

America is especially liberal compared to only a few generations ago. We are now living on a planet where diverse social influence has great sway over how we think and act. Social media can create a great deal of pressure on what we believe or give credence to. But as adults, we should ask ourselves why we cultivate certain concepts and reject others. Perhaps we are unduly loyal to someone from the past. Could it be that popularity has influenced our judgment? We may even think that we are living our own truth. But living our own truth will turn out to be the most deceptive lie of all. Have you ever asked yourself if the basis for what you believe is even rational? If we can't give a legitimate reason for our personal convictions, then it's time to reexamine our credo. And that couldn't come at a more critical time in the history of America. The hour has come for God's citizens to be more discerning and stand aright. Believers must be a sweet savor, the very fragrance of Christ, attracting all those plodding through the murkiness of Satan's devilry to the pathway that leads to the Savior. If we follow God's pattern for living throughout our lifespan, we will reap great rewards here and in the hereafter. Any recompense from the Almighty is far above the meager temporal gain offered by the latest craze in the world. God is gracious to all the children of earth, but especially so to His faithful and obedient disciples, who aren't ashamed or afraid to publicly carry their cross.

Regrettably, the number of faithful Christians worldwide is dwindling at a rapid pace as we come ever closer to the last days that the Bible talks about. That unfortunate situation is especially apparent in America, the nation formerly faithful and obedient to God. It's par for the course when superficial Christians pray to God when they have need of Him but pay very little attention to His righteous mandates. Other Christians choose to exhaust their own resources instead of first consulting the Lord. However, everyone should take stock of this one certainty. Almighty God remains in control no matter how dreadful things may look from our lowly vantage point. *Many are the afflictions of the righteous; but the Lord delivers him out of them all* (Psalms 34:19, RSV).

Commence to learn how, when and where the real problem begins to erode spiritual faith, especially among immature Christians. Taking their eyes, their thoughts, and their confidence off the One Who has the perfect solution to whatever problem they are dealing with, is the same stone that they continue to stumble over, time and time again. When will Christians take the hint? Every child of God must be fully equipped in sound doctrine while continuing in the faith, remaining earnestly focused and resolute concerning every principle and assurance of God. Only then will a true believer continue to grow spiritually and begin to flourish, even while persevering in life's hardships. That is faith in action. *The Lord is my rock and my fortress and my deliverer; My God, my strength, in whom I will trust; My shield and the horn of my salvation, my stronghold.* (Psalm 18:2, NKJV). God should be our first line of defense, not our last desperate effort. Why wait until we've come to the end of our rope before reaching for the hand of God?

Now I realize that not everyone has begun life in the same lap of love and luxury that others may have been fortunate to enjoy. Indeed, everyone has their own story to tell. And that story contributes significantly to their ideology. The front cover of your life may look very different from the back cover, or vice versa. But it's the pages between the cover that really tell the story. No doubt there are some very tragic circumstances among us. No doubt there are people that have endured much suffering ultimately, while their counterparts have been indulged in opulence from the very beginning of life. Life isn't always fair. But God never promised that life would be fair. He instructs His children to avoid covetousness and to be content with what He provides.

God will never forsake His children (Hebrews 13:5). He has promised a future and a hope for a brighter tomorrow. The Almighty Father gave His Son to the world so that we could partake in the joy of heaven for all eternity with our Savior and Creator. That is why He has offered us a practical guide referred to as the Bible. It would be very foolish to visit a foreign country without the proper preparations. Such things as a map, possibly a translator, and maybe a hired guide to facilitate the newcomers' arrival and help set them on the right path. Our spiritual journey is just such an expedition. Christians have not traveled this way before. God knows each person far better than any good parent knows their child. He is omniscient. He knows the past, sees the present, and has exact knowledge of each person's future. He is our Bible and trusted Guide through those uncharted waters.

Scripture is a faith builder given to prepare us for all future probabilities. Furthermore, God would never leave His creation defenseless. So, in addition to the Bible, God has offered us His own armor for our complete protection. *Therefore, take up the whole armor of God, that you may be able to withstand in the evil day, and having done all, to stand* (Ephesians 6:13, NKJV).

Now maybe you're asking, why in the world would we need any armor? Well, you can be sure that if God Said we need armor, then we need armor. And if we need armor, we had better be properly fitted for a battle. There is an evil day slowly encroaching upon us. And if that wasn't bad enough, the god of this world roams around looking for easy prey to devour. Be on the alert and ready to defend your ground. And having done all you know how to do, then just stand! *So remain strong in the faith. Put the belt of truth around your waist. Put the armor of godliness on your chest* (Ephesians 6:14, NIRV).

In the beginning, God Provided Adam with an easy Life. He was given a wife and a fully producing garden in which to establish their home. What more could a man ask for? But sin changed everything. The first man chose to throw it all away for a world of ungodliness and constant tribulation. God has made it very clear through His Word that we live in a world of adversity. That is why God provided us with a practical guide to prepare us for any antagonistic probabilities. And in the event we suffer impairment, God will rehabilitate anything that has been broken. *He heals the brokenhearted And binds up their wounds* (Psalm 147:3, NKJV).

Haven't we all enjoyed recognizing or comparing the similarities and resemblances in the family tree? Many characteristics may indeed follow us from generation to generation, but maybe not all those characteristics would be considered favorable. Some of us know a family member who has led a life of rebellion that has given rise to great sorrow. Often generational weaknesses still exist within a family and can lead a person entirely in the wrong direction. It is important to identify any such propensities and immediately make the proper corrections. Otherwise, instability, discord, and grief are sure to follow. God has given us a wise and foreseeable path to follow. In the book of Galatians, we are given a list of immoral actions that lead directly to eternal death. *When you follow the desires of your sinful nature, the results are very clear: sexual immorality, impurity, lustful pleasures, idolatry, sorcery, hostility, quarreling, jealousy, outbursts of anger, selfish ambition, dissension, division, envy, drunkenness, wild parties, and other sins like these. Let me tell you again, as I have before, that anyone living that sort of life will not inherit the Kingdom of God* (Galatians 5:19–21, NLT).

The Bible cannot describe sin any planer than that. Scripture is a fantastic chronicle of prudent practices and Commandments that are beneficial to all mankind regardless of culture or the color of one's skin. When God's mandates are applied, there is harmony and tranquility among the people wherever they dwell. God's wisdom, when followed, served our ancient brotherhood well in their day. And that same guiding Light is especially suitable for modern society. God has chosen for us a far better direction than the one we might unwisely choose for ourselves.

Modern civilization should learn a lesson from historical societies that have tragically tried to usurp God's Commands by their own set of common standards or ethics. America has now become one of those societies. And although God is patient by nature, we must never consider Him lenient in any of those areas that defile His strict standard regarding sin.

God has a deliberate reason for exacting such a strict standard upon His people. The Almighty views everything much differently than we do, including time. Everything in our world is in accordance with God's precise timing. All life's events are at the behest of God alone, and we must therefore accept the decisions He makes on our behalf. Remember that His Words will never fail. Almighty God is dependable. *And we know that God causes all things to work together for good to those who love God, to those who are called according to His purpose* (Romans 8:28, NASB). It will never be the Lord Who aborts a promise. That will be determined by our own heart for whatever precarious or ill-chosen reason.

There are certain edicts that have been unchanged from the beginning of creation, and they will be applied to everyone alike. The Lord's paradigm is firmly placed, and nothing is ever going to change it. The Lord is no respecter of persons; therefore, He will never controvert His truth. God's kindness provides for the just and the unjust equally. *God said to Moses, "I will show kindness to anyone to whom I want to show kindness, and I will show mercy to anyone to whom I want to show mercy"* (Romans 9:15, NCV).

God of the Old Testament has acquiesced marked authority to His Son Jesus; He is the Lord and King of all the earth. Jesus is now Commander in Chief. *"The Father doesn't judge anyone. He has entrusted judgment entirely to the Son so that everyone will honor the Son as they honor the Father. Whoever doesn't honor the Son doesn't honor the Father who sent him* (John 5:22–23, GW). In the Old Testament, Jehovah showed Himself in astonishing ways, displaying powerful signs and extraordinary wonders. Some of those methods were so frightening that the people were often terrified of the Lord. Then Jesus was born. God's Son began His Life in very humble beginnings. As a matter of fact, throughout His human ministry, Jesus displayed many graphic and picturesque examples of humility as a template for us to emulate. Just for your information, a definition of the word humility includes the absence of pride and self-assertion. Humility is also defined as unpretentious and submissive to the divine will of God.

The book you are holding is merely a limited attempt to illustrate how the Holy Bible avails itself in our lives when we adapt the practices and advice it recommends. Notice I used the word *recommend*. That is because God is gracious in allowing everyone to decide for themselves what road in life to follow. But for anyone desiring to seek the way, the truth, and the Life that Jesus calls them to, they must be fully persuaded to do it faithfully. The Holy Bible is our model and pattern for fellowship with God and peace among men in our society. Hopefully, anyone reading this has already established a kinship with God and a productive, well-disciplined relationship with the Lord Jesus. Nevertheless, just keep in mind, whether it is true of you or not has no bearing on God's truth or His ordained principles in the life of each human being. Life is decidedly better with God than without Him.

Chapter 21

Stand Firm for What You Believe

Prayers are a Christian's staple. Just like bread and water sustain life. Prayers speak to God of relationship, dependence, and trust. Many years ago, just prior to the carpet being laid in the new sanctuary, several members of the church wrote prayers and scripture verses upon little pieces of paper and placed them all over the floor where the carpet would be installed. It was an intercessory action of spiritual underpinning to the foundation of God's house. The same concept was established when the Founding Fathers of America sanctified the land and its government to God. They dug deep in prayer to lay a fathomless, indestructible infrastructure in the governing body of our nation. Their sincerity and devotion to God secured our rights of freedom, liberty, and justice for all Americans, then and in the future. So how was this liberty to be interpreted? Under the Constitution of the United States of America, providing the people remained within the limits of the law, no legitimate authority had the power to impose upon society any oppressive restrictions, inequality, or biases.

Any sovereign nation built upon the firm foundation of God's Scripture is rather self-governing. In other words, holding on tightly to God's standard in all things unconditionally. God's ideal for treating all members of society decently is in accordance with His foreordained pattern. Love is the only custom of brotherhood acceptable. But unfortunately, it's the greater number of people that will ultimately prescribe the policies that set in motion the truculent behavior that we are seeing all around us today.

If the wayward nation of America continues down the road it's on, we could wind up like China, or worse, governed by China. Their Christian churches are being closed by government order, and many of the Chinese are being brutalized and killed for their faith in Almighty God. America has become weakened by the inefficiency of the Biden-Harris administration, and China is fully aware and ready to take advantage of America's incompetence. It's no secret that China aspires to take America's place as the number one superpower throughout the entire world. Maybe you can't imagine that, but it is a credible threat. You don't have to take my word for it. You don't even have to watch the fake news. Just read your Bible. Many predominant and influential nations of their day were every bit as superior as America once was. Where have they all gone? One by one, they were all pulverized into the dust by forces mightier than they and many times at the designated hand of God. It seems that Americans have forgotten that God has always been a stronghold over this nation. Even now, God's ascendancy prevails over America, and whatever the Lord wills for the future of our homeland will indeed be accomplished according to His sovereign decree and schedule.

China already has a grip on this nation, thanks to a lax governmental policy. They've had one foot in the door for a long time now. Stop and ask yourself: does America's administration have the clout to stop China from an invasion? Or would they even have the desire to do so? Are they doing anything to prevent the millions of migrating foreigners from violating America's borders? There is your answer. If the day ever comes when China occupies this nation, look out. And, just in case you weren't aware, let me remind you: there are no options when China sets the rules.

Let me say to the non-believer, should that day materialize, hang on to that rabbit's foot; you will need something to hold on to. As for the Christians in America, our faith is in God alone. He is our Bulwark. It is God Who is holding on to us. But this I will add. I pray you have hidden the Word of God in your heart where it cannot be stolen. Because more than likely, your Bible will be one of the first things confiscated by the Chinese government. And they won't stop there. They will permanently close down churches, remove all crosses and symbols of Christ, and freedom in America will be exactly what the Chinese government determines it to be. Christians in America will come face to face with actual life-threatening persecution for the very first time. Be prepared to live by the cross and die by the sword.

If the modern church had done what was expected and followed the pattern laid out by Jesus and the disciples in the New Testament, we wouldn't be in this position today. Did our Christian leaders fail us, or did we fail our Christian leaders? In any case, if we had been diligent concerning our Father's business, we would have made it a priority to do the will of God as Jesus Instructed. The Words of the Lord are the same today as they have been for centuries. *Then He said to them all, "If anyone desires to come after Me, let him deny himself, and take up his cross daily, and follow Me* (Luke 9:23, NKJV). If you are wondering what it means to pick up your cross and follow Jesus, I'll tell you. Sinful deeds are conceived in the darkened and depraved mind of the flesh. Sin hates the purity of light. The Light of righteousness exposes the degenerate evil for what it is. Therefore, at the beginning of your walk with Jesus, your flesh will fight you tooth and nail. It wants to resist the things of God and return to its own way. But the cross is a symbol of death by crucifixion. Therefore, take all those old habits, desires, and thoughts and nail them to the cross. You can't follow Jesus and carry around all of your old baggage. Lay down your burdens in exchange for the cross and your new Life of righteousness. Our cross is no burden to carry. The overriding burden was upon the shoulders of Christ. It was the Lamb of God Who was laden with the exacting sins of the world.

One very critical question on the minds of many today is, who or what should we believe? Well then, that begs the question, who or what have you been listening to? Is it family members, friends, your stylist, or maybe some self-appointed guru on social media? Much too often, those people we keep close company with today are just as confused and lost as the next person. Maybe you are trusting the unscrupulous news media for the answers you seek. Heaven forbid! And if anyone is foolish enough to think the current administration of Biden-Harris is being straight with the nation of America, or looking out for their best interest, then, unfortunately, that person isn't substantiating the claims expressed by the president or his delegated spokesperson.

As appalling as it sounds, the current White House administration is very likely carrying out someone else's instructions. For the extremists on the left to achieve their hidden agenda, they have underhandedly done everything possible to pull the wool over the eyes of the unsuspecting public, blinding them from the verifiable truth. How many times have our leaders subtly leaked a contrivance to throw us off the scent? I would suggest many more times than we are aware of. Far too frequently, the activity of those in authority intentionally deceive their constituents concerning the true nature of their calculated and diabolical intentions.

There is an old but valued expression: if it looks too good to be true, it probably is. If you glance out over the shimmering surface of a calm body of water, it may appear very serene and inviting. But many times, lurking beneath the surface is where the real obscure dangers lie in wait. How often have you purchased a medical prescription on the advice of your trusted physician, only to discover an encyclopedia of dangerously potential side effects from it? But if you have blind confidence in your physician and take the medicine without reading the small print on the package, what seemingly was the answer to one problem, has now created a whole new assortment of secondary conditions that you weren't prepared for. And the same analogy holds true for the rip tide at 1600 Pennsylvania Ave. in Washington, D.C. Would you make the same decision today as you did in the presidential election of 2020? For the majority of American voters, it's called buyer's remorse.

Please take the next moment to ponder King David's impassioned words of influence upon the nation of God's people. It's no wonder he was the apple of God's eye and beloved ruler of his citizens. *The God of Israel has spoken. The Rock of Israel said to me, 'When one is right and good in ruling over men, ruling in the fear of God, he shines on them like the morning light. He is like the sunshine on a morning without clouds. He is like rain that makes the new grass grow out of the earth through sunshine after rain'* (2 Samuel 23:3–4, NLV). Is there the least bit of semblance between King David's idea of rule and President Biden's leadership?

Let me offer this unpretentious piece of advice. Arrogance often impedes the perception we have of ourselves, believing that we are incapable of being defrauded. Then only after the fact will we find out how terribly wrong we were. There is a well-founded expression from the past: they can't see the forest for the trees. Sometimes it may be necessary to take a step back and look at things from a different perspective. It's never wise to take something as crucial as the leadership position of a nation purely at face value. It's always a good idea to seek out an unbiased or second opinion in matters of uncertainty. On the one hand, wisdom is indispensable. On the other hand, there is no accounting for stupidity, and ignorance is a shortcut to a great sense of regret.

America has entered a vast crucible of extremes. Each of the different inflammatory elements—fear, hate, and hopelessness—is exacerbating the chaos unfolding in our homeland day by day. Our very own government is devastating its citizens with harmful propaganda and overwhelming legislative power. There is a deadly pathogen spewing out from the White House maligning our beautiful America. This is a powerful and menacing conspiracy that is endangering our long-established and highly virtuous constitutional system. Our Founding Fathers developed an exemplary structure of balanced government promoting equality for all. It's every Christian's responsibility to actively labor in prayer to defend and preserve our God-given rights. We ought to pay closer attention to the winds of change. The present powers in control are simply using the ole shell game to draw us off the Rock of our foundation with their gravitational pull to the extreme left. Their use of enticing language is only a smokescreen to induce the average citizen into conceding to legislation blindly. But we must be discerning and prepared against every storm in life, including those intended to eliminate our bedrock principles and freedom. We mustn't wait until the tornado is across the street to act. The time to act is prior to the danger.

Modifications in society are to be expected over the ages. But wrong will never be right in God's economy. Neither will sin ever be sanctified. When an emerging generation attempts to change America's foundational norms on the pretense of adapting congenial laws to accommodate the needs and habits of an immoral evolving society, their intentions are enormously flawed and deceptively corrupt. Let me repeat. The edicts mandated at the underpinning of America were predetermined by the Holy Spirit of God and placed deep within the soil of America by the prayers of God-fearing men dependent upon the unfailing grace of God. Trying to sever the roots of America's articles of faith is inordinately foolish, not to mention ineradicable. Does anyone remember what happened when the Egyptian Pharaoh pushed back against God's authority one too many times? The personal carnage suffered throughout Egypt was unimaginably devastating.

Take for instance what is occurring in this country right now. Whatever happens to stir up strife or be thought of as outright contemptible by a few mutinous individuals immediately becomes the main feature on the nightly news. How many times have we seen America's beautiful national anthem disrespected by someone's demonstration of twisted ideology? The American flag, the tenacious symbol of this nation's patriotism, is often contemptuously disgraced. It's hard to imagine that there would come a day in America that the traditional red, white, and blue would be desecrated by the very citizens who benefit from all the rights and privileges that the stars and stripes symbolize. Haters can deface the cloth, but the embodiment of its fabric is representative of the service and honor in which untold American men and women courageously sacrificed to keep Old Glory flying in impassioned esteem.

Then there are the transgenders. They want to be recognized and validated on mere claims. They demand special consideration for their chosen identity, willfully exchanging their physiological orientation for one they like better, often by means of fashion or medical modification. Adding to the list of bizarre foolishness is the cancellation of all personal pronouns. Who would have ever dreamed that the words boy or girl would be offensive? Or addressing someone by sir, miss, or madam would be considered a violation of someone's rights. Any person without a variance in skin pigment—otherwise referred to as Caucasian—is now considered inequitable and xenophobic by the yardstick of the rule-setting extremists. Children's harmless books are targeted, candy is being refashioned, toys and cartoons are suddenly inappropriate by the subversive standards of the power-driven fanatical left. In addition, there seems to be an inordinate amount of pressure to surrender spiritual ideals that Christians have long regarded as highly sacred and most virtuous.

One of the most recent inclusions to the persecution complex of the woke psychosis is the magic kingdom, once thought to be the last bastion of healthy fantasy for children of all ages. However, since 1991, visitors identifying themselves other than heterosexual or conventional have descended annually upon the park in massive numbers. Conservative and Christian groups tried to oppose those events, but their censure fell on deaf ears. Amid the criticism, the park officials denied sanctioning what later became known as *gay day* but did nothing to discourage it or put an end to it. Therefore, since 1995, gay days have been an unofficial get-together at the park. It's all about what consumers demand. The bottom line is revenue.

For the time being, the militant hard-liners are satisfied by using intense coercion and all-out banishment, canceling what they deem improper. "Might makes right" is an erroneous saying that asserts: right and wrong will be decided upon by those who wield the greatest power. All this is leading up to a much bigger series of harsh measures and monumental burdens upon society through clever, deceptive campaigns, artful tactics, and outright bullying. Unfortunately, most Americans are under the mistaken impression that eliminating capitalism is the best way to exhibit fairness and equity to all ethnicities. Sadly, many passive Christians agree. What a bunch of gobbledygook! That nonsense is the first step toward complete government rule. God gave us freedom by way of His Son's death on the cross at Calvary. And now we're just expected to stand idly by and let the government take away that precious gift of independence in exchange for human subjugation? Not a chance! Liberty contributes to capitalism, and private enterprise promotes societal strength within the nation.

The fifth Roman Emperor, Claudius Caesar Augustus, better known as Nero, also used his powers of persuasion through tyranny, debauchery, and excessive spending funded by a high rise in taxes. He was perhaps considered one of the most oppressive rulers of his day. That corrupt despot also began a campaign to eradicate Christians; how analogous! And, it has been suggested that he may have beheaded Paul during his second imprisonment in Rome. God help us if the day of stark tyranny ever materializes in America. But if it does, how many of us will bear our cross with distinction? I would say this to those Americans who no longer consider Christendom fashionable. There is no argument there! Putting on the robe of righteousness was never meant to be a fashion statement. It is a robe that affirms the servant of Christ has been washed in His sinless blood and justified to the Father, Almighty God. *For whosoever will save his life shall lose it: but whosoever will lose his life for my sake, the same shall save it* (Luke 9:24, KJV).

God expects Christians to speak the truth in love. Of course, there will be occasions when it is necessary to courageously confront injustice or a lie. But that is the essence of true faith in action. Faith is a mighty tool in the hand of a courageous Christian. God's truth is for the pulling down of strongholds in the lives of a lost society. Only the truth of God Almighty will set us free from demonic destruction or governmental tyranny and lead us forward peacefully in the love of Christ.

The high standard that faithful Christians live by is set

before us by the great Almighty, not a dictatorship government. Nevertheless, be assured, God is always in control. There are no limitations in the spirit. As long as the children of God just keep following the Lord's pattern for living, they will reap rewards far beyond the temporal benefits this world or the government has to offer. The Lord is exceedingly gracious to those who will rest in the knowledge of Him. His overwhelming and charitable expressions of love and generosity flow lavishly into the lives of those who call Him Abba Father.

Chapter 22

The Deadly Dangers of Doubt and Delay

Although Job wasn't a Christian, he was indeed a righteous man. Satan did his level best to utterly trounce Job's spirit into the dust but was unsuccessful in all his attempts. Nevertheless, Satan's methods of destruction were merciless. He destroyed Job's family, his property, livestock, and most of his servants. Yet Job remained faithful to Jehovah.

The Lord gave Peter notice that Satan was going to sift him like wheat. Jesus tried to caution Peter by telling him what the devil's intentions were. Jesus warned Peter to stay alert and pray against the strategies of Satan. Unfortunately, Peter failed in that responsibility and paid a dear price for his negligence.

Satan roams around like a lion, looking for someone to devour. His roar is like that of a jungle cat, using a threatening territorial call to announce his mighty status. It's his symbol of power. So, consider yourself warned. If anyone is caught sleeping as Peter was, you've left yourself open to the wiles of the devil.

However, it was an entirely different story when it came to the Son of man. Satan used three of his best techniques on Jesus, trying to tempt Him after His forty days in the wilderness. But Satan failed miserably each time. Jesus was not enticed by the wiles of the devil. But Satan wasn't the only challenge Jesus would be faced with. The Messiah was rejected in His own homeland by His own people. In fact, Jesus met with constant adversity, but none of the scorn would stand in the way of His love and plan for man's salvation. And when that perfect hour had come, Jesus was nailed to a cross as God's Lamb, sacrificially crucified for the sins of humanity. His execution procured man's freedom from sin and reconciliation to the Father. But not even death could hold Jesus. Three days later, He removed His burial clothes and walked out of the tomb to claim His victory over hell and the grave.

Children of God, please remember why Jesus was referred to as the Man of Sorrows and what proceeded the amazing triumph of our Lord and Savior. He was treated insufferably, humiliated, ridiculed, beaten, and afflicted to the depths of His mortal soul. He received all that appalling trauma and never uttered a word of protest. That is until that dark moment came when the sin of the world was thrust upon Him. Christians, please realize the incontrovertible price Jesus paid for the redemption of your soul. Only at the very moment when Jesus realized for the first time in His Life that He was separated from the Father, did Jesus Cry Out in agony. In the desperate throes of torment, the Son of God could be heard. Exclaiming, "Eli, Eli, lama sabachthani, My God, My God, why have You forsaken Me?" It was the heavenly Father Who offered His only begotten Son for the propitiation of man's sin. But it was the Eternal, Almighty God, Who was loathed to look upon the Sacrifice that became the Sins of man.

Christians must understand the cost of discipleship under the Lord Jesus. God's children will encounter their own form of persecution at the hands of haters. Not haters of you necessarily, but Who and what you stand for. *But Jesus replied, "Foxes have dens in which to sleep, and the birds have nests. But the Son of Man has no place to lay His head"* (Matthew 8:20, NLT). Jesus is letting His followers know in advance that there will be harsh and unpleasant times ahead. Persecution frequently goes with the territory when contending with evil in today's malevolent world. You might get your feelings hurt. You might not have a bed to sleep on for a night or two. Ask the missionaries about hardships. So, in essence, it takes resilience and courage to be a Christian. That is what Jesus was advising in the preceding Scripture.

In addition to dedication, Jesus is clarifying something else. His stay on earth was only temporary. It made no sense for Him to set up a permanent residence; He was only visiting. It goes without saying, but I will say it anyway: earth is the planet that Christians only temporarily inhabit. At the point of spiritual rebirth in Christ Jesus, believers become citizens in their new heavenly kingdom for all eternity. Earth then becomes a temporary residence while colonizing the lost sinners. When sinners receive Christ as their Savior, everything about them begins to change. The whole sequence of their future is refashioned, and for the better. From the first day of salvation unto the day of demise, travel light and continue steadfast in faith no matter the cost. The saints of God must never take spiritual matters for granted, especially salvation. It's too precious a gift to lose over a few inattentive and careless choices.

God knows His children by their name. He knows their heart and which ones are serious, hardworking, committed servants on behalf of His kingdom. On the other hand, God knows every lost soul by their name also. God's heart longs for the unreceptive and wayward, the Christian who is half-hearted, indecisive, unassertive, and hesitant. Don't be like the Israelites who feared entering into the Promised Land. Fight the good fight of faith. We've been told beforehand that it's going to take a sturdy backbone to stand against the evil impetus in today's world. *So take a new grip with your tired hands, stand firm on your shaky legs, and mark out a straight, smooth path for your feet so that those who follow you, though weak and lame, will not fall and hurt themselves but become strong* (Hebrews 12:12–13, TLB).

Jesus exposes one such proclivity in the following story. The Lord began by describing some of the many hardships encountered in the pursuit of righteousness. Then Jesus explains to His potential disciple the importance of immediacy when the invitation to follow the Lord is presented. How very interesting were the reservations of this would-be follower. He wasn't willing to forgo his family inheritance and commit to the lifestyle that Jesus proposed. Therein lies the problem. Instead of laying up treasure in heaven, many unbelievers and even some passive Christians clutch ever-so tightly to the material things of this world instead of commandeering the better choice, life eternal. Observe the conversation between Jesus and His would-be apprentice. *Disciple: "Jesus, before I do the things You've asked me to do, I must first bury my father"* (Matthew 8:21,

VOICE). *Jesus: "Follow Me! And let the dead bury their own dead"* (Matthew 8:22, VOICE). Jesus graciously extended the invitation of salvation to the young man. However, his response was the same as many people today. They have too many other important matters to attend to. They'll get around to it one of these days.

In the following story, notice the reaction to the father's invitation. Can you see the similarities between that society and our modern-day society? Jesus is describing a father's invitation to come for a special dinner and gaiety. Unfortunately, the reluctance that Jesus describes is altogether too familiar. *"A certain man hosted a large dinner and invited many people. When it was time for the dinner to begin, he sent his servant to tell the invited guests, 'Come! The dinner is now ready.' One by one, they all began to make excuses. The first one told him, 'I bought a farm and must go and see it. Please excuse me.' Another said, 'I bought five teams of oxen, and I'm going to check on them. Please excuse me.' Another said, 'I just got married, so I can't come.' When he returned, the servant reported these excuses to his master. The master of the house became angry and said to his servant, 'Go quickly to the city's streets, the busy ones and the side streets, and bring the poor, crippled, blind, and lame.' The servant said, 'Master, your instructions have been followed and there is still room.' The master said to the servant, 'Go to the highways and back alleys and urge people to come in so that my house will be filled. I tell you, not one of those who were invited will taste my dinner'"* (Luke 14:16–24, CEB).

That beautiful symbolic story is nevertheless a revealing picture of today. The heavenly Father's initial invitation was to His people, the Hebrews. God was preparing a wedding feast for His Son Jesus, but they refused their invitation. They wanted no part of Jesus, the Messiah. So then, to fill up the banqueting hall, the Father made an open invitation to the public. Since the nation of Jews gave Almighty God the brush-off, it opened the spiritual Door to the Gentiles. God even provided every wedding guest with a clean article of clothing, fitting and proper for such a noteworthy and joyous event. Soon after everyone was seated, the Father arrived to greet His guests with a welcoming gesture of hospitality. *"But when the king came in to look at the guests, he saw there a man who had no wedding garment; and he said to him, 'Friend, how did you get in here without a wedding garment?' And he was speechless. Then the king said to the attendants, 'Bind him hand and foot, and cast him into the outer darkness; there men will weep and gnash their teeth.' For many are called, but few are chosen"* (Matthew 22:11–14, RSV).

This is an illustration of the future banquet to be held in the kingdom of heaven in honor of the marriage between Jesus and the bride of Christ; those born-again Christians who accepted the Redeemer's blood-bought gift of salvation and everlasting Life. Only those souls washed in the cleansing blood of the Lamb of God are permitted into heaven. They are the adopted children of the Father, the overcomers. Their name written in the Lamb's Book of Life is evidence of their relationship to the King. The Father then furnishes each of His children with a robe whiter than snow, some of the hidden manna, and a white stone with a new name known only to the recipient. There is no other Name under heaven by which mankind can be saved. Jesus is the way, the truth, and the Life. The crucifixion of Jesus was a propitiation to satisfy God and the rabbinical law, which required a blood sacrifice by death for the cleansing of sin. Jesus' death permanently canceled the sin debt that was inherited from Adam when he fell from God's grace. Adam went from the garden into the world. The blood-bought children of God go from the world into heaven.

Those historically sad excuses and tragic examples are very similar to the busy people in today's modern society. No time for God, church, or the Bible. Most people are just too busy or preoccupied with other activities. God, by all recognized standards, is the indisputable essence of unfeigned love and patience. And yet, He is often put aside and treated as though He was an inconvenience or troublesome annoyance. Imagine the Almighty Creator being cast aside as though He was a common intruder, interrupting in someone's private domain and interfering in their vital itinerary. From the beginning of ancient times as we know them until this very day, the Bible confirms those very same attitudes, generation after generation.

We've all heard it said many times: we are what we eat. And there is ample evidence to support that reality. Additionally, one's environment is thought to have a direct impact on an individual's habits and lifestyle. Whether it is good or bad, it is generally considered a natural human phenomenon to assimilate with the people we spend the most time with. We find our identity first in the home; then it advances in grade school, on the playground, and in the cafeteria. Later, with various groups or organizations, the workplace, social media, bars, or nightclubs. These are the situations that set the pace of our life and attachments. Or, in some cases, entanglements. The more time we spend around these kindred spirits, the more we will talk like they talk, dress like they dress, and enjoy the same interests. It's just natural to embrace or mimic those dominant influences that we admire.

There are some individuals that are very stealthy and fly under the radar. Humans can sometimes be very chameleon-like. They'll do whatever is necessary to remain well camouflaged. This is quite the practical tool in the cold-blooded world of reptiles. Lizards often use this technique as a defense mechanism for their survival. They borrow from their natural surroundings for protection. Therefore, it should come as no surprise that many people today are having to adapt using this same method. It's especially advantageous for self-preservation. It doesn't take very long before people change their behaviors and even their opinions to blend in and identify with whatever environment they happen to find themselves in. But, if belonging means having to lose your personal identity by changing your own point of view, basic principles, or even the most sacred held beliefs, you had better run. Furthermore, God made individuals, not cookies.

However, the animal kingdom being what it is, such tactics might not always fair that well in nature. Suppose a little lizard decides to camouflage itself upon a beautiful and luscious green leaf atop a tall tree somewhere in the Serengeti. All is peaceful until a giraffe comes along and takes a big bite for lunch. What a delightful surprise in the daily special, a little protein along with the salad. My point here is merely to express how dangerous the conditions can sometimes be, even in one's very own environment. These circumstances may not be the same for everyone. It takes a strong resolve and a powerful mindset to retain what distinguishes you from everyone else. And for those of you who march to the beat of your own drum, get comfortable with being out of place when determining to hold on to your real Christian identity.

People's differences are easily distinguished on the outside. But it is an entirely different matter to perceive what is in someone's heart. What used to be buried down in the deep mire and gutters of America has bubbled up to the surface. And the stench is appalling. Most young Americans haven't been alive long enough to know from experience what a defective democracy can do to a nation in only one or two short generations. The white hairs of wisdom and common sense are no longer valued. Solomon was right on point when he said, "There is nothing new under the sun" (Ecclesiastes 1:9). Human nature being what it is, puts me in mind of a circumstance very similar to that of today.

Upon the death of King Solomon, his son, Rehoboam, reigned in his stead. He wisely sought the counsel of his father's advisors on a matter of leniency upon the citizens in the kingdom. From their many years of combined experience, the elders recommended that the new king use a kinder pathway and improved judgment than that of his father, thereby making the king's subjects loyal, contented servants forever. But then, King Rehoboam decided to consult the opinion of his friends. Their opinion was shockingly opposite. They recommended harsher directives and greater punishments. And the king chose to heed the recommendation of his peers. *"And now, whereas my father put a heavy yoke on you, I will add to your yoke; my father chastised you with whips, but I will chastise you with scourges!"* (1 Kings 12:11, NKJV) But never fear; God will always have the last word. And the following Scripture makes His anger very apparent. *You have committed far greater sins than those who ruled before you. You have rejected me and have aroused my anger by making idols and metal images to worship. Because of this I will bring disaster on your dynasty and will kill all your male descendants, young and old alike. I will get rid of your family; they will be swept away like dung* (1 Kings 14:9–10, GNT).

And then there are other incompetent elders in government that should have retired to the rocking chair a long time ago. But they simply refuse to let go of the power they're addicted to. It matters not to them what kind of harrowing circumstances lay ahead for the future generations, just as long as their security and prosperity aren't affected. And this reminds me of Eli, an Old Testament priest who refused to correct the greedy, dishonest, and evil ways of his two sons, Hophni and Phinehas, also priests. *Now the sons of Eli were evil men who didn't love the Lord. It was their regular practice to send out a servant whenever anyone was offering a sacrifice, and while the flesh of the sacrificed animal was boiling, the servant would put a three-pronged flesh hook into the pot and demand that whatever it brought up be given to Eli's sons. They treated all of the Israelites in this way when they came to Shiloh to worship. Sometimes the servant would come even before the rite of burning the fat on the altar had been performed, and he would demand raw meat before it was boiled, so that it could be used for roasting. If the man offering the sacrifice replied, "Take as much as you want, but the fat must first be burned as the law requires," then the servant would say, "No, give it to me now or I'll take it by force." So the sin of these young men was very great in the eyes of the Lord; for they treated the people's offerings to the Lord with contempt* (1 Samuel 2:12–17, TLB). What was even worse, Eli was fully aware of his sons' wickedness and did nothing to correct it. *Eli was now very old, but he was aware of what was going on around him. He knew, for instance, that his sons were seducing the young women who assisted at the entrance of the Tabernacle* (1 Samuel 2:22, TLB). When Eli heard the news that Israel had been defeated in battle by the Philistines and both his sons were slain, there was little reaction. But when Eli was told the Ark of God had been stolen by the Philistines, he fell over and died also. God's ways are past finding out. His methods of correction are far beyond our ability to comprehend. Nevertheless, no one escapes the judgment of God. No one!

Hopefully, you were able to grasp my purpose in sharing the story of God's priest Eli and his two dishonest sons. Any official holding a high-ranking office of authority should themselves be above reproach and never, under any circumstances, turn a blind eye to the unscrupulous behavior of their offspring.

Of course, it would be naïve to suppose that modern humans would be permanently content to remain restricted indefinitely by the Bible's virtuous societal norms. History bespeaks of that. Although it may have been inconceivable a few generations ago, the inevitable has happened. Contrary to America's long-established ethical roots, our homeland is headed in a downward decline that this once proud nation may never recover from. Recognizing the unfortunate truth is a terrible shock to the system. Scores of irreproachable dogmas are no longer accepted by one-half of the society in which we live. Then it should come as no surprise when conservative orthodoxy is no longer welcomed or acceptable in the social community; thereby making ample room for Satan himself. America, long regarded as a watering hole to the nations, is being contaminated by laws that are in direct disobedience to the Commandments of God.

When ridiculousness is carried to the ump degree of absurdity, then rational heads must prevail. This is where we should glean some well-established wisdom from the apostle Paul. *Let no one be under any illusion over this. If any man among you thinks himself one of the world's clever ones, let him discard his cleverness that he may learn to be truly wise. For this world's cleverness is stupidity to God. It is written: 'He catches the wise in their own craftiness'* (1 Corinthians 3:18–19, PHILLIPS).

A very long time ago and on more than one occasion, I heard it said, "If you can't beat them, join them." In other words, just throw in the towel and surrender even before engaging the opposition.

Apparently, that is today's philosophy. But before you make the decision to surrender your God-given right of emancipation, here me out.

In times past, regardless of what state Americans lived in, they were bonded together in unity and with a spiritual cohesiveness and love for each other. Notice how drastically unethical standards have reshaped this nation through the leadership of one reprehensible man, whose fraudulent bait-and-switch claims have tranquilized half of America while the rest of its citizens are fighting to block a totalitarian power grab.

Wouldn't you at least try to fend off someone who was attempting to overtake your home, your spouse, or your children? Common sense dictates it is what anyone would do under similar circumstances. It's considered responding responsibly to a threat in order to protect the things and people you care about and that are dependent on you. But that is not at all what is happening. People nowadays are being carelessly content with regard to their liberty. Wake up America! Smell the abhorrent stench reeking within our system of jurisprudence. It's time to acknowledge the bigger picture. Be cautious of the real deception. The government is determined to take complete control of American lives. Let me refresh your memory with the term "Nanny State." That is the government's interference in the personal choice of its citizens.

If there was ever a reason to stand your ground, it's now. That is when someone absolutely refuses to give up and defend what belongs to them. I'm certainly not advocating violence in any form, but occasionally, there may be sufficient cause to push back when appropriate. Just how much of the very essence of individualism are you willing to relinquish? Those freedoms are every bit as tangible as any other of your possessions. And nobody, not even the government, should have the right to take them away. If our children's future is worth securing, if our convictions are worth defending, if this nation is worth saving, then we should stand in allegiance with the Lord God Who gave us these rights and privileges to begin with. Make a personal decision to stand in incorruptible solidarity for life, liberty, and the pursuit of happiness for all future generations. Don't give in, don't give up, don't betray our God or our nation.

The tremendous advancement of this country didn't just happen by accident or even because of the resourcefulness of man alone. From the beginning of conception, America has been upheld by the mighty hand of God. I can't help but contrast America's growing pains to the frog in the kettle story. If you put a frog into a kettle of hot water, the frog will immediately recognize the danger and leap from the kettle. But, if you put the frog into a kettle of cold water before turning up the flame, he will slowly cook to death. Let's not be ignorant of the government's stratagem against the people of America.

America is like the Promised Land spoken about in the Bible. A land flowing with milk and honey. God made sure that everything needed or required by the early colonists was made available to them. Not only would the pilgrims survive, but they would thrive in a nation that was thoroughly self-contained to allow for their independence and societal growth. It was the benevolent hand of God that supplied the necessities of Life to those God-fearing settlers. Their survival was reliant on the good graces of God alone. And the survival of modern America is no different.

Chapter 23

From a High Horse to a High Calling

This would be a good time to observe an amazing phenomenon in the exceptional life of a man whose entire life was transformed by the adoration he had for the Lord Jesus. This man was none other than the apostle Paul. Paul was born to Hebrew parents in the metropolitan city of Tarsus. His birth name was Saul, and he was a proud Pharisee and the son of a Pharisee. At some point, Paul studied the law under the great teacher Gamaliel, considered the most prominent rabbi of his era.

Saul's broad understanding of the Torah and his dedication to long-held national customs and historical conventions seemed to extend far beyond ordinary superficial comprehension. He was a deep thinker and vehemently impassioned for national compliance and eager for the continuation of his heritage and traditions to remain intact. Furthermore, Saul also had an intense understanding of the prophets, literature, and philosophy. In all that, he wasn't afraid of hard work; in fact, during his ministry, he earned his living as a tentmaker. Which, given his background and education, is somewhat peculiar. But in all this, Jesus saw Saul's potential and knew he would make a great candidate for the ministry of the Lord. Which eventually proved to be unreservedly true.

During the early rise of Christianity throughout Jerusalem, Saul was an intolerant activist against the church movement. He was truly a daunting militant. Saul was exceedingly zealous in apprehending those who became believers. He was doing everything within his power to eradicate any followers of the new way. In today's language, Saul was very much a conformist. He persecuted any believer he found observing the new way. It didn't matter to him, man or woman. Saul was even named among those persons that condoned and witnessed the stoning of Stephen in Jerusalem, which marked Stephen as the first of many martyrs.

Saul seemed to take great pleasure in persecuting Christians. In fact, it was believed that Saul had arrest warrants from the chief priest in Jerusalem to take into custody as many believers as he could find in Damascus. But then, that's when it happened.

Along the journey to Damascus, Paul had a life-changing encounter with the Messiah. His travel was interrupted when an imposing Light from heaven shone down upon him. This startling phenomenon was so intense that it caused Saul to fall off his horse. While he laid upon the ground, stunned, he heard a Voice saying to him, "Saul, Saul, why are you persecuting Me?" Overwhelmed by this experience and blinded by the Light, Saul asked the following question. *"Who is speaking, sir?" Paul asked. And the voice replied, "I am Jesus, the one you are persecuting! Now get up and go into the city and await my further instructions"* (Acts 9:5–6, TLB).

All the men accompanying Saul were astonished by what they had witnessed. Each of the men traveling with Saul heard the Voice but didn't see the Man Who was speaking.

The Lord's orders were immediately followed, and Saul was taken to Damascus. There Saul remained sightless and went without food or water for three days, praying to the Lord. After those days, the Lord Spoke instructions to another one of His disciples. Ananias was told to go to a street called Straight in Damascus and restore Saul's sight by the laying on of hands. This rather concerned Ananias, for Saul was notorious for having those of the faith arrested and brought before the chief priests in Jerusalem. But Ananias set aside his unease and obeyed the Lord's Command, and Saul's sight was returned to him, and he was also filled with the Holy Spirit.

Saul, then referred to as Paul, remained in Damascus an additional three days, after which he immediately began preaching the good news of Jesus, the Son of the living God. Those that heard him were amazed at Paul's transformation but nonetheless uncertain of his legitimacy. It was a considerable length of time before Jesus' other disciples were sure of Paul's intentions. Despite the skepticism, Paul's message and works couldn't be denied. The Lord picked the right man for the job of church planting. All of Paul's zeal, tenacity, and skill were directed toward the building up of the kingdom of God. Paul would be God's ambassador to the Gentiles, to kings and the children of Israel. Even with a great many hardships and extraordinary travails, Paul persevered and succeeded in his mission. The apostle faithfully followed the Lord's directions, wherever His directions would lead.

Christians today have much to be thankful to Paul for. His early life and education became the groundwork for the New Testament church that all Christians are a part of today. Anyone can change their life's course from a Saul to a Paul. But getting knocked off your pedestal isn't the most preferable introduction to Jesus. A far less dramatic encounter would be to pray for forgiveness and ask Jesus to open your blind eyes. After that, follow all the instructions the Lord gives you.

After the Lord's resurrection, the disciples had two exceptionally important possessions to guide them in their commission to build upon the foundation of the Lord's church. Their personal witness to share with others and the Holy Spirit to usher them in the right direction. Despite that, according to the New Testament accounts, every day must have been an uphill battle. Amid the danger of persecution, the disciples were nevertheless changing lives through the message of salvation, healing the sick, and casting out devils. And because they were meticulously aware of the lasting and great importance of their work, they took the needed time to carefully record their acts. That's where the book of Acts in the New Testament originates from. The apostle's enthusiasm to spread the gospel was tremendously fruitful due to their fervor and perseverance. Every experience was rich with reward, intense with danger, but fervent in love and goodwill. Although they often met with considerable resistance from every direction, they refused to be discouraged and persisted diligently out of their gratitude and tremendous love for the Savior Jesus.

The Lord's apostles were well taught through the examples modeled by the Lord Himself while He walked among His creation. Unafraid and stouthearted, they risked their very lives to bring the gospel into existence. Apart from rejection, they faced death in their everyday missionary duties. The early church had a great many adjustments to make. Those rugged men weren't indestructible, just unequivocally loyal to Jesus and their deep commitment to defending Christ's purpose. Evidence of their diligent labor and unreserved dedication remains with us today. Praise be to God that the exploits of Jesus and His disciples were written on scrolls, preserved, and transferred into modern-day Scripture for our edification. The apostles laid the framework for many subsequent generations to build upon. We have the easy part. The gospel pattern has been formulated for us to follow. A model of faithfulness and bravery. Especially when it comes to clashing head-on with the religiously defiant governmental authorities.

For it is time for judgment to begin at the household of God; and if it begins with us, what will be the outcome for those who do not obey the gospel of God? (1 Peter 4:17, ESV) Who would have thought that in the 2021st year of our Lord, we would have our chance to stand up in defense of our sovereign authority? But that is exactly what the church nation did. After the second lockdown order to slow the spread of the coronavirus, John MacArthur, Pastor of Grace Community Church in Sun Valley, California defied the states orders. Not only did He open the church doors, he sued the State of California and won a sizable settlement in August of 2021.

God's Word Said, don't touch His anointed and do His prophets no harm (Psalm 105:15).

The Covid-19 virus took this nation by complete surprise. But the attack upon God's church was totally unexpected and unconstitutional. How dare civil authorities threaten God's clergy with arrest if the church doors weren't closed and all religious activities stopped immediately, including in-home gatherings. And the most absurd mandate of all, no singing. Who could have imagined that a day would come in America when pastors would be menaced with jail for opening their church doors to worship Jesus Christ, Lord of all. And why all the fuss over a plague anyway? Has everyone forgotten Who is in control over everything that happens in this world God created for us? The good and the bad are at the behest of the Lord God Almighty. Including plagues. Maybe we should learn the same lesson God taught His rebellious people during their time in the wilderness. *"But if you will not listen to me or obey me, but reject my laws, this is what I will do to you: I will punish you with sudden terrors and panic, and with tuberculosis and burning fever; your eyes shall be consumed and your life shall ebb away; you will sow your crops in vain, for your enemies will eat them. I will set my face against you and you will flee before your attackers; those who hate you will rule you; you will even run when no one is chasing you! "And if you still disobey me, I will punish you seven times more severely for your sins. I will break your proud power and make your heavens as iron and your earth as bronze. Your strength shall be spent in vain; for your land shall not yield its crops, nor your trees their fruit. "And if even then you will not obey me and listen to me, I will send you seven times more plagues because of your sins* (Leviticus 26:14–21, TLB).

The Words of God in the previous Scripture are disturbing indeed. But don't think for one minute they are idle threats. God doesn't make idle threats. God says what He means and means what He says. And may I remind the reader: God is the same today as when He first Spoke those Words. *Be still, and know that I am God: I will be exalted among the heathen, I will be exalted in the earth* (Psalm 46:10, KJV). Amen!

Part 4: Chapter 24

When God Chooses to Test Your Faith

In today's modern society, there is a reluctance to believe in the intervention of God in our lives or the nefarious activity of Satan among the living. In other words, the supernatural. Is any of it real? And the answer is unequivocally *yes*, as we will soon see. Miracles are confirmed in both the Old and New Testaments. We tend to believe that all miracles are favorable, which isn't always the case. God displayed His dynamic powers in various ways and for many different reasons. Most of those reasons we haven't the mentality to understand. But in every circumstance, God has a divine purpose. Nevertheless, God doesn't manifest miracles just to entertain us or prove His existence. We need only to be alive to recognize there is a loving Sovereign doing wonderful and often unexplained things ceaselessly in our lives. That Sovereign's Name is Lord.

The miracles of God surround us on every side. Many of God's children might experience some form of a supernatural event without ever realizing it. We live our everyday lives amid miracles without taking the time to acknowledge the creative Power behind them. The wonder of our very environment, which God amply provides, further attests to the Lord's phenomenal benevolence on behalf of mankind. Sadly, we give very little credit to God for the good or the difficult events we encounter from day to day. Yes, I said difficult. But first, let me emphasize to those of you reading this book that the Lord Jesus is, first and foremost, the epitome of love and compassion in the lives of all men. His affection, benevolence, understanding, tolerance, leniency, and His clemency prove it. And that is only a tiny fragment of the graces that God extends to His creation. On top of all that, God's mercies are new every morning. God's generosity is extravagant. There is no lack, no end, no limit, no depth, no length, no height He won't go to to shower His love upon us. *It is because of the Lord's loving kindnesses that we are not consumed, because His tender compassions never fail. They are new every morning; Great and beyond measure is Your faithfulness* (Lamentations 3:22–23, AMP).

There is a very important reason for emphasizing the benevolence of God so strongly. Many unbelievers aren't interested in learning about God, and too many Christians only identify with Jesus in terms of salvation, neglecting to explore the extent and complexity of how His Life and Lordship enriches and controls everyday Life. Therefore, in essence, some shallow believers know very little about the Sovereign Who governs over them and the world in which they live. And because of that misperception, let me caution you on the next element of the gospel to be shared. This is where a darker rudiment emerges, giving us a narrow glimpse of innocence and ignorance within a supernatural event in the early days of antiquity. However, what the outcome reveals is spiritually enlightening. God's excellent standard is the criterion that we must adhere to. Each believer must securely anchor God's morals and code of behavior down deep into their heart, giving them time to take root. The principles of God must be rehearsed repeatedly until they become a permanent part of your soul and used in your daily vocabulary. That is where faith in God is first established, and from there, it only intensifies with diligence and faithful regularity. It's very important to understand how God operates in the lives of everyone He has brought into existence. You're not here by chance. You weren't an accident, no matter what the evidence appears to suggest. You are the intentional masterpiece of the ubiquitous Sovereign. Somewhere up in heaven, there is a diagram that describes you perfectly, even down to the number of hairs on your head. Why am I telling you this? First, because God loves you and He wants to share His kingdom with you throughout eternity. Secondly, most people haven't a

clear and proper understanding about the Lord's legitimate influence over the universe and all its created beings. Every detail in the Life of each individual is influenced and controlled by God. And because that is something most people just shrug off, I hope these next few chapters are a revelation into the real world of the invisible living God. An author has no idea in whose hands the Lord may put their book; therefore, it's vital to give a vivid rationalization of God's interrelationship with mankind. I hope by sharing this profound account of one man's encounter with the all-powerful and merciful God, it will put someone in closer touch with the unseen reality of Yahweh-Roi, our Shepherd.

There is a distinctly different book within the Old Testament named for the man that it centers around. Although the book's author is in question, many biblical scholars consider the volume of Job to be the first and oldest book in the Bible. The intricate details are best understood from the book's own historical account. At times the book of Job is deeply complex and, other times, very somber. But there is one single, all-powerful lesson that should be seared into the heart of every reader. And for that reason alone, we shall stick closely to the most obvious lessons. How is Job going to deal with so much loss? What practical knowledge can we learn from this book? And most importantly, how do we rightfully and respectfully worship Almighty God in the midst of our own trials. In the final analysis, we must understand that sometimes suffering is for a greater purpose. Job is just such an example. The patience of Job produced a closer relationship and higher level of spirituality with the Almighty. What we call suffering, God considers merely reshaping by molding His children into a more effective *vessel* than before. A vessel according to His purposes and not our own. Therefore, if you are suffering in some area of your life, give thanks to God and give yourself over to the Lord entirely, so He can complete His purpose in you.

All Christians must firmly and emphatically welcome the notion that God is not only sovereign but He is also Omniscient. Meaning, God has absolute mastery and knowledge over every detail of His world and complete proficiency in managing all things, from the earliest beginning to the historic end. Absolutely nothing is concealed from God. Nothing. The Father knows each sparrow that falls to the ground (Matthew 10:29). He is the God of immediacy and thereby called "I AM."

Before continuing with the events of the story, let's remember that Job's conquest over Satan occurred many centuries before the birth of Jesus. And although there was a great deal of history between the two events, as far as we know, Job had no spiritual pattern to follow, and still, God referred to him as a man of upright moral standing. Throughout his entire ordeal, Job remained righteous. And even though Job was oblivious to the particulars of his ordeal, Job's moment of triumph was when he stated the following. *And he said, "Naked I came from my mother's womb, and naked shall I return. The Lord gave, and the Lord has taken away; blessed be the name of the Lord"* (Job 1:21, ESV).

Finally, at the climax of Job's testing, He was justified by God Almighty. I would ask you to think about this profound occurrence for just a moment. Here is an average fellow, like many of us, just minding his own business. Enjoying a prosperous life one day and the next, his entire life spirals out of control. It's difficult to imagine the depth of Job's despair. All this unfortunate man has been left with is his wife and a handful of servants. No doubt we've all had our share of calamity in this life. But in case you might be someone who has gone through any similar misfortune, I pray the God of restoration is healing you now. Whatever trial befalls us in life, faith in the Lord God Almighty will always prevail.

Satan ultimately lost his intended conquest of righteous Job. But we must understand the deeper heart of the matter. No matter what, Job continued to honor God and never harbored any bitterness toward the Almighty. Job glorifies God even further by acknowledging that everything, even our children belong to the Lord. All we've acquired in this lifetime is because of God's blessings, yet all of it is merely on loan. It's within God's right to do what He chooses with what belongs to Him.

The book begins by giving the reader a bit of background about the main character. He is probably the wealthiest and most prosperous man of his time in the region of Uz. In those days, a man's assets were not only measured by acreage but according to the number of his children, a reckoning of his livestock, fowl, and the servants under his care. In addition to Job's prosperity and excellent reputation, he had something greater on the inside than all his outer qualities put together. That something will prove to be profoundly indispensable and far more enduring than any material substance.

The sequence of events recount a story of one man's spiritual trials. Job may be one of the very first examples encapsulating an explanation of an all-powerful God in relation to man's fragility. The scene unfolds with a pleasant picture of Job's serene wealth and affluence. But the progression that follows is a truly horrifying spectacle of heartache, brought about by who else but Satan himself. This is the same diabolical character we must guard against today. He is known as the prince of the power of the air (Ephesians 2:2). And his capabilities are cruel and tormenting. He is the fallen angel referred to as the god of this world.

Although Job lived many hundreds of years before our time, the principle that he set for us is well beyond that of our gold standard. Job shows us his foremost veneration of God through his earnest piety and secure perception of God's unending presence.

Job feared that his children's lifestyle may sometimes be offensive to the Almighty. Therefore, it's Job's custom, on behalf of his grown sons and daughters, to offer sacrifices to God for each one of his ten children. Thus, hoping to sanctify them from any sin in their heart they may have committed against God. That is a beautiful portrait of a father of adult children continuing as head and spiritual priest of the family.

On one eventful day in the life of Job, Satan came to stand before God, confident that he was dominant over the thoughts and affairs of mankind. The accuser of the brethren is another label attached to Satan, and we shall soon see how he earned the name. But be assured, in the final chapter of the Bible, the Lord God has the last say (Revelation 12:10, TPT).

Now for reasons that we aren't quite capable of understanding, God presents Satan with a challenge that He knows the devil can't possibly win. Unbeknownst to Job, God consigns His servant to the most horrific and unexpected test. God describes Job as an upright, God-fearing man that shuns sin and avoids evil. God is advocating for Job by declaring to Satan that His servant would remain loyal to Him regardless of any circumstance that would befall him. Hear then how favorably Almighty God speaks of His servant Job. "No one in the world is like him. He is a decent man of integrity."

In response to God, Satan rails against Job, claiming that he has every reason to fear the Lord. He has been greatly blessed on every side, and everything he owns has a shield of protection around it. That's when the most profound thing happened. God lifted His hedge of protection from Job's Life and gave Satan liberty with one exception. He wasn't to lay a hand on him.

Chapter 25

Glorifying God in the Ashes of Life

Now we return to examine the heart of Job's story. Every aspect of his life has been totally ravaged to the ground. The experience of Job is a testimony in credence and steadfastness. Through the life of Job, he helped us to better understand how very important it is to resist the devil. How to cope with intense tribulation. And, above all else, he reveals how to trust God through every hardship of life. *But whoever denies Me before men, him I will also deny before My Father who is in heaven* (Matthew 10:33, NKJV).

Can you imagine the audacity of Satan to even suggest that God should be the One to devastate Job's life? The Bible tells us that Satan is the father of lies. And when you discover further escapades of Satan, you will soon realize he is also the master of dirty tricks. Satan has used every possible deception in order to mislead Job into thinking that it is God behind all of his afflictions.

It wasn't long before one of Job's servants, who narrowly escaped death, came running to tell Job that they were attacked while plowing in the field. The marauders killed all the servants and stole the oxen and donkeys. That messenger hadn't even caught his breath when another servant came running, proclaiming a sudden fire fell from heaven and completely burned up all the flocks, and none of the servants survived but him. Still another bearer of bad news came and told Job that there had been a raid upon his camels, and again the servants were killed, but he alone survived. And finally, the worst of all possible messages that any parent could conceivably hear. A rare and violent storm arose without warning and swept across the desert, striking the house where his sons and daughters were celebrating. The entire house collapsed upon everyone inside, and they were all struck down and killed. That lone messenger was able to escape and tell Job what had happened. *Many are the afflictions of the righteous, but the Lord delivers him out of them all* (Psalm 34:19, NKJV).

Job's second messenger unwittingly told Job that it was fire falling from heaven that destroyed his flocks and servants. He was only describing the best he could what he had witnessed. And even though that may have been the case, that tragedy wasn't delivered by the hand of God. In the book of Ephesians, Chapter 2, verse 2, we are informed of Satan's status and influence over the disobedient children in the world. Although Job wasn't disobedient, Satan had permission from God to put him to the test. Therefore, it was one of Satan's projected delusions upon Job's mind to torment him into thinking that God was angry with him and his children. God would never, never do anything to harm one of His own. But maybe now you're asking, then why did God allow Job's suffering? Well, I can't answer for God, but I can reason with what is written in Scripture.

Even at the deepest point of Job's desolation and suffering, he chose not to strike out at God. But instead, Job expressed his lamentation by tearing his own clothing and shaving off the hairs of his head to symbolize his living nightmare and immense emotional pain. But still, this humble man took those blows and demonstrated his profound, incorruptible character before God and Satan. Job's moral qualities were deeply rooted in every fiber of his being. He refused to allow himself to be corrupted. It would seem that everything Satan could do to Job has been done, and he has finally finished devastating the man in every possible way. However, there was one exemption to Satan's rampage upon Job. Satan wasn't permitted to lay a hand on him.

We've learned of one crisis after another and how Job responded in the midst of tragedy. But that wasn't the end of the story. The devil returns to God for double or nothing. Satan isn't satisfied with ending the existence of all Job's children, killing most of his servants along with his flocks, in addition to suffering the loss of his herds. Satan has another strategy up his sleeve. Satan suggests to God that it's an entirely different matter when one's own flesh is exposed to something physically overwhelming. And this time, he is convinced that Job will crumble and curse God. *Satan answered the Lord, "Skin for skin! Certainly, a man will give everything he has for his life. But stretch out your hand and strike his flesh and bones. I bet he'll curse you to your face"* (Job 2:4–5, GW).

Even with Satan's last challenge, God stood firmly on the side of His servant and repeated His assessment of Job's principled integrity. Despite that, God once again permits Satan to do to Job what he will, but he must spare his Life. Then Satan left the presence of the Lord and struck Job with painful boils from the top of his head to the bottom of his feet.

What must Job be imagining at this point? Sitting there in a pile of ashes, Job takes a piece of broken pottery and begins scraping the sores on his flesh. His physical pain must be literally unbearable, in addition to his persevering anguish over his children, servants, and everything that his life once amounted to. All gone. Yet, Job refuses to acknowledge any sin in his life. Then, to add to his already miserable condition, his unsympathetic wife proposes that he should curse God and die. In other words, just get it over with; there is no reason to continue in faith, prolonging the inevitable. That was the devil talking for sure. At her ill-chosen words, Job referred to his wife as a fool, chattering on as though she were a godless woman. And still, without knowing God's reasoning, Job reflects on all the good they have received of the Lord. Then Job put this question to his wife. Shouldn't we accept the bad also?

When Job's friends came to console him, they were appalled at Job's unrecognizable figure. No one could bring themselves to speak a word for seven whole days. Then Job broke the silence by cursing the day he was born. Having never been born would have spared him from the wretched condition and un-merciless pain he's been dealt. He longs for death, but it evades him. He has no peace, no rest, and no comfort.

Then Satan lets Job have it with a double whammy, and his troubles just keep piling up. This time he uses Job's friends to pour salt into his wounds. His companions were just another unpleasant pill to swallow. Eliphaz breaks the silence by telling Job that only guilty people suffer. The entire situation is one pathetic insinuation after another. Job is told that he should not despise God's correction. He responds by expressing his torment and bitterness of soul. He serves no purpose in his present condition and doesn't understand why God just won't let him die. His body is covered with maggots and oozing sores, and he feels as though he has every right to complain.

Then Bildad speaks out. Instead of offering solace to a man that has just lost everything, including his health, Job's claim of innocence is rejected, and it's further intimated that his children must have been guilty of sin also. Bildad is defending God's judgment on the actions of an unrepentant sinner. *Does God distort justice, or does the almighty distort righteousness? If your children sinned against him, he allowed them to suffer the consequences of their sinfulness* (Job 8:3–4, GW). *Certainly, God does not reject a person of integrity or give a helping hand to wicked people* (Job 8:20, GW).

Bildad has not only interpreted the situation wrongly, but he has also judged Job unjustly and severely. Unfortunately, Satan has put those very same imputations into the minds of many believers even today. How is Bildad benefiting his friend by implying so harsh a censure? Fortunately for Job, God knew Job's heart and, therefore, the truth. Fortunately for us, we've been given the facts concerning the trials of Job. We learn how this man's friends wrongly accused and charged him guilty on the basis of appearances and without evidence. They have pronounced a verdict on Job by supposition only.

Let me point out that Job has not retaliated against either of his accusers. Furthermore, Job didn't waste any time or energy avenging himself against Bildad's allegations. Job knew there was no justification for Bildad's remarks. Man to man, Job stood his ground in righteousness. But before God Almighty, Job humbly assents to God's judgment, knowing that flesh could never achieve perfection on this side of heaven. No one alive can measure up to God's holy standard. New Testament believers live only because of the Lord's patient love and His desire to bring as many as will come into unity through the blood of His dear and majestic Son Jesus.

Though his soul is cast to the dust, Job maintains his dignity and continues to speak well of the Almighty. Job declares the many virtues of God. He is wise in heart and mighty in power. *He does wonderful things, even confounding things, and performs an infinite number of miracles. Still, if He passes right by men, I don't see Him; if He brushes past, I don't notice Him* (Job 9:10–11, VOICE).

Up to this point, Job was holding his own. In order to enlighten his colleagues, Job is trying to assert a truth they simply were unwilling to accept. In reality, God's temporal judgments often fall on the just and unjust alike. Many times wicked people prosper while the lives of the upright are frequently shattered. However, his friends had their minds made up, and there was no convincing them otherwise. They were determined to believe that Job's guilt is what brought about God's harsh judgment upon him.

Sometimes the only recourse in that kind of situation is to give it a rest. But then Job makes a serious error in judgment. Despite the fact that Job remains resolute of his innocence, in his despair and frustration to be believed by his friends, he says some things he probably wished he hadn't said. While God isn't likely to overlook Job's charge against Him, He is nonetheless true to His nature and especially considerate of Job's fragile state. Hear the frustration in Job's verbal expression. *How then can I answer him or choose my arguments against him? Even if I were in the right, I could not answer I could only beg my Judge for mercy. If I summoned him and he answered me, I do not believe he would pay attention to what I said. He batters me with a whirlwind and multiplies my wounds without cause. He doesn't let me catch my breath but fills me with bitter experiences. If it is a matter of strength, look, he is the powerful one! If it is a matter of justice, who can summon him? Even if I were in the right, my own mouth would condemn me; if I were blameless, my mouth would declare me guilty* (Job 9:14–20, CSB).

In response to Job's diatribe, Zophar replies with oratory eloquence, recounting the awe-inspiring character of the Almighty. But, as in the case of Job's other friends, Zophar locks horns with Job over his unwillingness to repent the guilt he insists on harboring. Zophar describes God's forbearance and compassion and how such a merciful God would most certainly forgive a righteous man who is willing to repent and confess his sin. Job has to agree with Zophar concerning God's magnificence; nevertheless, he stands firm against the latter. Job now makes a decision to rebuke his peers for their high-minded attitudes and hard-hearted verdict of him. Christians should be very considerate when they council their friends in need. If they are already broken and damaged, what they require first and foremost is compassion for their circumstance, regardless of how it materialized.

Job's erudite companions weren't as smart as they thought they were. In fact, they often proved themselves quite ignorant about God's ways. It usually takes a great deal of self-control not to strike back defensively, especially when guiltless. This again is where Job proved his temperance. In the Old Testament book of Ecclesiastes, the reader is advised of the importance of timing. *A time to tear; A time to repair; A time to be quiet; A time to speak up;* (Ecclesiastes 3:7, TLB).

But finally, the time had come. Job was filled to capacity with his friends' condescending attitude and pious display of virtue. He speaks to them as an equal and not as their inferior. Here Job uses sound doctrine to put his contemporaries in check. Job uses tact in a way that conserves friendship and yet lets them know that his wisdom is in no way substandard to theirs. Job further cautions them concerning their enthusiasm to convey their spiritual superiority over him. Additionally, Job emphasized his friends' dissension may indeed be contrary to their undertaking by declaring that their prideful boasting is actually a lack of objectivity.

He further disdains their deceitful and corrupt assertion that they are communicating on God's behalf.

Chapter 26

Never Jump to Conclusions

Compassionate Christians must think and act as Jesus did in every circumstance. One situation that comes to mind is the woman caught in the very act of adultery (John 8:4). That woman was taken by force into the temple by the scribes and Pharisees and placed before the crowd of people that Jesus was teaching. This lesson comes down to law and mercy. True, she was guilty and subject to death by stoning. Jesus didn't contradict the law but very wisely acquired her freedom by designating the man who was without sin should cast the first stone (John 8:7).

Jesus didn't pummel her with the law as Job's friends did. He didn't bombard her with guilt and berate her with shame. Instead of castigating her with humiliation, Jesus showed compassion for her. One by one, each man walked away. When everyone was gone, Jesus looked at the woman and inquired, "Where are your accusers? Has no one condemned you?" The woman answered, "No one, Sir." Then Jesus Said to her, "Neither do I condemn you. Go and sin no more."

Since Job's friends have failed to provide him with any consolation, moral support, or empathy, he directs them to hold their peace, allowing him the privilege of answering. Job proceeds with a reprimand to his friends by expressing his own knowledge and wisdom of God through years of relationship. *Yes, God's riches are very great, and his wisdom and knowledge have no end! No one can explain the things God decides or understand his ways* (Romans 11:33, NCV). *Even if God kills me, I have hope in him; I will still defend my ways to his face. This is my salvation. The wicked cannot come before him. Listen carefully to my words; let your ears hear what I say. See, I have prepared my case, and I know I will be proved right. No one can accuse me of doing wrong* (Job 13:15–19, NCV).

Job is nothing if not courageous and unshakeable. Even in

the depths of his agonizing despair, his friends remain adamant, refusing to show any glimmer of mercy, only callous disregard for a man who stands by his conviction and refuses to abandon his righteous course. Satan has obviously put his friends up to victimizing Job even further. They are relentlessly cruel in insisting that Job is guilty of a considerable number of great offenses. Not because of evidence, but because of what appears to be God's judgment of Job. Despite that, rather than a confession, Job testifies of a distant Man of the future, certifying how serious and Life-changing it is to hold on to righteousness in the face of adversity. He is indicating that those whose hands are clean will only grow stronger and stronger. Job upholds this commitment in his next declaration. *I will never agree you are right; until I die, I will never stop saying I am innocent* (Job 27:5, NCV).

Job goes on to explain to his disputers that he made a covenant with his eyes never to look upon a maid. He insists that his heart has never been deceived by a woman, nor is he guilty of desiring his neighbor's wife. He knows that God sees his ways and counts his every step. Job further indicates that he has at no time neglected the poor or the widow and always opened his doors to the stranger in the street and provided for the fatherless. He has clothed the poor and warmed them with the fleece of his own sheep. Job also reflects on the fact that he has never wished destruction on another person or rejoiced at someone else's hardship. In fact, he has prayed with many tears on behalf of others. He further states that he has always made God his hope and never his riches or gold. Finally, Job's first three friends abandon any further attempt at discrediting him, concluding that Job's remarks were only a sanctimonious attempt to adjudicate his own cause.

Next, Elihu, the fourth and youngest in the group, finally speaks out, condemning Job for his pride and pious exaggerated claims of virtue and kindness. Elihu undiplomatically convicts Job of being laden with guilt. And instead of taking responsibility for his sins, Job is holding God responsible for his situation. Elihu is totally unconvinced of Job's assertions, insisting that Job's hypocrisy is only making matters worse for him. He simply wants Job to realize that God is endeavoring to pull him from the flames of hell. Elihu continues by telling Job that he won't be able to buy or bribe his way out of tribulation this time. Elihu further expresses God's compassion and willingness to forgive if Job would only confess his sins. Elihu may have had the best understanding of God but nevertheless was still of little benefit to Job. Consequently, even Elihu fell short in his attempt to coerce Job into a false confession.

At one point, Job refers to his friends as enemies. Frankly, it seems as though they were there merely to win a debate rather than deliver any compassionate aid or mercy to their companion. It's absolutely shameful how Job was treated by the men whom he considered to be his friends. Not one of them gave him the benefit of the doubt. All their assumptions were based on what they saw with their eyes in the natural. How is it that they just conveniently failed to remember anything good about their friend's former life? If any one of them could have provided something to substantiate their claim, they would have provided it. Nonetheless, they persisted in their own rationalization of Job and how the Almighty deals with defiant and unrepentant sinners. What is the single common denominator in all their analytical discord? One by one, they verbally bludgeoned their friend until he was grieved to the depths of his soul. On top of that, what was the weapon they used to magnify Job's trauma? They used Almighty God against him!

The reader of Job isn't given any information on the actual duration of Job's suffering. But it is made clear that Job is never apprised of the conversation between God and Satan. Therefore and understandably, Job was invariably under the impression that God necessitated judgment upon him and was nevertheless willing to accept the verdict. Yet, Job was impervious to any such reproach or transgression he was culpable of. Evidently, it never occurred to him that Satan had orchestrated the whole undertaking, and with God's permission, of course. Job feels isolated and alone. He opines that his wife is avoiding him and his relatives have forsaken him. What adds to his pain is knowing that his friends have turned against him, and even his remaining servants are neglecting him.

Then God makes His appearance through a whirlwind, quizzing Job to answer if he is able. *"Who is this that questions my wisdom with such ignorant words?"* (Job 38:2, NLT) God continues with a list of His stirring accounts during creation's early events. God offers Job a brief history of measuring the earth and setting its foundations. Separating light from dark, Commanding the rain when and where. He questions Job in his knowledge of snow, hail, and dew, and the seas' boundaries. His narration continues with a chronicle of various wildlife and even the early living creatures of the Mesozoic era, from 245 million to 65 million years ago. God Speaks of many beautiful images, such as wrapping the evening light in a scarlet robe. The positioning of the stars and planets. This is just a short list of the attributes God conveys to Job. But what is the most interesting aspect of God's dialogue? He never once mentions any of the characterizations inscribed by Job's so-called friends.

In the simplest of terms, God is declaring to Job that His ways are higher than man's ways. His knowledge has no limitation, and His intellect is without boundaries. God not only cares deeply for what He creates; He advocates for those who depend upon Him. The Almighty wasn't as concerned with Job's past ignorance as He was with Job's future comprehension of Himself. Above all things, God executes appropriate justness and inexhaustible provision. *"Shall the one who contends with the Almighty correct Him? He who rebukes God, let him answer it"* (Job 40:2, NKJV). *"Would you indeed annul My judgment? Would you condemn Me that you may be justified?"* (Job 40:8, NKJV) Job persisted no further. He humbly placed his hand over his mouth.

The book of Job is a wealth of prudent understanding and the embodiment of man's misjudgment concerning the Almighty. When we look into the lives of earth's early inhabitants, it's like looking through a glass darkly. *In the same way, we can see and understand only a little about God now, as if we were peering at his reflection in a poor mirror; but someday we are going to see him in his completeness, face-to-face. Now all that I know is hazy and blurred, but then I will see everything clearly, just as clearly as God sees into my heart right now* (1 Corinthians 13:12, TLB).

Each of the historical characters has a sense of the Almighty and a sense of righteousness, but none are capable of understanding the deeper degrees of God. Everything God decides is ethically just, spiritually enlightening, and socially advantageous. Who is able to distinguish the way in which God may choose to relate to an individual spirit or a nation or the entire world, for that matter? Job's friends were quick to jump to conclusions and convict both Job and God incorrectly. Their only interest was in getting their friend to admit to a serious offense against God.

If ever there was a book in the Bible that required astute meditation, it's the book of Job. Taking into account the interchange of dialogue, unkind opinions, and the mixed perception of God. Overall, the book of Job is a banquet of cognition and vulnerability that is sometimes obnoxious, unpalatable, and at other times valiant and delectable. It provides far more than just insight into relationships. There are many rewarding perspectives on matters that we ourselves are predisposed to. Learning the value of keeping one's presence of mind and recognizing the distinction between being right-minded and high-minded. Easing tension among friends, remaining even-tempered under duress, and especially the need for perseverance. But of everything we glean from the ancient past, none is better appreciated than the intricacies of God. How comforting it is knowing that the Almighty exceeds anything we could think or imagine. *For as the heavens are higher than the earth, so are my ways higher than your ways, and my thoughts than your thought* (Isaiah 55:9, KJV).

The Almighty has painted a vivid portrait of Himself for Job's benefit. And when God concludes conveying His thoughts and fundamental truth, Job realizes, maybe for the first time, a greater depth of the Person of the Almighty. The following is Job's humble response to God. It is the same lesson every believer needs to secure for themselves, ideally, without having to go through the severe trial that Job encountered. *Before I knew only what I had heard of You, but now I have seen You* (Job 42:5, VOICE).

God made no mention of Elihu, but the Almighty's anger was aroused against Eliphaz and his two friends. They were not only harsh and unsympathetic critics; they also castigated Job while misrepresenting their knowledge of God. Thereupon, the Almighty ordered the three men to go to Job and present a burnt offering, and His servant Job would pray for them. Otherwise, He would chastise the three for their irresponsibility. Twice God made mention of their ill-spoken words, but when God referred to Job's observations, the Almighty's review was remarkably different. Therefore, Job was never judged for his words.

In the end, Job was remorseful over his misjudgment of God and repented for his remarks, but he never became bitter over his ordeal. He maintained his dignity and righteous standing before God. Job's Life was completely rehabilitated. God gave His servant eight more sons and three daughters of unmatched beauty. His extended family returned, as well as his former friends and acquaintances.

Any remnant of remorse was culminated by the Almighty's additional blessing of fourteen thousand sheep, six thousand camels, one thousand yoke of oxen, and one thousand female donkeys. After all Job went through, God gave His servant one hundred and forty additional years of Life. Job's latter years were even more fulfilling than the first. He lived with a new understanding of the wisdom of God while enjoying four additional generations of grandchildren.

Two vitally important things declared by Job that should always be remembered. *For I know that my redeemer lives, and He shall stand at last on the earth; and after my skin is destroyed, this I know, that in my flesh I shall see God, whom I shall see for myself, and my eyes shall behold, and not another. How my heart yearns within me!* (Job 19:25–27, NKJV) *And this is what he says to all humanity: 'The fear of the Lord is true wisdom; to forsake evil is real understanding'''* (Job 28:28, NLT).

Chapter 27

Last Will and Testament

All living things will die. At some point in time, thriving will cease, and death becomes inevitable. However, not everyone prepares for death. But those that do usually have something legally drawn up to express their last wishes after their demise. Those humans put a great deal of thought into their preplanning. How they want their stuff dispersed, who gets what, and how much. Although our possessions mean a great deal to us, everything acquired over a lifetime is left to another. We leave this life exactly the same as we entered. Naked. But what about the preplanning of the soul? How much thought has gone into preparing for your eternal future? Think about all the other events that have been meticulously planned for. We plan for tomorrow, next week, even next year's vacation. There is nothing wrong with planning if we keep a bright focus on what lays beyond this earthly existence. Securing our eternal home is the most important decision we will ever plan for in this lifetime. Will our eternal Life be spent in the presence of the Lord in heaven or spent in outer darkness, somewhere in hell? We mustn't leave the most important decision we will ever make to chance. No one had a choice about their birth, but God offers everyone an opportunity to decide where they will live for all eternity.

I certainly don't want to be the voice of gloom; nevertheless, there are some basic facts everyone must consider. God has not promised that any one of us will see tomorrow's sunrise. Have you ever experienced the shocking news that someone you recently spoke with is no longer among the living? That is precisely why we must value and not squander each day that is on loan to us. One important element in preplanning is to avoid any unfinished business or leave any loose ends lying about. And in keeping with judicious knowledge, we must remember that regardless of what took place yesterday, the current events are profoundly more significant. We can't take back what was said or left unsaid, done, or left undone. Lamenting over the past is futile. If there is a fence to be mended, then attempt to repair what was damaged in a timely manner. Yet, many of those situations are easily avoided when we follow the golden rule. Do unto others as you would have them do unto you. Nevertheless, our yesterday is gone, and nothing can change what did or did not come about. Therefore, we mustn't worry over things that are beyond our control.

But there is another side of control. That is the part of any situation that we have jurisdiction over. The problem arises when pride interferes with a genuine motivation to change circumstances. Pride can be as hard and painful to conquer as El Capitan in Yosemite National Park. Here is where one of the most powerful words in the Bible comes into play. It's the word, repent. Repent is far more than just an acknowledgment of regret. When there is honest lamentation, it is shown by some outward expression of grief or sorrow that bubbles up from the heart. But far too often, a meaningless apology of empty words reveals no distinct change in true feelings. If there is no appreciable behavioral change, that person is obviously insincere and unrepentant. However, the healing balm for both parties is forgiveness. It releases the injured party from having to carry around a cancerous grudge and stops the continuous licking of their wounds. And freedom for the conscience-stricken who is filled with remorse and heaviness of heart. Forgiveness is both mercy and compassion. I speak from personal experience.

Springtime is a particularly invigorating season of the year. Especially for Jews and Christians around the world. The dead of winter is past, and a new stage of life arises, announcing that spring is in bloom. And along with the first season of the year emerges the greatest celebration Christians look forward to commemorating, as they have for thousands of generations. The Life, death, resurrection, and Pentecost, immortalizing the Lord Jesus. For Christians, the observance begins with Palm Sunday, the day Jesus formally entered Jerusalem. The following Friday is Good Friday; Jesus was beaten and crucified. Resurrection Sunday—or Easter, as referred to by many—was the day Jesus was restored to Life. Seven Sundays after Easter is Pentecost. The Jewish nation observes Passover in and around the same time of the year. God provided Adam and Eve freedom. God freed His people from slavery in Egypt. The blessed Savior Jesus freed man from sin and death.

Let me briefly explain why the Christian Holy Week and Jewish Passover are so very significant to every living soul today. When God created our first parents, they were given freedom. With liberty comes enormous responsibility to continue making righteous decisions, thereby avoiding the bondage of sin that Satan would happily ensnare you. Unfortunately, that wasn't the case with Adam and his wife, Eve. Their choice robbed them of their freedom. If you're wondering how they were robbed, I will tell you.

Eve fell prey to Satan's lie. In her desire to be equal to God, she dismissed God's Command and ate from the only tree in the entire garden she was forbidden to eat from. While under the influence of Satan and still holding the forbidden fruit in her hand, Eve enticingly offered it to Adam, and he too consumed what was forbidden by God. Since both Adam and Eve refused God's warning to never eat of the tree of knowledge of good and evil, they were immediately condemned to eternal death and banished from the Garden of Eden. As a result of their choice, God mercifully allowed them to resume their life temporarily in the fallen world outside the presence of their Creator. That unfortunate episode affected us all. Our first parents had one choice to make. Stay in the everlasting presence of God in the Garden of Eden or forfeit eternal Life and live in an evil world governed by Satan. They chose the latter. But let us remember, the fallen world is only temporary. Decide today where you want to spend all eternity. It's not complicated. But if you don't choose Life in heaven, hell is your destination by default.

Now I can't say with any certainty that the Garden of Eden

still exists. But God has given us an alternative to that. God's heavenly kingdom can be an eternal home for anyone who chooses Life through the shed blood of God's Son Jesus, the Christ. And I know according to the Word, the Tree of Life is there. The apostle John explains: *Then he showed me the river of the water of life, bright as crystal, flowing from the throne of God and of the Lamb through the middle of the street of the city; also, on either side of the river, the tree of life with its twelve kinds of fruit, yielding its fruit each month; and the leaves of the tree were for the healing of the nations* (Revelation 22:1–2, RSV).

Let me break it down even further. At some point, we are all destined to die a physical death. That brings us to the question, where do we want to spend our eternity, in heaven or in hell? Well, there is good news. We all have been given a choice where we spend our continued eternal existence.

When Jesus surrendered His Life on the cross, it was to take your place and mine. Because Jesus was completely sinless, it legitimized His sacrifice unto the Father on behalf of the human race. Jesus was described as the Lamb of God because of His tender age, His meekness, His gentleness and purity of soul. Jesus had no imperfections. The word Christ is not our Savior's last name. The word *Christ* is what God Almighty determined His Son Jesus was qualified to become. Our Redeemer. When Jesus died on behalf of mankind's sin, His chaste blood washed away all the sins of the world. Without the sacrifice Jesus made for us, we would have no hope or future home in the kingdom of our dear Lord Jesus.

When someone desires citizenship in another country, the normal procedure is to make a request. Then an application must be submitted to the authorities of that nation for review. That is the widespread customary procedure, and citizenship in the kingdom of heaven is no different. So, if you want to become a citizen in the eternal kingdom of God, you must apply for occupancy. There are no papers or forms to fill out. No test to take or swearing-in. Almighty God has a different criterion. Since salvation is a Life-altering experience, the petitioner must be wholeheartedly sincere and prepared to honor their covenant with Christ Jesus. *Everyone who asks receives what he asks for. Everyone who looks finds what he is looking for. Everyone who knocks has the door opened to him. What man among you would give his son a stone if he should ask for bread? Or if he asks for a fish, would he give him a snake?* (Matthew 7:8–10, NLV).

It's essential for the person seeking salvation to humbly confess their sins before God and ask Him for forgiveness. That makes the soul eligible to be washed by the cleansing blood of the Lord Jesus. This simple but vitally important gesture is an indispensable spiritual formality. The blood of Jesus makes the blackest garment white as snow, thereby birthing a new child of God and resident in the kingdom of heaven. God will remove your filthy old heart of stone and give you a brand-new heart of flesh. The new heart then becomes the temple of the living God. That's right. The Holy Spirit of God will live in your heart from then on. Don't ask me how this happens; that too is a mystery only God knows. When the flesh expires, and you have remained fully committed to God, you will resume your residence in the magnificent kingdom of heaven with Almighty God and His Son, Jesus, the King of kings and Lord of lords. What a joyous victory that day of celebration will be.

I imagine that you might be wondering why salvation for the soul must be done this way. It is because earth is considered the fallen world that Adam and Eve chose by their rebellion against the Commandment of God. A secular world of carnality, profanity, and materialism. A place thoroughly corrupt, sensual, and sordid. It is written that Satan and one-third of the angels were ejected from heaven and thrown down to earth because of their insurrection. The Bible tells us that Satan is the god of this world. He and his cohorts, the fallen angels, are busily trying to obstruct everyone's lives with fake news and allurements into sinful behavior, just as he did back in the Garden of Eden. It matters not where one lives on the earth; by God's standard, it's a fallen world. ...*because the evil god of this age has blinded the minds of unbelievers. As a result, the light of the good news, the radiant glory of the Anointed—who is the very image of God—cannot shine down on them* (2 Corinthians 4:4, VOICE).

Since earth is considered a fallen or sinful world, everyone born of the flesh is by nature sinful. Again, it doesn't matter how young you are or how good you think you may be. Here is how we are described in the Bible. *We are all infected and impure with sin. When we display our righteous deeds, they are nothing but filthy rags. Like autumn leaves, we wither and fall, and our sins sweep us away like the wind* (Isaiah 64:6, NLT).

It's beyond foolish to argue the point with your Creator. He is God, and if He says that you need a cleansing and a change of heart, then that's final. Accept the judgment God demands, or else accept the death sentence that Jesus died to free us from. God is merciful. He wants His creation to remain free for all eternity. That's why there was a Passover, and the cross. The Lord freed His people from their Egyptian bondage and slavery. Being a slave to any kind of sin is a heavy yoke of bondage. You are in shackles and chains to whatever holds you prisoner. Drunkenness, sexual perversion, thievery, murder, pornography, and the like. It's just another kind of slavery. But freedom from every bondage is possible with the Lord God. For hundreds of generations, beginning with the very first Passover that night in Egypt, freedom has been celebrated as a high holy day for God's people. This is how it all began.

Initially, when their own land was given over to drought, the shortages forced the tiny band of Israelites to seek refuge in the prosperous and fruitful nation of Egypt. But all too soon, God's people became accustomed to the sumptuous and lucrative lifestyle offered in the thriving empire. After a time, they forgot their heritage and even their God. But things began to change when a new Pharaoh feared their great numbers and started treating the Israelites badly. They were no longer considered citizens; they had become slaves exploited for menial work and hard labor. The years intensified their sorrow, and their burdens escalated their plight until their cries were heard by the Lord. By then, their Egyptian bondage had lasted four hundred years.

Eventually, God sent Moses and his brother Aaron to deal with Pharoah, demanding that God's people be set free. Unfortunately, by the time Pharoah saw the light, freedom came at an exceptionally high cost.

In an overly simplified understanding of the meaning of Passover, it is the annual remembrance and celebration associated with the freedom of God's people after four centuries of persecution endured at the hands of the Egyptians. God gave Pharaoh every opportunity to release Israel from their bondage, but Pharaoh stubbornly refused to do so, demanding to know, "Who is this Lord, that I should obey His Voice to let Israel go?" (Exodus 5:2, KJV) Uh-oh, that was obviously the wrong answer!

Here is where our God showed temperance and might. He could have easily exterminated such an indignant source of annoyance with a puff of His nostrils. But God never executes vengeance as we might expect Him to. The Almighty had a better plan. God chose to harden Pharaoh's heart instead. Therefore, each time Pharaoh refused to allow Israel's release, the Lord would demonstrate another one of His spectacular and imaginative powers. Those became known as the ten plagues of Egypt. And by the last and most foreboding of all the plagues, the Egyptians couldn't get rid of the Israelites fast enough. But there was another purpose in God's mighty display of authority. By revealing His tremendous commanding powers, God Almighty, Creator and Ruler of all heaven and earth, wanted to instill in His chosen people their complete confidence in Him. This mighty show of power was God's assurance to the Israelites that nothing could ever, or would ever be able to frustrate either His purpose or His will.

Meanwhile, Pharaoh refused every opportunity to release God's people. Plague after plague and still Pharaoh refused to be dissuaded from his ironclad position. Anyone who is foolish enough to provoke God by insisting on their own course of action will eventually be affected in some unfortunate way. In Pharaoh's case, it was the final plague upon Egypt that no one saw coming. The last plague may have been God's judgment and final retribution upon Pharaoh for all the Hebrew male babies that were drowned at birth in the Nile River.

The Lord is well known for His extended patience and ever-enduring love of mankind. For that reason, the imminent event that was about to unfold in Egypt was a harbinger of the coming Messiah, Jesus the Lamb of God. On that definitive day in history, God gave the Israelites explicit instructions regarding their safety during the night of visitation by the death angel. God's people would not only escape the angel of death but they would finally be released from under Pharaoh's control.

Moses instructed the Hebrews on how to go about preparing themselves for freedom on that momentous night. God's guidelines were strict and precise. They were to remove all the leaven from their household. Select a Passover lamb on the tenth day of the month and keep the lamb in the house until the fourteenth day, and then kill it in the evening and take the blood, striking it upon the side and upper door posts. Roast the lamb with fire and eat it all quickly with unleavened bread and bitter herbs. They were to follow these instructions fully dressed so that they could make a hasty departure.

The following Old Testament account in Exodus clearly establishes the Lord's sovereign power over Life. As it was said by Job, "God gives and God takes away; blessed be the Name of the Lord." Then the Lord told Moses that He would go out at midnight and bring one final plague upon Pharaoh and Egypt. *And all the oldest sons shall die in every family in Egypt, from the oldest child of Pharaoh, heir to his throne, to the oldest child of his lowliest slave and even the firstborn of the animals. The wail of death will resound throughout the entire land of Egypt; never before has there been such anguish, and it will never be again. "But not a dog shall move his tongue against any of the people of Israel, nor shall any of their animals die. Then you will know that Jehovah makes a distinction between Egyptians and Israelis'* (Exodus 11:5–7, TLB).

Notice the last sentence in God's final and prevalent Declaration. Jehovah made a clear and decisive distinction between the Egyptians and the nation of Israel. What made that statement so pivotal? It was the blood's Seal upon the doorposts that proclaimed God's sovereignty. The Israelites were His chosen people then, just as the Jews are still. God faithfully intends to honor His long-established covenant He made with Abraham, Isaac, and Jacob. Then here is one final thought for you to gravely consider. Although the death and resurrection of Jesus is celebrated only one time a year, salvation is not a seasonal event. Salvation is a now action. When Moses told the children of God that it was the day of their deliverance, they obeyed immediately and were set free. When you know in your heart, it's time, that's when you must take the initiative. Jesus is waiting for you even now. Who knows what tomorrow will bring? *For God says, "Your cry came to me at a favorable time, when the doors of welcome were wide open. I helped you on a day when salvation was being offered." Right now, God is ready to welcome you. Today he is ready to save you* (2 Corinthians 6:2, TLB).

God gave the nation of Israel the special distinction of belonging to Him. They became His firstborn. And Jehovah would do whatever it took to free them from captivity. We in modern culture might not be Egyptian captives, but we are nonetheless the captives of sin. The lamb's blood on the doorposts of the Israelites proclaimed God's supremacy over every man, woman, and child. The blood of the lamb is what saved them and their animals from the death angel. At that time, it was all about the blood sacrifice offered by the lamb. For everyone else, it is the sacrifice offered by the Savior Jesus, the Lamb of God. He made atonement to God on behalf of all who would believe. Confessing the Savior Jesus as Lord will safeguard from eternal damnation in the lake of fire. Jesus is our High Priest. Those who confess their sins and profess Jesus are washed in the blood of the beloved Son. That is what is meant by being born-again. It makes us joint-heirs with Jesus and sons and daughters of the great Almighty. The church nation will have the honor and pleasure of living forever in the kingdom of our dear Lord, but only if we continue to follow Him worthily and in all righteousness. Historically, the Israelites were physically liberated by the Passover event. But the atonement Jesus secured upon the cross set true believers free for all eternity. *The Lord says, "All you who are thirsty, come and drink. Those of you who do not have money, come, buy and eat! Come buy wine and milk without money and without cost. Why spend your money on something that is not real food? Why work for something that doesn't really satisfy you? Listen closely to me, and you will eat what is good; your soul will enjoy the rich food that satisfies. Come to me and listen; listen to me so you may live. I will make an agreement with you that will last forever. I will give you the blessings I promised to David* (Isaiah 55:1–3, NCV).

Epilogue

Upon salvation, a Christian's mission is to serve their Lord and Master. To worship God is to recognize Who He is. Giving the Almighty honor as Creator and Lord commemorates the relationship we have with the Holy Trinity: Father, Son, and Holy Ghost. God in three Persons, the Omnipotent-all-powerful, the Omniscient-all-knowing, and the Omnipresent-ever-present Godhead. Service and obedience to Him is our obligation as a member of the family of God. Just exactly as Jesus once Said, "I must be about My Father's business" (Luke 2:49). If you are also a child of the Almighty, then it's your responsibility to continue in the great commission of our dear Lord and Savior. We are building the church daily by saving the lost and dying. By faith, we stand strong in unity, beautifying the bride and body of Christ, that she may one day be presented to the King, her Groom, perfect, without spot or wrinkle.

From the earliest days of ancient past, there has been bloodshed. Cain slew his own brother Abel. Later the Bible gives us multiple glimpses of the unconventional suffering of God's people. There was Joseph, sold by his own brothers; King David, persecuted by Saul; God's prophet Elijah, the prey of evil Jezebel; Paul, beaten, stoned, and shipwrecked. God's Son was rejected by His own people. And that certainly is not an exhaustive list by any means. The fact that none of us are completely out of harm's way should cause each of us to recognize our eventual exposure to some manner of pain or suffering. Do I have your attention? The very life we live exposes us to inevitable harm, mentally, emotionally, physically, and most assuredly spiritually. And because you are a child of Almighty God, you no doubt have a bullseye on your back. I'm just being perfectly honest.

But let us look at misfortune and tragedy from a different angle. Suppose you made some dreadful choice that turned out badly. And because of that decision, you and perhaps others are suffering the woeful consequences. Many times God will use the very situation that you fabricated to deliver an impactful lesson and turn a tragedy into a significant blessing. Our principled Father never turns His face away from a blameworthy child. However, He may use those episodes as a favorable time to teach, using the experience as an opportunity to make the necessary changes in His child's Life. Such is a picture of our wonderful, loving Father God.

There are only two kinds of cultures in this civilization: the saved Life through the blood of Jesus or the life that is damned and going to hell, separated from God for all eternity. There are no other choices. The misery within the unregenerate community is Satan's territory, and he can do whatever gives him the most pleasure. If anyone is in partnership with the devil and lives according to his standards, their future is in dire jeopardy. Although Satan has certain restrictions and limitations from God, nevertheless, he can do a great deal of damage in a short period of time, just as in the case of Job's affliction.

The nature of suffering for the righteousness of God can be two-fold. Just because a sinner has confessed Jesus as their Savior doesn't exonerate that believer from being persecuted by the devil or tested by the Lord. The difference being, Satan despises Jesus, and he is doing everything within his power to discredit Him by getting the bulk of the world to repudiate Him. In other words, when Satan initiates a scheme attempting to devalue the Lord's dominion in the hearts of men, he deludes their thoughts, causing them to doubt the Lord's indisputable divine Supremacy. When effective, whole societies will walk away from Jesus as others have done for centuries. John the Baptist baptized Jesus. He saw the heavens open and the Holy Spirit descend upon Jesus. John heard the Voice of God announce His pleasure in His beloved Son. And yet, while in prison, John sent one of his disciples to ask, "Are You the One, or should we look for another?" Satan only needs to create a small uncertainty. Doubt does the rest. It kills! Satan has pulled the wool over the eyes of millions. Never let it be said of you. Satan can't destroy Jesus, so he does the next best thing and destroys the world's exploitable victims. And sadly, there are millions and millions of defenseless individuals convinced of his lies. But remember this. God may use Satan's lies to test our veracity. But God will not allow us to be tested beyond our spiritual comprehension. Moreover, God is for us, even if He does decide to test us to the brink of our faith. He is consistently pulling for our triumph over sin and Satan. That's not to say that God will coddle us, no sir. We must hold our own and hold fast to our integrity for all it's worth because our heavenly home is at stake in the testing. And if you can pass the test, there'll be no trial. God has never asked anything of mankind that was destined to fail. And His promise to us is in the first book of Corinthians. *Any temptation you face will be nothing new. But God is faithful, and He will not let you be tempted beyond what you can handle. But He always provides a way of escape so that you will be able to endure and keep moving forward* (1 Corinthians 10:13, VOICE).

BOOK 2:
Fundamental Pillars of Honorable Wholesomeness

In all seriousness, please allow me to ask you this question. Do you have a deep desire to enjoy more of God's kindness? Maybe it's His peace that is absent in your life. There is no supernatural mystery to reaping the benefits and blessings of God. But first, you must make a significant effort to know Him. And then to know Him intimately. God is the Word. The Word became our Teacher in the flesh. You must demonstrate your interest in holy Scripture. The more involved you are in the Word, the more knowledge you acquire, and the easier it is to discern the things God wants you to know. Believe me; God is anxious for us to learn of Him in a personal sense. That is when He will begin to bestow His greater goodness upon us. The more we position our lives in Jesus, the broader our spiritual dimension. *Next, learn to put aside your own desires so that you will become patient and godly, gladly letting God have his way with you. This will make possible the next step, which is for you to enjoy other people and to like them, and finally you will grow to love them deeply. The more you go on in this way, the more you will grow strong spiritually and become fruitful and useful to our Lord Jesus Christ. But anyone who fails to go after these additions to faith is blind indeed, or at least very shortsighted and has forgotten that God delivered him from the old life of sin so that now he can live a strong, good life for the Lord* (2 Peter 1:6–9, TLB).

Hopefully, you will begin to notice how the following pillars flow interactively with each other. They resemble a beautiful adornment of precious pearls consisting of integrity, merit, courtesy, geniality, clemency, and benevolence, enhancing the loyal Life of the Savior's servant.

Chapter 1

Pillar of Faith

Every age presents its own set of challenges. And usually, the growing pains experienced in youth will arise purely from a sense of exuberance with little acquired wisdom. Youth is anxious to take the reins of adulthood in order to prove their capability in managing their own life. But life is a long journey, full of ups and downs, successes, and failures. A prudent student under the tutelage and direction of the Lord will learn from each hurdle encountered. Even when it looks in the natural as though something has failed, God evaluates our efforts by His own specifications. His ways are past finding out (Romans 11:33). One thing you can be certain of; when God gives a Command to do something, He is the Guarantor of the outcome. His children offer their best, and He fills in the rest. Many challenges are to test us, to grow mightily in His strength, and bear much good fruit. Lay a firm foundation upon the Rock of your salvation and build your Life from there.

Don't get discouraged if a pitfall somehow interferes with your early dreams. Many times, a disruption in daily life can feel like a detriment, but with just a little persistent effort, it can prove to be a truly worthwhile experience. See those obstacles as God's way of challenging your faith. The Lord's interruptions in your daily routine can seem like an annoyance; nevertheless, there is something worthwhile that God wants you to invest your time in.

Maybe someone surrendered their ambitions because of a wrong turn or unforeseen occurrence. Don't lose heart or hope. There just might be greater and more rewarding aspirations up ahead. Don't look at obstacles as dead ends. Keep looking to God for the answer or the solution and never stop asking, seeking, and knocking. Life with God is full of mystery, intrigue, treasure, and intimacy. He arouses our curiosity, deepens our understanding, and fortifies our faith in His ability to bring something to pass.

But if we are unwilling to take the risk, we might never discover what heavenly favors we're forfeiting. Blessings can materialize in hidden forms. Our own agendas often keep us far too busy to lend ourselves to the purposes of God and His many blessings that would come from obedience. For me, it was writing my first book. It just seemed all too intimidating. We should never discount our capabilities or underestimate God's advantages merely because the circumstances don't conform with our preconceived notions. That's what dealt a death blow to my early potential as a writer. The fate of my would-be book fell between the extraneous cracks in my life. But never throw the baby out with the bath water. Often what we see as hopeless in our own strength, God considers perfect for His glory.

This is a good time to share a bit of good ole Christian advice. Little is much when God is in it. That's a lesson worth remembering. If some of you happen to be stuck between a rock and hard place, then maybe you aren't leaving any room in your life to partner with "the Rock." Self is a lonely place. Never leave God out of the equation. And you can be sure; if anyone allows the devil to invade their thoughts, it will be a death blow for certain. As for me, instead of focusing on God, my own inadequacies were all I could see. I felt incapable, too inexperienced for the task. Which, as it turned out, was all a big fat deception of the devil. I swallowed Satan's lies hook, line, and sinker for years. That was how he was able to cripple my talent and keep me restrained from sharing the good news of the gospel with others.

I speak from experience when I tell you that there will be times when God asks you to do something that leaves you terror-stricken. Stop right then and ask yourself: is this fear reasonable? And if your answer is "probably not," then assume the devil is somewhere close by, trying to discourage you from fulfilling your service to God. But, on the other hand, if your fear is reasonable, all the better. It's very likely that God has a plan, and you're His hand-picked instrument to orchestrate it. Do not hesitate. Do it afraid if necessary. It's those very occasions when you begin to learn just how significant your work is for the Lord Jesus. Every inch of labor for the Lord is another milestone added to the kingdom of God. Furthermore, it's important to remember: if the Lord asks you to do something, you can be sure that He will equip you in every possible way. Thereby, His purpose will be one-hundred percent achievable and entirely perfected. God would never set one of His children up to fail. He wants you to be every bit as victorious as you see yourself to be. If you see yourself a failure...you guessed it, you'll fail. Stop seeing yourself and see God.

When the Israelites arrived at the border of Canaan, their promised legacy, God instructed them to go into the land and see everything that had long been promised. God wanted the Israelites to see for themselves the immensity of what they were about to inherit. God described to them a land flowing with milk and honey. Fortified cities and houses they didn't build. The land was rich and producing abundantly. This territory offered everything pre-established for the Israelites to possess for their very own. The land was just exactly as God portrayed it to be. But some of the Israelites saw God's proposal quite differently.

God instructed Moses to select twelve leaders from each of the tribes that made up the nation of Israel. They were instructed to spy out the land of Canaan. This was the same country that God promised to give to Abraham and his descendants even before the nation of Israel actually existed. This territory was referred to by God as an abundant place rich in prosperity and would eventually become the permanent homeland of God's people. There was just one little hang-up, something the Israelites hadn't considered. There were giants still living in the land of Canaan. Here is but one story from the Bible that has an indispensable lesson attached. One that we should all be eager to embrace.

The twelve chosen leaders were directed to spy out the land and bring back a report on everything they could discover about the land's condition and its people. Was the land boundless and good or meager and barren? Were the cities well-fortified strongholds or tent dwellings? Everything that existed prior to the Israelites' possession would be greatly serviceable for God's people well into the future. God thought of everything for His people in this land of prosperity.

The spy's covert operation consisted of forty days of intelligence gathering. Upon returning from their exploration, they brought proof of the land's generous abundance. Just one sizable bounty of grapes was so massive that it took a pole hoisted upon the shoulders of two men to transport them. In addition to the grapes, the men brought even further evidence of the land's goodness by producing a hefty quantity of pomegranates and figs, proof of the land's productiveness. The land of Canaan was indeed a very prosperous substance from God. Not some uninhabited run-down uncultivated wasteland in the middle of nowhere. This was ready-made prosperity. Oh sure, maybe they did see a few giants, but they weren't unconquerable. And what if their cities were well fortified? That didn't mean that they were unassailable. None of the things that terrorized the cowards were insurmountable. No, it wasn't the size, strength, or number of giants that the Israelites would come up against that did them in. They left their faith in God out of the undertaking. The perception of how those leaders imagined themselves in the enemy's eyes was what really unnerved the entire nation. They weren't leaning on the incomparability of the Lord.

Before continuing with the story of the Israelites, I would ask that you consider certain aspects of their story similar to the condition that Christian Americans face today. There are some vexing giants that have invaded our homeland, but with the help of God, we can drive them out, reestablish our principles of right and wrong, and save our precious children from having their little minds corrupted. But it will take courage and strength to face those giants. We can't do it without the Lord's help. But with God, we can do all things. *"And all those gathered here will know that the Lord doesn't save by means of sword and spear. The Lord owns this war, and he will hand all of you over to us"* (1 Samuel 17:47, CEB).

How is it possible that a small handful of cowardly men could turn away the hearts of an entire nation? Why did they fear the giants? Because of how they saw themselves, incapable little grasshoppers. And that's exactly what fear reduced them to. They were defeated by their own imaginations because they were unwilling to trust God and go forward in the power and strength of the Almighty. So, the consuming fear of ten cowards spread like wildfire among the nation of Israel, totally convincing God's people that it was too dangerous and entirely impossible to overcome the giants in the land.

However, not everyone was of the same opinion as the men who lacked courage. Joshua and Caleb were completely convinced that they could overtake the giants that were occupying the territory. It wasn't that Joshua and Caleb were without fear; they simply placed their confidence in the promises of God. Together with God, those two men showed a fighting spirit, not one of defeat. They were completely prepared to endure the possibility of unpleasant conditions in order to gain victory over the prize. Nothing ventured, nothing gained. Besides, they knew it was God's good pleasure to give them this land by enabling them and providing whatever means necessary to achieve their goal. Obviously, Joshua and Caleb had a completely different spirit and mindset. They tried to assure the assembly that it was just as God Said it would be. But as the people listened to the full report of the spies, some of the other men began to express their foreboding about entering Canaan. And that's when it happened. A spirit of terror started to well up amongst the people, proliferating to such a degree that the entire nation was beginning to encounter great apprehension about going forward.

The more detail the fearful spies recounted, the more alarmed the people became. There was no denying that Canaan was everything and even more than what God promised. And none of the men were willing to deny that. But because they had taken their eyes off God, their courage had wilted, and the only thing left was what their own reasoning was imagining. That is precisely what is meant by looking at things through one's limited natural senses.

Regrettably, after all God had done for them, they still refused to trust the Lord to bring their nation safely into their new homeland. Those few cowardly spies were supposed to be the nation's premier leaders—Israel's principal commanders responsible for implementing God's will and Commandments. Instead of preparing the people and encouraging them to trust God for a conquest, they discouraged the people and instigated rebellion among the entire nation. And consequently, that lamentable event led to the eventual death of every cowardly grumbler involved. *And Joshua the son of Nun and Caleb the son of Jephunneh, who were among those who had spied out the land, tore their clothes and said to all the congregation of the people of Israel, "The land, which we passed through to spy it out, is an exceedingly good land. If the Lord delights in us, he will bring us into this land and give it to us, a land that flows with milk and honey. Only do not rebel against the Lord. And do not fear the people of the land, for they are bread for us. Their protection is removed from them, and the Lord is with us; do not fear them." Then all the congregation said to stone them with stones. But the glory of the Lord appeared at the tent of meeting to all the people of Israel* (Numbers 14:6–10, ESV).

God was angered by the lack of confidence His people had in Him. But unfortunately, the damage at that point was irreversible. The apprehension of the Israelites was so great they stood stubbornly upon their fearful objections and refused to enter into the Promised Land. They grumbled against God and Moses and even wanted to return to Egypt. Imagine that!

Sadly, mass hysteria had spread throughout the camp, and their only desire at that point was to stone Joshua and Caleb. This, of course, exasperated God and He was ready to strike them with pestilence and utterly destroy them all with only a few exceptions. But Moses boldly reasoned with God on behalf of the entire nation. God heard the heart of Moses, and instead of putting a complete end to the rebellious society right then, God chose a more merciful way of dealing with those who were openly defiant and resistant to His authority. As a consequence of God's judgment, the entire nation was redirected back into the wilderness to live in profound regret every day for nearly forty years.

God gave the people a beautiful gift, and they threw it right back in His face. One of the very first lessons that we must learn about God is His gracious, benevolent love. We can have everything our hearts desire if it is within His will. And we must know without a doubt that God only wants what's in our best interest. The more we include Him in our everyday life, the more we will come to know God and understand the goodness of His love.

God cannot fail. But it's interesting to note that every unsuccessful initiative undertaken and written about in the Old Testament was due to man's refusal to comply with God in a complete manner. Notice I used the word *complete?* Half measures will never do with God. Anything less than a one-hundred percent commitment to the Lord Jesus is a dereliction of spiritual duty.

Each one of us has taken a wrong turn in life at least once. Whether it was the wrong place to live, the wrong job, maybe even the wrong mate. Although there may not be an immediate solution to life's blunders, the consequences we may be forced to live with should be an invaluable lesson. Sometimes there might seem to be delays in the various implementations of God's will, but He will always succeed in having His way, no matter how long the interval. Let me interject something of monumental importance here. Whatever God has done or is doing in your Life or the lives of others that you know about, exclaim His goodness enthusiastically and tell everyone who will listen. The Lord God is loving and good. He deserves to be recognized for Who He is and for all the marvelous works He continues to do in the lives of His creation. People of God, we should be thinking of the Lord's goodness continually and talking to others about Him far more often than we do. We never know who may be listening and yet struggling in silence, wanting desperately to find their way out of the darkness but can't seem to summon the words to ask. If you're willing to share God's providential love with others, it just might help turn someone else's life around. Keep this in mind. God and Satan cannot occupy the exact same place. So, if your mind and heart are filled with the benevolence of Almighty God, there is no room left for Satan. Know for certain there is only room for one god in your life. Therefore, which god would you prefer to govern your life? The god of the flesh or the God of the Spirit?

Faith in God provides such a peaceful existence no matter what the conditions are around you. Faith is believing that our God, our Sovereign, the One Who created us in the womb, loves us beyond anything we can think or imagine. Therefore, we don't have to figure out how He does what He does. All we have to do is receive it, appreciate it, and give Him thanks for it. Then we can simply enjoy all the equanimity the Lord Jesus has provided us.

Often when God does those amazing things we call miracles, they aren't really miracles at all. It's the goodness of God, being God. He takes the heavy circumstances in Life, rearranges the outcome, and brings about a divine conclusion to lighten a person's oppressive load. It's through the love of God that we receive favor, compassion, and mercy. We just call them miracles because they are so astonishing to us when they happen. Every impossible detail coming together right at the precise moment. Everything falling into place at exactly the right time to arrange what seems impossible to us. Those seemingly unattainable things happening in such a spectacular way, we have no other explanation. People will think what they want to think or what Satan influences them to disbelieve. But I tell you from years of personal experience with God: there is no such thing as a coincidence in this life. Everything that appears to be a chance occurrence, fluke, or providence is by divine intervention, period.

Take Jacob's son Joseph for example. His older brothers were so jealous of him, they sold him to a caravan going to Egypt. When Joseph arrived there, he was sold as a slave to Potiphar, the overseer of Pharaoh's guards. Egypt is where Joseph spent the remainder of his life. From outward appearances, no one could have imagined or recognized God's divine intervention for the Israelites' greater good. But it was Joseph's faith in God that turned every negative circumstance into a providential opportunity for Joseph to glorify God in the trials he faced. As a result of Joseph's faith in God, the nation of Israel was increased innumerably. Thereby, what was meant for evil, God reversed direction and made something good come of it. *As for you, you meant evil against me, but God meant it for good, to bring it about that many people should be kept alive, as they are today* (Genesis 50:20, ESV).

Chapter 2

Pillar of Virtue

During this modern era in which we are living, *virtue* is not a word we hear a lot about or frequently see among our fellow man. Maybe that's because it is not an inherent quality; therefore, it does not always make itself known early in life. Moreover, virtue is a highly desired but rare quality that must be cultivated, thereby stimulating inner goodness to increase over time. So, let's scrutinize that analysis a bit further. The word *virtue* is interchangeable with the word *goodness*. Either word is defined by righteousness, morality, propriety, and decency, et cetera. A virtuous person is always warmhearted and charitable.

Virtue incorporates several wholesome attributes, including but not limited to the broadest meaning of honesty. Therefore, if you wanted to describe someone's good character in a single word, virtuous would be an excellent stand-alone portrayal, clearly defining that person's distinguishing high merit in the most complementary terms. But, if you ask just about anyone to evaluate their own character, you will very likely hear, "I'm basically a good person." Basically? That describes the barest minimum required. Basically doesn't make the cut in the virtuous standard set forth by the Lord God.

We all know someone who is less than virtuous. It's a negative characteristic that makes itself known in any number of irreverent ways. All too often, some of the nicest people have the least amount of integrity. In the Old Testament book of Judges, there was a man named Samson. He was a Nazarite, consecrated to the service of God, known expressly for his beautiful uncut hair and tremendous physical strength. But when it came to virtuous character, Samson just didn't measure up. Virtue had eluded Samson in many ways. His outward strength was his only claim to fame. Due to his weak morals and wanton flesh, Samson's unrestrained principles caused him a bitter and somewhat tragic end to what might have been a very effectual Life in service to God.

There are many descriptive words that define the good characteristics of virtue. Strength is a word that would describe the inner conviction of someone's virtuous character. When faced with the opportunity to do something wrong, virtue is the compulsion to resist that temptation and do the right thing, even when no one would be the wiser. Being truthful is an absolute necessity. Have you ever heard someone say about another that they'd rather tell a lie even when the truth comes easier? Or have you ever walked away from a conversation scratching your head, wondering if anything that was said had the slightest bit of truth to it? See what is on God's list of things He hates. *A false witness who breathes out lies even under oath, and he who sows discord among his brethren* (Proverbs 6:19, AMPC).

That is a sad commentary of someone's character. Human beings can easily become creatures of habit, good as well as bad. The more anything is done, the easier it is to repeat. Unfortunately, dishonesty has become the new normal these days. But if we want to change from the wayward deception of sin, we must take a virtuous stand against lying. Remember, everything in life comes down to one thing and one thing only. Choice. And choice has consequences. *To the victors will go this inheritance: I will be their God, and they will be My children. It will not be so for the cowards, the faithless, the sacrilegious, the murderers, the sexually immoral, the sorcerers, the idolaters, and all those who deal in deception. They will inherit an eternity in the lake that burns with fire and sulfur, which is the second death.* (Revelation 21:7–9, VOICE).

A word of caution when reflecting on the interpretation of the word deception. Please be aware that sometimes even the noblest of persons can be misled. Some very high-profile people most admired for their religious posturing can oftentimes be a deluding influence and tool of deception. Regardless how sweet the sound, if even one soul is misled by erroneous religious doctrine, it's one too many. Whether by inference or postulation, the views of people vary greatly when it comes to religion, and what's being expressed may not necessarily be biblically accurate. Admittedly, circumstances and situations may differ greatly and are often very tricky to detect, especially for loving gullible Christians. Christians immediately shy away from the need to judge. The last thing any sincere Christian wants to be guilty of is chastising another Christian. But much too often, in the absence of doctrinal inerrancy , the naïve are then beguiled. And the results of that tragedy can be deadly. Therefore, let's use a different analysis. I'm not suggesting anyone judge another's reasoning; that remains in the hands of the Almighty. I am, however, challenging all my Christian family to know expressly what the Bible says on everything. There is no better way to detect an error than knowing the accuracy of a subject. A comprehensive study of what's authentic will immediately expose the counterfeit. Take three tiny newborn babies and blindfold the mother of one of the infants. Ask her to detect the identity of her own child using only her bare hands. It's a no-brainer. Once you become knowledgeable in Scripture, you will know immediately what is untrue.

Sometimes the truth can be painful. Sometimes the truth can be totally devastating. I'm relatively sure that we all have been on one end or the other of a bitter truth. Either circumstance can be unpleasant. Painful for the one telling the truth and pain to the one hearing the truth. Either can be an awkward and uncomfortable position to be in. But truth always takes the high road. It deals swiftly and cleanly, causing far less damage than a lie would. Furthermore, in the end, truth will leave a much cleaner wound and smaller scar, and honesty will promote speedier healing of the injury.

Scruples is an old-fashioned word that defines the moral code of ethics that we should endeavor to live by. The word may not be used much in today's language, but the significance of the word has never changed over time. Simply stated, scruples are the internal perceptions of conscience letting us know what is right or seemingly wrong. It is like a flagman on the road ahead, warning us to slow down and proceed with caution; we are approaching something questionable up ahead. Be alert; heed those warnings. Prudence and vigilance will forgo many painful regrets.

Fortitude is an additional facet of someone's virtue. It is the single most indispensable asset that drives resilience and courage when challenged with uncertain circumstances. Fortitude will never back down in the face of fear or opposition but will proceed straightforwardly with absolute integrity and undiluted veracity. When the power of this rare and beautiful quality is at work in us, everyone will be far better off. *Brothers and sisters, continue to think about what is good and worthy of praise. Think about what is true and honorable and right and pure and beautiful and respected* (Philippians 4:8, ERV).

In the Old Testament book of Ruth, there is a beautiful story of a woman by the name of Naomi, the mother-in-law of Orpha and Ruth. The narrative account portrays the embodiment of virtue as it unfolds through a twisted pattern of pain, love, and loyalty amid a great hardship in an unavoidable circumstance. These three women were all widowed and left all alone in the land of Moab, without sufficient resources for their survival. Hearing that the Lord had provided adequate bread in the land of her nativity, Naomi decided to return to Judah. At Naomi's insistence, Orpha returned to her relations, but Ruth refused to leave her mother-in-law under any circumstance other than death. Moreover, she vowed to go wherever Naomi went and to adapt to Naomi's lifestyle, her people, and even serve her God, the God of Israel.

The motivating force behind Ruth's decision was never declared openly or distinctly. But as the story develops, we begin to see the hand of God in the picture. Ruth's steadfast determination to follow Naomi throughout the remainder of their lives was not just a noble gesture. Her fidelity to Naomi went far deeper than either of them might have imagined. In all actuality, Ruth was denouncing her past life to follow in the direction of righteousness.

Ruth's unselfish determination to remain attentive to Naomi and accompany her to Bethlehem proved to be the sovereign will of God and a heaven-sent blessing for them both.

So, it was decided that Naomi and Ruth would journey to Bethlehem, where Naomi's wealthy kinsman Boaz had just begun the work of harvest in his barley fields. Ruth was gleaning the remains in the field after the servants were finished reaping. It was there that Boaz noticed her and inquired among the servants about her identity. When it became known to Boaz that his cousin Naomi had returned to her homeland and was attended by her widowed daughter-in-law Ruth, this man of integrity stepped in to maintain proper care of the widows. Boaz was a principled man and provided sustenance according to the Hebrew law pertaining to a kinsman. Once Boaz received word from within the community that Naomi's daughter-in-law Ruth was a virtuous woman, he became smitten with her. From then on, his intention toward Ruth was honorable, hoping that he could lawfully redeem the widow and make her his wife. As it turned out, that was God's plan all along.

Virtue has great rewards. Boaz took Ruth as his wife, and when their nuptials were formalized, the Lord caused Ruth to conceive. As per judicial law and family tradition, the son she bore named Obed would be the continued heritage of Mahlon, Naomi's son and Ruth's deceased husband. And so, the Lord provided Naomi with a restorer of Life. Then Naomi embraced her grandson tenderly and became a nurse to the child. The virtuous love Ruth had for her mother-in-law and the upright virtuous principles Boaz held for the tradition of family made a clear pathway for the birth of Jesus through the descendant of Obed, who became the father of Jesse, who was the father of King David. That is a magnificent testimony of the goodness of God.

Chapter 3

Pillar of Knowledge

One of the Psalms that King David wrote begins as follows: the fool has said in his heart, there is no God (Psalm 14:1). The Hebrew translation for fool is stupid, wicked, or evil. That is very explicit language. Even so, there is a large segment of society that flat-out refuses to believe the truth. These unbelievers are willing to overlook the fact that there were countless eyewitnesses in both the Old and New Testaments that interacted with God in one way or another.

The repudiation of God's truth begs the question: who or what could be behind such an extraordinary deception for so many thousands of years? Especially if there is nothing to be gained from it in the end. If it were not true, what would be the point? And furthermore, let's not fail to remember and mention the many martyrs that have died for their faith, both past and present day. Will their lives be discounted also? Pray-tell then, what was the purpose behind all the unfounded and meaningless forfeiture of each one of those lives? To all the fools who would say there is no God, let me put them in mind of this Scripture. It's a very fearful thing to fall into the hands of the living God (Hebrews 10:31). In addition to that, here is another Scripture for the unbelievers to ponder; God says, *"They will all be condemned because they did not believe the truth and because they enjoyed doing evil"* (2 Thessalonians 2:12, ERV).

Have you ever known someone who seemed to be smart but at the same time incapable of logical reasoning? Their skepticism and stubbornness have hardened their hearts and blinded them from believing the truth. It is one thing to be ignorant of the facts, but it is an entirely different matter to know the facts and refuse to acknowledge what is the plain bona fide truth. This is not meant to be disrespectful, merely to point out that there are a great number of bright people all over the world who simply refuse to acknowledge what historical evidence has factually substantiated.

In the New Testament book of Acts, there was a respected teacher of the law named Gamaliel who thought to quill the students of the law who were uprising over the new doctrine being introduced by Jesus and His disciples. This was the very same Gamaliel that tutored Saul prior to his conversion to Christianity. In the following Scripture, Gamaliel gives his students some unscholarly and offhanded but prophetic guidance. *And so in the present case, I say to you, stay away from these men and leave them alone, for if the source of this plan or movement is men, it will be overthrown; but if the source is God, you will not be able to overthrow them; or else you may even be found fighting against God"* (Acts 5:38–39, NASB).

And so, there's your answer. The gospel message has continued to spread like wildfire throughout the entire world, and it hasn't been restrained yet.

When God made His covenant with Abraham and his descendants, He was intent on establishing Himself as their only true God. During that time, other nations worshiped all sorts of gods and idols. Many atrocities and degenerate acts were enacted for those false deities. Therefore, Jehovah God needed to insulate and protect His chosen nation from participating in similar barbarous acts of sin while at the same time establishing their continued trust and dependence exclusively upon Himself. God's people experienced His mighty power and generous sustenance, right along with His many marvelous acts of protection and supremacy. At other times, they witnessed God's majesty to such a terrifying degree they feared having any personal contact with Him directly.

For God the Father to have a closer relationship with mankind, He determined to send His Son Jesus in the form of a Man to lead His creation in the way of righteousness and receive everlasting Life. The Son of man revealed many astonishing signs and wonders that demonstrated His deity, but in a remarkably different way from Almighty God. How many eyewitnesses will the agnostics, atheists, and the greatest percentage of the Jewish population continue to deny? God gave us His beloved Son Jesus as Living proof of His committed love to all those who would believe on Him. Therefore, Messiah came as the promised Deliverer to the nations. At His first incarnation, Jesus brought a message of love that had to be spread across the regions and embedded deep within the hearts of all men everywhere. *Satan, who is the god of this world, has blinded the minds of those who don't believe. They are unable to see the glorious light of the Good News. They don't understand this message about the glory of Christ, who is the exact likeness of God* (2 Corinthians 4:4, NLT).

Regrettably, all those souls who refused to believe will have a rude awakening at the time of their judgment or the Lord's second coming. Be warned: either day is clearly appointed without advance notice.

There are only two ways into the arms of the Savior Jesus. By way of the grave or the rapture. Everyone who perpetuates their reluctance to receive the salvation offered by Jesus continues to be under a strong delusion by none other than Satan, causing them to potentially forfeit the loving embrace of the Lord, whether by death or rapture. The final day of familiar life, as we know it, is approaching. That day will culminate with seven and one half years of tribulation. A time of great difficulty and significant suffering. When the tribulation comes to an end, the next earthly appearance of the Lord Jesus will not be a social call. The imminent occurrence of Jesus will not be a replication of His first visit of love, compassion, and tolerance. This return will be to adjudicate the wicked world of sin and sinners. On that day, Jesus will distinguish Himself as Lord and King over all the earth. Then, every eye will see His indisputable Transcendence, and every knee will bow. His second coming will be with condemnation, wrath, and severe judgment. The unregenerate sinner's fate will then be sealed.

There is a powerful display of Jesus' justifiable but controlled anger in the book of John. When Jesus entered the temple and saw the desperate need to cleanse His Father's house of its atrocious conditions and immoral conduct, He was enraged. The example illustrated by John was but the minutest admonition of the Son of God. Jesus was seething on account of the reprehensible attitude and indifference toward the Almighty Father and the deplorable condition of His house of prayer. *In the temple he found people selling oxen, sheep, and doves, and he also found the money changers sitting there. After making a whip out of cords, he drove everyone out of the temple with their sheep and oxen. He also poured out the money changers' coins and overturned the tables. He told those who were selling doves, "Get these things out of here! Stop turning my Father's house into a marketplace!"* (John 2:14–16, CSB)

However, if anyone still chooses not to believe the eyewitness accounts in the Bible or continues to ignore the intelligence that leads to the knowledge of truth and a personal relationship with Christ, then so be it. Jesus would be the last One to suggest that anyone should accept the gospel truth blindly. Each person should be well informed before deciding on such a critical matter as eternal Life or unrelenting death. Every individual should open those portals for themselves. Maybe your doubt is simply a lack of proper data and traceable evidence that would dispel those uncertainties. Therefore, I'm suggesting the cynic give Christianity a chance. Ask yourself: what is there to lose? Your justification, to be sure! No one is capable of learning anything with a closed mind. Open a Bible and ask God for understanding. If any seeker is sincerely after the truth, they are sure to find the answers that will open their eyes. The Lord has already made certain of it.

This next Scripture is a quote from King David's son Solomon, the wisest man during the time of antiquity. *Fear of the Lord is the foundation of true knowledge, but fools despise wisdom and discipline* (Proverbs 1:7, NLT). The Solomon quote may sound somewhat brash, but the truth is, revelation knowledge of the gospel can only be endued through the power given by God's Own Holy Spirit.

The following Scripture is the evidence of that gift. But such a powerful and glorious manifestation of God will never be imparted frivolously. *A manifestation of the Spirit is given to each person for the common good: to one is given a message of wisdom through the Spirit, to another, a message of knowledge by the same Spirit, to another, faith by the same Spirit...* (1 Corinthians 12:7–9, CSB)

It is God Who has equipped the saints with faith to believe. If you are one of His chosen, regardless of how faint your voice may seem in this vast cosmos, worry not; the angry opinions of others will never drown out the truth of the gospel. The Lord's truth continues to flourish in the hearts of Christians all over the world. Even the softest whisper that proclaims Jesus as Lord of lords and King of kings will continue to echo throughout the entire universe forever. You do not have to holler or try to shout down the voice of someone who might disagree with you. Just stand on your evidence. Stand on the Word of the Lord. His truth is a mighty foundation that will never be shaken. When God's truth is on your side, you know the Lord Jesus will honor your courage. God knows the heart and weighs the actions of men. *At one time you were separated from God. You were his enemies in your minds, and the evil things you did were against God. But now God has made you his friends again. He did this through Christ's death in the body so that he might bring you into God's presence as people who are holy, with no wrong, and with nothing of which God can judge you guilty. This will happen if you continue strong and sure in your faith. You must not be moved away from the hope brought to you by the Good News that you heard. That same Good News has been told to everyone in the world, and I, Paul, help in preaching that Good News* (Colossians 1:22–23, NCV).

Chapter 4

Pillar of Self-Control

Temperance is a word we seldom hear much of these days. It is a word that defines the control we have over our behavior. Americans have been indoctrinated into thinking that if a little is good, then a little more must be better. Therefore, we give ourselves permission to indulge excessively in whatever provides us the greatest pleasure. However, the unfortunate aftermath of excessive self-gratification is the danger of what it might eventually lead to. Quite possibly a health concern, uncontrolled violence, or any other habitual condition commonly referred to as an addiction. Another big slice of pumpkin pie won't kill me. What difference will a couple more dollars in the slot machine make? The truth is, a bottle of beer never hurt anyone, right? How about one more for the road?

Nevertheless, if anything that was once occasional has turned excessive, it may be time to question its disproportionate use and, if necessary, seek competent help. Whatever the concern might be, diagnosis in the early stages may indeed prevent a bigger problem in the future. Rage, immoral or illegal exploits, or anything that would cause property damage, harm to self or anyone else must be addressed. Regrettably, if failure to harness any of those unmanageable desires early on, they will no doubt escalate into more major concerns. Step by step, those exploits will often and tragically become the catalyst to a disastrous end. Whatever the proclivity, whether excess, perversion, or pattern, just one more time might be the last time forever.

Without self-control, it is easy to overindulge in all sorts of practices. Sometimes we fool ourselves into thinking: where is the harm? If it's legal, it must be okay. If the doctor prescribed it, it must be safe. It's Friday, a holiday, or that old standby, it's five o'clock somewhere. Those are simply statements for justifying unsuitable or excessive behavior. That is precisely what Adam did when God found him hiding in the garden and questioned the reason for his infidelity. Instead of Adam taking responsibility for his sin, Adam blamed God for giving him the woman. *The man said, "The woman you put here with me—she gave me some fruit from the tree, and I ate it"* (Genesis 3:12, NIV).

Adam's effort to escape responsibility had a devastating effect on the entire human race. I can't help but wonder how things might have been different if Adam had told God the truth. And frankly, Adam's lie reverberates the same travesty of familiar deceit all too common today. People may think they are getting away with shirking their responsibility for doing wrong, but reparation cannot be avoided.

Culpability for evil conduct will never be overlooked by God. Those pathetic excuses are just another way of deflecting responsibility for self-gratification. We cannot place blame for our problem on another human being. And it's just as ridiculous to condemn a vice such as alcohol, food, gambling, pornography, illegal drug use, anger, or any other abuse that has the individual entrapped. It's the person behind the activity who is relinquishing their authority to a lessor entity—their flesh. Take the right to bear arms for instance. A firearm never harmed anyone on its own. The damage only occurs when the impetus of a human holds it, loads it, points it, and then pulls the trigger. The gun is only the device by which the agent used to channel the destructive action. If everyone allows their flesh to dictate their actions, then clearly, it's the individual's lack of self-control that contributes to most of the world's upheaval. The apostle Paul once said, "*I don't understand why I act the way I do. I don't do the good I want to do, and I do the evil I hate. And if I don't want to do what I do, that means I agree that the law is good. But I am not really the one doing the evil. It is sin living in me that does it*" (Romans 7:15–17, ERV).

The sin that Paul talks about is common to the flesh of mankind. There is nothing unique about sin. Our flesh often behaves like a spoiled child when it is denied. It will have a tantrum of sorts and persist peevishly until it gets its own way. Everyone must deal with this intrinsic characteristic throughout their lifespan. All too often, instead of taking the moral high road, we take the path of least resistance by simply giving in to those weaknesses, just to calm the beast within, usually without considering the consequence to ourselves or those we love or society in general. Don't be naïve. If those first steps are leading in a subversive direction, they may well stumble you into a great catastrophe. Or worse, catapult you headlong into a nightmare of long extended devastation, heartache, and misery. Thus, causing those you love to inadvertently accompany you through the experience. Take the better pathway and travel through life according to God's direction, thus conquering all your adversities utilizing the vanquishing pillar of temperance.

Temperance can play a pivotal role in eradicating any unwholesome or damaging behavior. Many human beings will listen to their internal voice that cautions. It's the voice of temperance telling you that a perilous situation will likely present itself. It is an inner knowing that implores the person at risk to reconsider their intended action. The practice of self-discipline will help everyone maintain a sensible balance in all the dicey areas of life. *It's clear that our flesh entices us into practicing some of its most heinous acts: participating in corrupt sexual relationships, impurity, unbridled lust, idolatry, witchcraft, hatred, arguing, jealousy, anger, selfishness, contentiousness, division, envy of other's good fortune, drunkenness, drunken revelry, and other shameful vices that plague humankind. I told you this clearly before, and I only tell you again so there is no room for confusion: those who give in to these ways will not inherit the kingdom of God* (Galatians 5:19–21, VOICE).

Regrettably, when taking the easy route too often, it will just prolong the inevitable. Each action, good or bad, will cause a subsequent reaction, just like a line of Dominos. Then the question should be asked: in what direction will this behavior lead me? Take the use of an automobile for instance. It's harmless just sitting there.

But when we get behind the wheel, it responds to our commands. The vehicle doesn't have a will of its own. The motorist has total control. If the driver is careless or decides to misuse the vehicle in any manner, it will fall upon the operator to face any resulting consequence. But it's a different story when someone impaired through the use of drugs or alcohol gets behind the wheel. That normally harmless machine then becomes a potential weapon of destruction endangering life and property, thereby resulting in lawsuits, the possibility of criminal charges, and perhaps a prison sentence or funeral. Negating good sense in order to drive in a diminished condition is a willful and irresponsible decision of the flesh.

Once we identify the harmful weakness or defect corrupting our otherwise healthy behavior, then it's time to take affirmative action and face the culprit head-on. If preventative measures aren't imposed, we will be held responsible for whatever occurs as the result of our Achilles heel. If we do not acknowledge our faults, we cannot correct or eradicate them. Just as soon as we have been made aware of a menacing activity, regardless of our own faulty justification, it is time to take control. Know when to apply the brakes. If your heart is beating, it's never too late to start over again. By controlling those excesses, you will be making today the first day of a brighter future.

Chapter 5

Pillar of Patience

Don't run from tests and hardships, brothers, and sisters. As difficult as they are, you will ultimately find joy in them; if you embrace them, your faith will blossom under pressure and teach you true patience as you endure. And true patience brought on by endurance will equip you to complete the long journey and cross the finish line—mature, complete, and wanting nothing (James 1:4, VOICE). I believe patience is the premier fruit of the Spirit. Not better in the sense of superiority, but more suitably able to give rise to each of God's other graces. Patience is typically multifaceted; therefore, it navigates without difficulty through many frustrating obstructions in life.

I cannot speak for anyone else, but patience was a word that I heard continually while I was growing up. Every time I turned around, someone was telling me to have patients. Have patients? How does somebody just have patience? I have since learned that patience is not something that always comes naturally. Patience is an exercise in willful forbearance. Even after the concept is grasped, it may still be difficult to wait for something wanted. Therefore, patience is something that must be practiced regularly to produce resoluteness. But anytime the word *work* is mentioned, the human psyche balks, anticipating some type of unappealing physical or mental labor. Therefore, patience is widely avoided.

Impatience is widespread, especially in this modern age of rapid technology. Many years ago, communication was done through hand-written letter writing. Then came the typewriter. Still, these forms had to depend on the snail mail to deliver the correspondence. But the real breakthrough came with the development of the first household computer. No one seemed to mind how long they had to sit staring at a line inching its way across the computer screen, waiting for the connection to the Internet. Why? Because even then, it greatly surpassed delivery by the United States Postal

Service. It was the same with the telephone. However, presently the computer and telephone have merged into the speed of lightning called cell service that we enjoy today. There is no more waiting. Everything is available to us almost instantaneously. Therefore, it's quite understandable that technology has obstructed our saught-after ability to be patient. Whether it is tolerance, self-restraint, or perseverance, these virtues no longer come easily in modern society.

Having patience is not only a personal endeavor toward greater self-control but also indispensable for Christians. Bear in mind: for a believer, patience is a spiritual discipline. A believer can do nothing apart from God. We must first recognize that self-restraint is a willing and applied application that is developed through the simultaneous work of the Holy Spirit. Nevertheless, it could very well take a good deal of time and concerted effort on the believer's part to attain a continual and desired amount of forbearance, especially if the impatient person refuses to apply themselves to that specific fruit of the Spirit. Nevertheless, as with anything worth achieving, the more it is practiced, the easier it becomes. Patience is an enrichment that offers its own reward. When patience is exercised, there is no demand on the duration of time, so then there is absolutely no shortfall of peace waiting in the interim. At other times, however, impatience is known to produce unwelcomed sorrow and misery, possibly lasting for several generations.

Patience is a practiced grace that everyone would benefit from if they were able to harness it. Practically everyone has heard of the patience of Job. The Bible tells of the many trials and extraordinary conditions he went through, everything that was lost to him, and the continued suffering he endured at the hand of Satan. Yet, at no time did Job lose confidence in the Almighty, always declaring his fidelity in the highest esteem. Regardless of what suffering Job endured, he persisted steadfastly in his commitment and loyalty to the Everlasting Father, Jehovah. Hopefully, none of God's children will ever have to suffer as Job did, but be assured, anyone in the faith will indeed be tested in one way or another. Patience is a character quality that will get us through life's trying times. Sometimes it takes a great deal of courage to hold on during a time of unpredictability. But the Lord never abandons His own when they are bearing a cross for Christ. Just keep holding on.

As in Job's case, patience just might be a rational conditioning strategy that God is using to help us appreciate the recompense that comes through waiting, especially when waiting on the Lord. How many occasions on any given day do we have the perfect opportunity to exercise that grace? In the natural world, practically everything we do requires us to be patient. I can think of dozens of frustrating moments every single day, just spent having to wait on someone or something. Many times, my flesh would prefer to think of waiting as squandered periods of fruitlessness. But with God, there is no such thing as waste. Think of it more as an alternative opportunity to make productive use of. Everything has a purpose, and the timing of everything belongs strictly to God's program. Therefore, if we take the time to analyze a few obvious facts about patience, we just might be able to see the value of endurance from a different perspective.

In addition to the work of patience, James, the brother of Jesus, speaks of perfect revenues associated with the practice of patience (James 1:4). That is a very powerful declaration. When I first pondered the word *perfect*, my thoughts shifted to a stunning work on canvas in the studio of any skilled or talented artist and how expressly important it is for that artist to recognize when the work is finally completed. When the artist's eye sees the work as utterly whole and entire, that's when the work is finished, and not one brush stroke before. If there is nothing more to add that would enhance the work additionally, then it is complete and, in that sense, perfect.

Think for a moment about the farmers of the world. I am very sure that God smiles upon every hard-working farmer who labors season after season in faith and patience. God and farmers must work together favorably. Timing is everything in their industry. If they sowed one day and the next day dug up what they had planted, where would the crops be? Consequently, if it were not for their patience, none of us would be enjoying the sweet fruit and grain of their labor.

Regardless of what circumstances may befall you, consider them all tests to greater endurance. Most of us have heard the story of the tiny butterfly and its struggle to leave the restrictive confines of the protective cocoon. If the butterfly's method of transformation is rushed or assisted during the process of preconditioning, it will impair the faultless work of nature. The only chance of survival the butterfly has is in the painstaking struggle that it must undergo to free itself.

Therefore, we too can learn from nature and use the difficulties of each day as our personal trainer, conditioning our character to sustain us in each aspect of every experience with patience. We should let every single frustration become our gym membership, using each negative resource to provide us with all the pointers necessary to help us refine better responses to impatience. One additional benefit would be to use any lag time to develop whatever skills are necessary to patiently persevere in all instances that would oppose peace and serenity. Remember also that patience is the virtue that will benefit all those that are waiting upon the Lord's return, should He tarry. He Said He would return on the last day. But the Father has never divulged that day to anyone, not even Jesus during His incarnation. So then, as believers, we must remain alert and watching ever patiently, remain joyful, and never become weary in well-doing along the way.

The Bible tells of a magnificent promise God made to Abraham, who is known to all Christians as the Father of faith. *And I will cause your descendants to become as numerous as the stars! And I will give them all of these lands; and they shall be a blessing to all the nations of the earth* (Genesis 26:4, TLB).

Abraham and his wife Sarah were childless at the time God

made that promise. Many years passed, and throughout the long years of waiting, Sarah remained barren. With the passage of time, Sarah advanced past the normal age of childbearing. Therefore, to underscore the importance of patience, let us remember what Sarah's frustration and premature zeal to have a child gave root to. Instead of waiting upon God to fulfill His pledge, she expedited matters by devising a scheme to hurry motherhood along. Sarah's meddling led to the birth of Abraham's first-born son, Ishmael, by her Egyptian bond woman Hagar. Yet, when Abraham asked if Ishmael could be the chosen son of promise, this was God's reply. *Then God said: "No, Sarah your wife shall bear you a son, and you shall call his name Isaac; I will establish My covenant with him for an everlasting covenant, and with his descendants after him* (Genesis 17:19, NKJV).

So, the birth of Ishmael was motivated by Sarah's misguided and impatient reasoning. Unfortunately, the product of that strategy became a grievous and permanent division of Abraham's historical lineage that continues even today. Despite Sarah's petulance and faulty judgment, God indeed fulfilled His promise to Abraham, and Sarah gave birth to the son of promise at around ninety years of age. According to God's instruction, the only child born to Abraham and Sarah was named Isaac. And it was through their descendant Isaac that all of God's assurances to Abraham would come to pass over time.

Moving along in history. Isaac and his wife Rebecca had twin sons: Esau, the oldest, and Jacob, the younger. The two babies struggled contentiously within Rebecca's womb. Her anxiety over this led her to seek God for an answer to her concerns. God informed Rebecca that her sons would represent two separate nations. God also Declared that the elder son Esau would serve the younger, stronger nation of Jacob (Genesis 25:23). For whatever reason, Rebecca became unwilling to wait upon the propitious hand of God to fulfill His pledge. Thereby, she and Jacob connived to deceive her husband, Isaac, into giving the birthright to Jacob rather than the customary first-born son, Esau. Which proved to be a moot point anyway, since God long before predestined His will upon the Life of Jacob. Furthermore, Esau placed no value on his birthright and traded it for a bowl of stew.

Because of the contention caused by this deception, Esau vowed vengeance upon Jacob. And since Rebecca was afraid for Jacob's safety, she sent him away to her homeland to stay with her brother Laban until Esau had a chance to cool off. But that stay became a period of practiced patience for Jacob, and he never laid eyes on his living mother after that. God had long-range plans for Jacob. He Declared as much even before his birth. But Jacob had some serious lessons to learn. The most frustrating and demanding of them all would be the lesson of forbearance. Patience is like a tree with many branches extending from one trunk. Although established and fed from a communal root, each separate fruit may be varied in size and development. God's timing is inevitable. Through many years of training in perseverance, Jacob learned tolerance, self-restraint, and long-suffering.

Since Jacob's uncle Laban proved to be just as cunning and deceptive as Jacob, God used Labin to authenticate the right qualities in Jacob, those specific to God's purposes. For example. Jacob fell in love with Rachel, Laban's youngest daughter, and agreed to work seven years for her hand in marriage. But the morning after the wedding, Jacob discovered Laban had switched his oldest daughter Leah for Rachel, claiming custom decrees that the oldest daughter must be the first to marry. That was Jacob's first lesson in reaping what he had earlier sown. So then Jacob agreed to work an additional seven years for Rachel. After many years of additional trials, tolerant conditioning, demands, and challenges through shaping, the vessel of God had become worthy, and Jacob was finally removed from the Potter's wheel. Now the much older and wiser Jacob began moving ever closer to God and onward toward his preordained inheritance. *Consider it a sheer gift, friends, when tests and challenges come at you from all sides. You know that under pressure, your faith-life is forced into the open and shows its true colors. So don't try to get out of anything prematurely. Let it do its work so you become mature and well-developed, not deficient in any way* (James 1:2–4, MSG).

Little children, you can't just say you have faith; you must prove yourself faithful. The forerunners of the faith didn't try to escape their spiritual trials or their fate. Throughout the Old and New Testament, there are countless stories of the kind of mettle it took for the saints to courageously stand in the face of adversity. In the book of Daniel, three young men from Judah—Shadrach, Meshach, and Abednego—were thrown into a roaring fiery furnace because they refused to bow down and worship Nebuchadnezzar's golden statue. But they came out of their ordeal completely unharmed.

Think of yourself as a lump of Ore, hidden within the deep confines of the earth. God sees your exact whereabouts, and when He is ready, He will bring you to the surface. Now, of course, God knows your immense value, but to the world, you look very much the same as any other lump. Nevertheless, you are ideal for the Lord's purpose; He has a plan befitting you. You may be filthy and encased in the natural compromising elements of earth, but that will soon change. All the pollution covering your true worth must be carefully removed without causing unnecessary damage to the treasure within.

In your original state, you're not much to look at. In fact, in your present condition, you're not worth much either. However, God sees the potential under all that defilement. And so, He will begin the process of purification. And it doesn't just happen overnight. There is a process. And in most cases, it will take many years to achieve God's desired results.

Each phase of the process is different for everyone. But the basics are very much the same. The first step is separating the clump of Ore from the crude matter around it. Then it's crushed and heated to such a great intensity that it further eliminates any remaining contaminants. After all the impurities have been removed, it is once again put into a furnace and melted into the proper shape and size for a specialized purpose. That purpose is determined by God. But the result of all that refinement brings out your true value. You've been tried and tested and purified into a vessel of golden honor. Such is the purification of the flesh, the temple of the living God.

Child of God, all the different refinements that you endure in this lifetime are to prove your faith in God under the severe pressures and adverse conditions of life. The Lord wants a sturdy vessel able to bear much fruit fit for the kingdom of God. Therefore, whatever form your purification process takes, permit it, do it, bear it, suffer it with joy for Christ's sake and the kingdom of God. Again, remember the sound words of James and prioritize them highly. *...for when the way is rough, your patience has a chance to grow. So let it grow, and don't try to squirm out of your problems. For when your patience is finally in full bloom, then you will be ready for anything, strong in character, full and complete* (James 1:3–4, TLB).

Chapter 6

Pillar of Kindness

Now, after learning of the trials and experiences in the life of Job and how his so-called friends neglected to provide him the slightest bit of compassion during his time of need, this next subject is one that will refresh the spirit and sweeten the mood and profit everyone equally. *Continue to love each other with true brotherly love. Don't forget to be kind to strangers, for some who have done this have entertained angels without realizing it! Don't forget about those in jail. Suffer with them as though you were there yourself. Share the sorrow of those being mistreated, for you know what they are going through* (Hebrews 13:1–3, TLB).

The act of kindness is something that usually takes very little effort. It's most pleasant to give away and should always be received with joyous humility. Before venturing into this theme, let me give a brief explanation of the word brotherly. For anyone not familiar with biblical terminology, please understand that this topic or the term brotherly is in no way gender-specific. It is precisely how God used the term in the Bible. Therefore, let us consider the word brotherly in terms of persons or neighbors.

First, let's define what brotherhood looks like. *Brotherhood* is a broad term for anyone who is part of the human race. They are our neighbors wherever in the world they happen to live; regardless of skin shade, the language spoken, style of dress, or any other diversity you could name. Folks must stop separating themselves by outward appearance. The separation discussed throughout the Bible has only to do with the sinful nature of a person or deviant religions. With that being understood, we can break down the structure of brotherhood even further. The nucleus family, of course. And we all know that we can't pick our own family members. They come from a garden of diversity. The church family is derived from many various backgrounds and social circumstances. Let me point out one hugely significant difference between the two families. The church family are born-again Christians serving the Lord God Almighty. That may not necessarily be the case with your immediate family members.

Many times, it feels as though very close friends are actually family. Military service personnel is referred to as brothers-in-arms. Colleagues and work associates might be considered brothers too. Comrades stem from many avenues. And let us not forget college fraternities and sororities. Anyone or any group where there is a commonality or close attachment will usually be thought of in terms of brotherhood. There is no hard and fast rule on the subject, except to say there should never be any exclusions or biases based on personal partiality. But God has His own standard of brotherhood. Christ's church is a spiritual family. His sons and daughters are adopted into the family of God by the shed blood of His Son Jesus, the Christ. That special group of saints are the born-again believers. It is the saved who will spend all eternity in heaven. But nonetheless, everyone else on the planet is our neighbor and should be regarded favorably.

All human beings are created in the likeness of God and therefore have the greatest capacity for benevolence, whether Christian or otherwise. When referring to any act of kindness—it is one of the most fundamental practices in any social society. You don't have to be a Christian to be a good neighbor and friend. The local church is a perfect example of a large-scale charity. They do a variety of wonderful works within and without the boundaries of the church and community. Often churches and religious groups band their forces together to provide support for many charitable causes. Frequently their contributions support poverty-stricken peoples in distant lands. Anytime anyone lends a helping hand to those in need, no matter where they are in the world, contributing in times of desperation is truly a benevolent act of love. Kindness has no boundaries or exceptions. Kindness is an unselfish action benefiting another human being, nation, or cause, irrespective of difficulty or rationalization of circumstance.

There is no specific formula for initiating kindness anytime or anywhere there is a need. Being kind does not always have to involve monetary resources; it might be something as natural as a smile to blow away the dark clouds in someone's day. Or something as simple as holding a door open for another. One day someone brought my trash dumpster from the street to the house. I never found out who offered that kindness to me, but I was certainly grateful. We never know what might be going on behind the scenes in someone else's life. Sometimes even the smallest gesture at just the right time can mean everything to a soul that is downhearted or hurting. Strike when the iron is hot, timing is everything. *A well-spoken word at just the right moment is like golden apples in settings of silver* (Proverbs 25:11, VOICE). Seize the moment; who can tell when another opportunity to do good may pass your way again? Furthermore, we never know if even our smallest contribution or assistance may have prevented a life-threatening tragedy. Unfortunate things can happen to anyone without notice. Empathy plays a central role in how we treat others, especially at a particularly devastating time. Life can sometimes be harsh, and certain events can often completely change the flow of life in an instant and test a person's faith severely.

There were many times in my young life that I heard someone declare, "There, but for the grace of God go I." Now think about that statement for just a moment. Every one of us can put our own name at the end of that sentence. Brotherly love opens the heart to kindness and resolves never to turn away from the broken, the suffering, or the impoverished. There might be times when you desire to lend a hand but don't know how or where to start. Prayer to God will find a way. The Lord is able to do more with the least amount than any of us could ask or think.

When we have reached our limitations, it is time to take the matter before the Lord. He can provide everything necessary for the relief of anyone's misery. The Lord God has no limitations! Here is just one example. *"All we have are five loaves of bread and two fish," they said. Jesus said, "Bring them here." Then he had the people sit on the grass. He took the five loaves and two fish, lifted his face to heaven in prayer, blessed, broke, and gave the bread to the disciples. The disciples then gave the food to the congregation. They all ate their fill. They gathered twelve baskets of leftovers. About five thousand were fed* (Matthew 14:17–21, MSG).

Kindness is a pure and compassionate work of the heart. How we treat others, regardless of their gender, appearance, political affiliation, or stature in life, is the real basis of love and unselfishness. There will always be situations where a helping hand can be offered to someone needing comfort or support in some personal way. That is when the Christian, the neighbor, the brother should step up and fill in the gap or take up the slack. *And the King will answer and say to them, 'Assuredly, I say to you, inasmuch as you did it to one of the least of these My brethren, you did it to Me'* (Matthew 25:40, NKJV).

God tells us that the poor will be with us always. Poverty comes in many different areas of life. Someone may be poor in health, penniless, friendless, lowly in heart, or spiritually empty on the inside and so forth. The deprived have been around since Jesus walked on earth. Every community is touched by poverty in some form. Homelessness, unfortunate circumstances, underprivileged, grief-stricken, and the worst of all possible penury is *Godlessness*. Add children to any of those difficulties, and it becomes even more tragic. Adults may need a hand up occasionally, but when children are involved in the equation, the necessity is much more urgent and complex.

Each individual is treasured greatly in God's eyes. He places tremendous value on every soul that He brings into the world. Keep in mind, whether someone lives in a mansion on a hill or in a hut at the bottom of that very same hill, God loves those persons equally. Peter declared that God is no respecter of persons (Acts 10:34). Therefore, we would do well to follow His example and regard others with mindful consideration.

Kudos to the generous and thoughtful volunteer force

throughout the nation of America. Think of the many hours they have donated by giving of their time and talents without any thought of personal remuneration. The incalculable hours that volunteers donate to the benefit of their communities are positively altruistic. Where would we be without them? The most recent example of compassionate humanity occurred after the tropical storm Ian profoundly devastated Florida in late September 2022. All of us have been touched by that special someone. That person is labeled kindhearted because there is not anything they wouldn't do for someone in need. That indeed is a special and wonderful characteristic. The whole of humanity would certainly benefit from more such kindhearted neighborly individuals. Maybe the recipients of such kind generosity might one day—as the saying goes—pay it forward. That would profoundly please the Lord. *Send your grain across the seas, and in time, profits will flow back to you* (Ecclesiastes 11:1, NLT).

There is an unusually true-to-life story in the New Testament displaying a markedly contrasting nature of personal character. Two of the individuals are insensitive and inconsiderate. The other is gracious and compassionate. This account describes a wonderful example of the kindness of one accommodating, generous man toward another. He is only referred to in the Bible as the good Samaritan.

A traveler on his way to Jericho fell among thieves. He was stripped of his clothing, beaten until he was half dead, and left by the roadside. A priest traveling upon the same roadway saw the man lying there and crossed to the other side of the road. Then a member of the tribe of Levi happened along. He took a look at the man and kept right on walking. But when a Samaritan happened upon the man and saw the condition of the poor soul, he had compassion for him. He tended his wounds and laid him upon his animal and took him to the nearest inn where he could better care for the man. The following day the Samaritan paid the innkeeper to look after the victim of violence and said he would settle any overage on his return (Luke 10).

The command that Christ has given us is this: whoever loves God must love others also. (1 John 4:21, GNT). Some time ago, I saw the most remarkable news footage of an individual police officer bravely facing the terror of a deadly situation. To the best of my recollection, that angel in uniform was courageously defending the lives of a small group of petrified and trapped hotel guests. The officer was attempting to lead this small group of patrons to safety. And the only option was to proceed through a maze of dangerous twists and turns during a terrible hotel calamity where there was an active shooter involved. Most of us will never experience that degree of adversity in our lifetime. But the image of that lionhearted messenger from God that day was spectacular. He knew that the clock of life and death was ticking, and he was the only lifeline of deliverance for those who were depending upon him to keep them safe. The action taken by that heroic policeman was daring and focused, nothing short of miraculous. But the sacrifice of love he conveyed to his fellow human beings was comforting in those horrific moments. He had two very important responsibilities to manage. To avoid danger and protect life. He spoke to his charges calmly. He repeatedly reassured them of his professional competence, telling them to remain composed and to trust him. He promised that he would get them to safety, and he kept his word. And for those watching the news coverage, it was quite simply breathtaking as well as heartwarming. There are times in life when going above and beyond the call of duty is an act of heroism. That day, one solitary policeman became a public hero, especially to those people he shielded from harm.

We should remember another brave and compassionate hero, Bishop E. Evans, age 22, who gave his life late in the month of April 2022. In an unexpected moment of life and death, Mr. Evans unhesitatingly jumped into the water at the Mexican border to save the lives of two illegals that were in danger of drowning. If it was not for the heroic and unselfish act of this young National Guardsman, the two migrating men might quite possibly have lost their lives. Did Mr. Evans stop to ask himself whether their lives were worth saving? Not for a single moment. Of course, he knew those men were illegally trying to enter America. But all he thought about in those immediate moments of desperation was the instantaneous need of his neighbors. The men's lives were spared, although the unfortunate aftermath caused the young guardsman to lose his own life during that courageous and dangerous gesture of kindness and heroism. Not much acclaim was offered on behalf of Mr. Evans' ultimate sacrifice. But, let me go on record as saying, the action of Mr. Evans demonstrated human kindness to the highest degree. And his spirit modeled the perfect example of brotherly love. The precedent set by Bishop E. Evans that day at the river's edge should always be remembered. God sees. *We know love by this, that he laid down his life for us—and we ought to lay down our lives for one another* (1 John 3:16, NRSV).

Chapter 7

Pillar of Love

Not long before the crucifixion of Jesus, He stood looking over the people and city He loved and came to reclaim and restore. But instead of humbly embracing their Messiah, they rejected Him with such hatred they sought to kill Him. But that had no effect upon the love Jesus perpetuated for them. *When the city came into view, he wept over it. "If you had only recognized this day, and everything that was good for you! But now it's too late. In the days ahead your enemies are going to bring up their heavy artillery and surround you, pressing in from every side. They'll smash you and your babies on the pavement. Not one stone will be left intact. All this because you didn't recognize and welcome God's personal visit"* (Luke 19:41–44, MSG). Those very same Words are ringing throughout the universe today. Wherever people exist in the world, Jesus' haunting Words echo in the wind. The Words Spoken by Jesus that day were not for a particular people or time. The Lord's Words are timeless and for all people.

There is nothing that I know of that could describe a more vivid characterization of love than the living portrait of God the Father and His Son, Jesus.

Thousands of years prior, the scene wasn't at all what one might think. There atop a mountain, at the Command of Almighty God, a loving father stood obediently over his beloved son with a knife in his hand. Abraham was fully prepared to plunge his knife into the heart of his beloved Isaac. Although the mood was solemn, Abraham had absolute confidence that God would give his son back to him. Abraham didn't receive an answer to his prayer for an inheritor until he turned one hundred years of age. And now, in his unwavering position of faith, as a sacrifice unto the Lord God, Abraham was fully prepared to slay that very same precious Life he loved and so long-awaited.

Imagine the father, looking into the eyes of his child without fear, without doubt, ready to slay his unquestioning son. At the very last moment of thrust, God calls out to Abraham. "Do not harm the lad." By consenting to God's Command, Abraham's faith in the promises of the Almighty passed God's assessment. Thereupon that mountain top, Abraham's powerful faith in the Almighty, created the pathway of descent to the Messiah. Just as God provided a substitute Ram for the boy, in the fullness of time, God would again provide a Substitute; but on that future occasion, His very own Lamb would die in place of sinful man. Forty-two generations later, the only begotten Son of God was conceived in the womb of a virgin by the power of the Holy Spirit. What were the words spoken by the angels at the birth of God's Son, Jesus? "Peace on earth, goodwill to men."

Fast forward in time to another hill and a gruesome scene in a city known as Jerusalem. On that day, another Father offered His only begotten Son as a Sacrifice. But in that instance, the Life of His Son was not spared. The heavenly Father's love for His creation was so profound that He allowed His only begotten Son to be sacrificed in exchange for the lives of many. The Father lovingly and charitably offered His Son, but then, His Son was viciously and brutally beaten and nailed upon a cross of crucifixion. And immediately, the first Life to receive Christ's salvation was granted to a thief on an adjacent cross. The sacrificial Lamb of God was Human Flesh and Bone. But His mission in the world was peace and goodwill, demonstrated by the purest form of love. That same prevailing love of God perseveres through the powerful and redeeming blood of Jesus.

Love rises far above the mere spoken word. Love is an action that is incorruptible. The following Scripture is the character of Jesus as He lived love through His short period of ministry. *Love is patient and kind. Love is not jealous, it does not brag, and it is not proud. Love is not rude, it is not selfish, and it cannot be made angry easily. Love does not remember wrongs done against it. Love is never happy when others do wrong, but it is always happy with the truth.*

Love never gives up on people. It never stops trusting, never loses hope, and never quits (1 Corinthians 13:4–7, ERV). The previous Scripture is a portrayal of the Father's attributes, confirmed in the Nature of Jesus. The Lord Himself Said, "He that has seen Me, has seen the Father" (John 14:9).

Even at the tender age of twelve, Jesus Declared it was time to be about His Father's business. It was then that young Jesus positioned Himself for His future undertaking. *And Jesus increased in wisdom and stature, and in favor with God and man* (Luke 2:52, NKJV).

At the age of thirty, the heavenly Father called His Son, Jesus, into ministry. When the Lord exchanged His robe of deity for a robe of righteousness, He would conform to much of the same limitations as any other flesh and blood human being. And for that reason, Jesus refused to compromise either His assignment or His common sense. But before He was allowed to minister in His office, He had to prove to the Father that He would be a competent Servant and convincing Leader and King. Therefore, God sent Jesus to be tested by Satan in the desert for forty days and forty nights. That illustration is one of the best possible examples Jesus gave to show us how to boldly use Scripture effectively to defeat Satan, the enemy of our faith.

Joining with God in a sacred covenant of unity is a serious matter and should never be taken lightly or in a moment of frivolity. It's actually a love pact similar to that of marriage. God has vowed to love you unconditionally, and we are to reciprocate faithfully. Anyone pledging their life's devotion to God should examine the personal cost of such a commitment. Someone taking that pledge is consecrating their very life to the Lord Jesus in complete surrender. This must be done without any uncertainty and with the purest intention to honor that solemn commitment without reservation for the duration of their time on earth. A covenant with the Lord is not a light action, and here's why. God's promise is eternal but conditional should you violate the agreement by persistent abandonment or adultery. Think this through carefully. *If you forsake him and worship other gods, he will turn upon you and destroy you, even though he has taken care of you for such a long time* (Joshua 24:20, TLB).

God's love is tenacious and perpetual. Thereby, committing oneself to Jesus is an eternal vow of exclusivity. *"Jesus said to him, 'You must love the Lord your God with all your heart and with all your soul and with all your mind'"* (Matthew 22:37, NLV). It is very clear what is expected by either party in such a solemn oath. Promising to remain forever faithful, unyielding, and devoted to one another no matter what. Even when the flesh dies and the spirit leaves the body. The covenant is still never, never broken. The result is what should be emphasized. It is an eternal promise of commitment. A pledge to remain forever loyal. The Lord promises to be with you always, even to the end of the world (Matthew 28:20). He will never leave you or forsake you (Hebrews 13:5). *I give them a life that is unceasing, and death will not have the last word. Nothing or no one can steal them from My hand. My Father has given the flock to Me, and He is superior to all beings and things. No one is powerful enough to snatch the flock from My Father's hand. The Father and I are one* (John 10:28–30, VOICE).

When someone decides to surrender their life to Jesus, it's customarily an act of humility and love. God then offers His own love in even a greater capacity. Each new babe in Christ receives the Holy Spirit in their brand-new heart. He is there to help, comfort, and direct the born-again child of God in the paths of righteousness. This is how Jesus explained it to His disciples. *But the Helper, the Holy Spirit whom the Father will send in My name, He will teach you all things, and remind you of all that I said to you* (John 14:26, NASB).

Without Bible knowledge, it's impossible to understand and appreciate the love and character of God and the Lord Jesus. When beginning a relationship with God, it's imperative to study Scripture. Not only will you begin to see the many virtues of God, but it is the key to building your spiritual nature and unlocking the holiness within. If you endure, soon your Life will take on a whole new significance. God will reward your persistence, and before long, you will develop greater faith and hunger for more of everything the Lord has to offer. Make God the center of your life. He has always made you the center of His.

A Christian's spiritual growth does not stop when they are born-again. That is only the awesome first step and initial preparation for the exciting journey that lay ahead. Although your sins have been washed in the blood of Christ, having a spotless character does not just happen automatically. There are no shortcuts to holiness. It is unattainable without the power of the Holy Spirit living in the heart of God's children. He is our moral Compass. But even then, if we have not been educated in the Word of God, we will be like a dry well. The Holy Spirit is indeed our resource to holiness, but if He has nothing to draw from, where then is the power? He can only dispense from a well that has been amply filled with the Living Water of Life.

The English language often lacks variations to certain words. One example of that is the word *love*. Americans use the word love for everything they adore, without emphasis on degree or measure. But in the Bible, there are definite distinctions for the word love. The Greek translation for the kind of love that describes pure love is the word *agape'*. It is indicative of God's perfect kind of immeasurable love. Jesus demonstrated His immense love on the cross where He was crucified. *Agape'* is a moral love that profoundly transcends the base or casual level of affection that is known in today's society.

To further clarify the point, in the original King James version of the Bible, the word *charity* is used to describe those feelings that Jesus articulated toward His traveling companions. But if *charity* was used here, it would give a whole different meaning to the characterization of our focus. Charity, in this sense, would give the impression of a type of assistance.

Those who speak the English language probably use the word *love* dozens of times throughout any given day. Sadly, it is the only word in our language in which to describe the affection we have toward someone or something. The single word love applies to positively everything from the very least of our affections to what we hold most dear. It's unfortunate that the word love is totally overused and completely inefficient when it comes to describing the level of emotional richness we sometimes feel and wish to communicate.

Being able to measure the level of love is significant, but unfortunately, our language does not allow for that. If love was expressed by a number equivalent, then there would be a differentiating assessment and value of true affection. It might be an interesting concept how those numbers would describe our love for people, different places, and many other things that we treasure in life. But for now, we must rely on the old standard. That is to attach a qualifying phrase at the end of a declaration of love. Something like, "I love you with all my heart," et cetera. Nevertheless, as heartfelt as that may be, it is still just words. But there is no greater love, no love that exceeds the love made public by Christ when He shed His own blood to cleanse the world of sin. *And here is how to measure it—the greatest love is shown when a person lays down his life for his friends; and you are my friends if you obey me* (John 15:13–14, TLB).

Love doesn't get any more real or passionate than what Jesus did for the world. Giving His sinless Life in place of the degenerate life of anyone willing to repent and receive the gift offered by the Son of man. His offer of love is an everlasting immeasurable love. We were the condemned ones. Jesus died so that we might have Life more abundantly and timelessly. Jesus became the Sacrificial Lamb that was given as a propitiation for anyone who would surrender their life to Him. Faithful love is believing on Him and following in the righteous direction He leads. And just as a little side note. Obedience is the only verifiable way to the heart of God and unconditional proof of our love for Him.

Of all the rules that Jesus wants His followers to observe, there is one that stands out front and center above all the rest. *Jesus answered him, "Love the Lord your God with every passion of your heart, with all the energy of your being, and with every thought that is within you.' This is the great and supreme commandment"* (Matthew 22:37–38, TPT).

There should be no mistake in what Jesus is saying to us. Anyone who is born-again ought to love Christ with every fiber of their being. He is the Owner of their redeemed soul and Keeper of the eternal flame. It's our duty to safeguard every thought, control every emotion, and be cautious of every action. *"Loving me empowers you to obey my commands* (John 14:15, TPT). And one of those Commands tells us to love our neighbor. Those aren't just the people that inhabit the house next door or the community in which we live. Neighbors are the inhabitants of the world we share.

Unfortunately, whenever there is disobedience to God's directives, especially brotherly love, it is an impertinent insult to the Lord Jesus. His love for everyone took Him to the cross. He died there to save even those who rejected Him and those who hated Him enough to kill Him. God uses a straightforward approach to a good and simple Life for all. His principles are basic and down-to-earth. Which quite simply means, on a level befitting us. The Lord never sets the bar higher than the least among men could attain. In other words, God always regards our ability to understand and achieve what is required to please Him. Let us follow the wisdom and edicts of God by utilizing the same respect toward each other as we want for ourselves. If all society would apply love and integrity to their character, those qualities alone might well change the entire culture of today's population.

Love is everlasting. Nothing surpasses the merit and magnitude of love, especially what it means to receive it and how it makes us feel to give love away to others. If we disregard the pure act of love toward others, then nothing we do will have any true meaning or lasting value in this world or the next. There will come a day when all our talents and gifts from God will come to an end. Regardless how charitable we may have been during our time on the earth or what works we may have accomplished, all will be valued as worthless without God's principle of love being authentically imparted to everyone on behalf of the Father. There is a timely and appropriate message in the book of Luke that should speak to all of us.

For if you give, you will get! Your gift will return to you in full and overflowing measure, pressed down, shaken together to make room for more, and running over. Whatever measure you use to give—large or small—will be used to measure what is given back to you" (Luke 6:38, TLB). If we are not fulfilling Luke's proclamation of love, then we have fallen short of the Commandment of God. Scripture tells us to owe no one anything except to love one another, for those who love others have fulfilled the New Testament law (Romans 13:8). Genuine love thrives without failure.

The epitome of love has never before been expressed the way Almighty God and Jesus displayed their profound love and what it achieved. Bible history records an unrivaled passion held by an unusual Man of valor Who suffered immense physical adversity for the vehement compassion He sustained for humanity. This Man had it all and relinquished it all. He surrendered His affluence, His opulence, and the nobility of His kingdom, His unsurpassed liberty, and unequaled power. He owned every beast of the forest. The cattle upon a thousand hills belonged to Him. He Called every bird and every creature of the forest and field by name. But that Man decided to give it all up to become a humble Human Being. That Man is Jesus, the Son of the living God. Jesus sacrificed everything for our sake. He was consigned to pain and torture, beaten unmercifully and physically marred like no other human being ever was. He was despised and rejected by His own people. And finally, His Life was purchased for a mere thirty pieces of silver by one of His very own disciples. But it was when Jesus died on the cross that He claimed victory over sin and Satan and received the keys to hell. And as a result of His resurrection, He defeated death and the grave. Yes, Jesus left it all so that He could give His all, that we might receive all that He had to give. Then at the conclusion of His triumph, Jesus returned to the Kingdom of Heaven, where He now sits at the right hand of the Father, reigning forevermore as King of kings and Lord of lords.

Postscript

Open your heart to God...

Blessed be the Name of our God and heavenly Father. Hear my prayer for the child that Your healing hand is upon this very hour. That special one whose name is written in the Lamb's Book of Life but has not confessed Jesus as Savior until now. Let there be no further delay in giving eternal Life to this weary soul. Hear the cry of this hopeless one pleading for God's forgiveness. Almighty Father, see into their penitent heart. Please, dear Lord, receive this person according to Your promise without reservation, without condemnation. Hear this person's prayer for absolution and permit the blood of Christ to wash over their inner being. Receive this desolate child who has stepped out of the shadows of guilt and shame to receive freedom from the bondage of sin. Remove the filthy rags that covered the old life, and clothe this born-again child in a robe whiter than snow. Lord, I pray You take the hand of this damaged mortal and lead them into newness of Life and keep their soul by the power of Your Holy Spirit for all eternity. Amen.

About the Author

Donna Dilbeck has discovered Satan's most effective and overlooked weapon against humanity, and she is sharing that knowledge with you in *Jesus the Forsaken, Occasional Christ*. Donna's unique writing style shines the marvelous light of Christ's righteousness directly into the dark corners of daily life. From her refreshing perspective, she expects her readers will discover something they may not have previously considered. Her prior works, The Price of Your Soul and The Imperceptible Raise or Siege communicates her zeal for humanity's need for the truth and the Savior Jesus. Although retired from the workforce, her greatest enjoyment is sharing her fiery passion for God's unfettered gospel and igniting in others those same spiritual flames.

Bibliography

American Standard Version (ASV)

Amplified Bible (AMP)

Amplified Bible, Classic Addition (AMPC)

Christian Standard Bible (CSB)

Common English Bible (CEB)

Complete Jewish Bible (CJB)

Contemporary English Version (CEV)

Easy-to-Read Version (ERV)

English Standard Version (ESV)

God's WORD (GW)

Good News Translation (GNT)

Holman Christian Standard Bible (HCSB)

International Children's Bible (ICB)

International Standard Version (ISV)

J.B. Phillips New Testament (PHILLIPS)

King James Version (KJV)

Living Bible (TLB)

The Message (MSG)

New American Standard Bible (NASB)

New Century Version (NCV)

New International Reader's Version (NIRV)

New International Version (NIV)

New King James Version (NKJV)

New Life Version (NLV)

New Living Translation (NLT)

New Revised Standard Version Updated Edition (NRSVUE)

New Testament for Everyone (NTE)

Revised Standard Version (RSV)

Tree of Live Version (TLV)

The Passion Translation (TPT)

The Voice (VOICE)

Worldwide English (New Testament) (WE)

Wikipedia

CPSIA information can be obtained
at www.ICGtesting.com
Printed in the USA
BVHW081944130223
658422BV00013B/187